AN EXEGETICAL GRAMMAR
OF THE GREEK NEW TESTAMENT

THE MACMILLAN COMPANY
NEW YORK · CHICAGO
DALLAS · ATLANTA · SAN FRANCISCO
LONDON · MANILA
BRETT-MACMILLAN LTD.
TORONTO

AN
EXEGETICAL GRAMMAR

OF THE

GREEK NEW TESTAMENT

BY

WILLIAM DOUGLAS CHAMBERLAIN

M.A., Ph.D., D.D.

NEW YORK

THE MACMILLAN COMPANY

1957

Sixth Printing, 1957

TO
MY WIFE,
COMPANION
IN
EVERY LABOR

6693

FOREWORD

This grammar has grown out of twelve years' experience in the classroom in presenting the facts of the grammar of the *koine* Greek and their bearing on the interpretation of the Greek New Testament. Experience seemed to indicate an unbridged gulf in the student's mind between a knowledge of grammatical facts and their application to exegesis.

To make a beginning, the author wrote an Exegetical Syllabus, which he has used in the classroom for six years with some degree of satisfaction. This Syllabus has been revised, corrected and enlarged into the present work. There has been no attempt to be original. The one objective has been to condense, arrange or simplify the works of the great pioneers in the grammatical field, so as to give a convenient handbook to the seminary student.

Exegetical grammar can have no landmarks until the work of historical grammar is done. Historical grammar cannot be put on a sound basis until the comparative grammarian has done his work, so the real beginning of scientific modern Greek grammar roots in Whitney's *Sanskrit Grammar* (1875), and the impetus that it gave to the student of comparative grammar. Out of this came Robertson's monumental work, *A Grammar of the Greek New Testament in the Light of Historical Research* (1914). There are many illustrious names in this field, such as Moulton and Deissmann.

In the last decade of the nineteenth century, Grenfell and Hunt discovered huge quantities of papyri in Egypt, the majority of these being written in a type of Greek very similar to that of the New Testament. About the same time, Deissmann's *Bibelstudien* (1895) and his *Neue Bibelstudien* (1897) produced further evidence that the New Testament was written in the everyday language of the Graeco-Roman world of the first century A.D. The long controversy as to whether the Greek of the New

vii

Testament was "pure Attic Greek," as some held; or a Jewish-Greek patois was settled. Neither group was right. The basic element of this vernacular, called ἡ κοινή, is the Attic dialect with admixtures of Ionic, Doric, Aeolic, Northwest Greek, etc. The vernacular received its stamp as the result of the intermingling of the soldiers from all parts of the Greek world in the armies of Alexander the Great. This discovery as to the true nature of the language of the New Testament has made many changes in its interpretation. These will be noted later. Many words that were thought to be "biblical Greek," i.e., a peculiar religious jargon, are now known to be the ordinary words of the shop, the street, and the home. In Thayer's *Lexicon of the Greek New Testament,* there are listed about fourteen columns of "biblical words," with an average of about sixty words to the column. Nearly all of these words have been found in the papyri. The list is constantly diminishing through new discoveries. This can leave no doubt about the nature of the language of the New Testament: the New Testament was written in the everyday speech of the Graeco-Roman world of the first century A.D.[1]

A word should be said about the practice of quoting only that part of the Greek sentence which is necessary for identifying the construction under discussion. This is designed to turn the student to the Greek New Testament, so that he will study the grammatical point involved in its context. This has a very real value, for, at the end of a semester, the student should have cultivated fair facility in locating passages in his Greek Testament. It has been a definite part of my classroom procedure to have the student look up in the Greek pertinent passages all over the New Testament. If the student learns to feel at home, as he leafs through his New Testament in the Greek, he is likely to continue consulting it later in his ministry.

Acknowledgments should be made to many whose works have been consulted, especially to the late Dr. A. T. Robertson, beloved teacher and friend; to Drs. Moulton, Deiss-

[1] For a fuller discussion of the *koine* Greek, see Moulton's *Prolegomena* and Robertson, *A Grammar of the Greek New Testament in the Light of Historical Research,* pp. 3-139.

mann and a host of others. I wish to express grateful appreciation to Mrs. A. T. Robertson for permission to use quotations from Dr. Robertson's work. My thanks are due to Professor A. Leland Jameson of Centre College, who read a part of the manuscript and made some constructive and highly appreciated suggestions. An especial debt of gratitude is due to my wife who has typed and retyped both the original syllabus and the present volume, and has been of inestimable help in the work of repeated revisions of the manuscripts.

For whatever errors of interpretation or of facts which may creep in, I take full responsibility.

Hoping that this small volume may be of use to other students of the New Testament, I send it forth.

W. D. CHAMBERLAIN.

Louisville, Kentucky.
February, 1940.

BOOKS REFERRED TO

Abbott, E. A., *Johannine Grammar.*
Abbott-Smith, *A Manual-Greek Lexicon of the New Testament.*
Barth, Karl, *The Epistle to the Romans.*
Blass, F., *Grammar of New Testament Greek.*
Calvin, John, *Commentary on the Epistle to the Romans.*
Deissmann, Adolf, *Light From the Ancient East, Bible Studies, New Bible Studies.*
Farrar, F. W., *Greek Syntax.*
Goodwin, W. W., *Greek Grammar, Syntax of the Moods and Tenses of the Greek Verb.*
Jebb, R. C., *Notes on Antigone.*
Liddell and Scott, *Greek-English Lexicon.*
Moulton, J. H., *A Grammar of New Testament Greek, Vol. I, Prolegomena.*
Moulton and Howard, *A Grammar of New Testament Greek, Vol. II.*
Moulton and Milligan, *The Vocabulary of the New Testament Illustrated From the Papyri.*
Robertson, A. T., *A Grammar of the Greek New Testament in the Light of Historical Research, An Introduction to the Textual Criticism of the New Testament.*
Robertson and Davis, *A New Short Grammar of the Greek Testament.*
Sanday and Headlam, *The Epistle to the Romans (I.C.C.).*
Thayer, J. H., *Greek-English Lexicon of the New Testament.*
Whitney, W. D., *A Sanskrit Grammar.*

I have, in general, omitted reference to books in German, for the simple reason that comparatively few undergraduate seminary students seem to be prepared to use German works effectively. As a student advances in New Testament studies, he will have very little difficulty in learning what German works are most useful.

CONTENTS

xi

Part III.

CONTENTS

PART IV.

PART V.

PART VI.

PART I

INTRODUCTION

A Definition of Exegesis

Exegesis, ἐξήγησις, is the science of interpretation. The word is formed by adding the action-ending -σις to the compound verb-stem ἐκ+ἡγέομαι, 'I lead out.' Exegesis, then, is the leading out of thoughts that the writer had as he penned a given document. No one can do this perfectly. The ideal, however, can be made quite clear and should be held clearly in mind, even though it can not be fully attained.

The governing principles of exegesis may be stated quite briefly. Dr. George A. Barton used to give his students the following:

Five Vest Pocket Rules of Exegesis:
1. Interpret Lexically
2. Interpret Syntactically
3. Interpret Contextually
4. Interpret Historically
5. Interpret according to the Analogy of Scripture.

To interpret lexically, one must know the etymology of the words, their historical development in meaning, and their usage in the particular document under consideration. This information is best secured from good lexicons. In using lexicons, one should notice carefully the meaning of the word under consideration at different periods of the Greek language and in different authors of the same period. The word δαιμόνιον is an example of this: in early Greek, it meant a departed spirit; in the case of Socrates, it was a sort of guardian spirit (almost his conscience); in the New Testament, it usually refers

1

to a malignant spiritual being (a demon) which produces mental or physical disorders in human beings. Josephus used it in the sense of a deity, a divinity. It is used in this sense once in the New Testament, Acts 17:18: ξένων δαιμονίων δοκεῖ καταγγελεὺς εἶναι, 'He seems to be a proclaimer of strange deities.'

Another example is ἀπόστολος. Do not be satisfied to equate this word with 'apostle.' Etymologically, it is derived from ἀποστέλλω, 'I send forth.' An apostle, then, is one sent forth. The history of the word is interesting: its technical Christian sense (apostle) is not its oldest usage.[1] In the papyri, ἀπόστολος means a 'grain ship' despatched on a commercial venture. In the New Testament, there is a rather broad usage. The most familiar usage is where it refers to the Twelve or to Paul, but Barnabas (Acts 14:14) and James (Gal. 1:19) are both called apostles. Epaphroditus (Phil. 2:25) is called an apostle of the church at Philippi. Jesus (Heb. 3:1) is called an Apostle of God. In Byzantine Greek, the word is always a technical term referring to one of the Twelve or to Paul. In second century Greek, ὁ ἀπόστολος refers to Paul. The article suggests that he is the apostle par excellence. Much learned debate has been expended to determine whether some men who are called 'apostles' in the New Testament were really apostles. A little more learning would have saved this effort. The word ἀπόστολος had not become a technical term in the New Testament: anyone sent on a mission might be called an 'apostle' of the sender.

Thayer's *Greek-English Lexicon of the New Testament* has long been the standard work in English, but it is now fifty years since it was revised. It happens that these fifty years have been very fruitful in New Testament study, so Thayer should be supplemented by Moulton and Milligan, *Vocabulary of the New Testament Illustrated from the Papyri;* Deissmann, *Light from the Ancient East;* the NEW Liddell and Scott (not yet complete); Abbott-Smith, *A Manual-Greek Lexicon of the New Testament.* For students who use German, Bauer, *Griechisch-deutsches Wörterbuch zu den Schriften des Neue Testaments und der übrigen urchristlichen Literatur* is good.

[1] A most thorough discussion of this word is found in *Theologisches Wörterbuch zum Neuen Testament*, Kittel. Band I, pp. 397-448.

To interpret syntactically, one must know the grammatical principles of the language in which the document to be interpreted was first written. This Grammar attempts to give in brief form the basic facts. It should be supplemented by the more comprehensive Grammars, such as Robertson's *A Grammar of the Greek New Testament in the Light of Historical Research,* and Moulton and Howard's *A Grammar of New Testament Greek.* The student must remember at all times that the function of grammar is not to determine the laws of language, but explain them. That is, language first developed as a means of expressing the thoughts of mankind, and then grammars were written to explain the laws and principles of language as it functions to express ideas. In one's native tongue, one senses the meaning of these constructions almost subconsciously, but in a strange tongue one must, by diligent toil, acquire the viewpoint of the language and follow its idioms closely to get its meaning.

To interpret contextually, one must keep in mind the trend of thought of the whole document, if it is a unified discourse. Then one must note the 'color of thought' immediately surrounding the passage, for this quite often shades the meaning of the words being interpreted. Much evil has been done to fair interpretation of the Bible by dividing it into verses as though they were separate entities of thought, unrelated to their context. Consequently, sometimes meanings are given to passages which are almost directly opposite that intended by the original author. A good example of this is Col. 2:21, which is often used as a text for a temperance sermon. As it stands in its context, it is a condemnation of asceticism. The document interpreted will supply what you need here.

To interpret historically, one must seek to discover the circumstances calling forth a certain writing. The introductory notes in a good commentary or an *Introduction to the New Testament,* such as that of Zahn or Moffatt, will be valuable here. In addition to this, it is necessary to know the manners, customs and psychology of the people among whom a given document is produced.

The psychology of a people will include their ideas of chronology, their methods of recording history, their use of figures of speech, and the types of literature which they used to express their thoughts. This information can be acquired by reading both particular and general historical material bearing on the writing studied.

To interpret according to the analogy of Scripture, one must use Scripture as an aid to understanding Scripture. A bizarre interpretation that clashes with the whole trend of Scripture is practically sure to be wrong. An accurate knowledge of the biblical viewpoint is the best help here.

In seeking to apply these principles, one must divest oneself of one's own prejudices and seek to see through the author's eyes.

EXEGETICAL PROCEDURE

Wrong Procedure

It is a common practice in exegesis to read what several commentaries say as to the meaning of a passage, and then accept the interpretation that pleases one most. This is bad exegetical procedure for several reasons. In the first place, it encourages one to seek an interpretation that fits in with one's own preconceptions. In the second place, one forms the habit of simply trying to remember the various interpretations offered. This, for the beginner, often results in bewilderment and mental resentment at the whole idea of exegesis. In reality, this is not exegesis: it is just another form of memory work, which is often very uninteresting. Some commentaries seem to be written from this approach. No doubt this accounts for what Prof. A. B. Bruce called "the sequacious habits of commentators." The most serious evil resulting from this procedure is that the student seldom learns to think for himself. Instead of turning to the passage of Scripture involved to see what it actually says, he runs from commentary to commentary. Finding them frequently not in verbal agreement, he decides that it is all a lot of academic silliness, or else that exegesis is a rather abstruse, impractical subject which he can never use in his ministry.

Correct Procedure

The interpreter should ask first, what does the author say; second, what does he mean by this statement. In Greek, the student will find many words of which he does not know the meaning, but in spite of that fact he should go over the passage to be interpreted, keeping these two questions in mind, and get all of the meaning possible out of it. This should be done before a lexicon, commentary or grammar is consulted. The next step should be to consult the best lexicons for the meaning of unfamiliar words. Great care should be exercised to get the meaning which suits that particular passage. After one has used a lexicon, then one or more good grammars should be used in order to understand the syntactical constructions accurately. In the verb, the voice-, mode-, and tense-signs should be watched for their contribution to the total idea. The same care should be exercised in dealing with the noun, participle, infinitive, etc. After these three steps have been taken, the interpreter should have a good idea of the meaning of the passage. Then commentaries should be consulted to check one's conclusions and to note thoughts over-looked in the previous steps. The exegete will need now and again to go back and re-examine the various processes as he advances in interpreting a passage. The purpose of this procedure is to discover what bearing the passage being interpreted has on Christian theology and Christian ethics. This procedure will result in new light constantly breaking on familiar passages.

THE USE OF HELPS

In using commentaries correctly, the student should keep in mind the theological climate out of which they come, for this invariably affects their interpretation.[2] A commentator may be able, in a measure, to avoid a bias and allow the document to speak for itself, but his emphasis on the various thoughts in the passage will be affected by the thought-currents of his day. The ideal is to preserve and reproduce, as accurately as possible, the balance of emphasis that the writer himself made as he wrote. If one changes that emphasis in interpreting, he should not only be aware of the changed emphasis, but should call attention to it.

In using grammars and lexicons, it is quite important to keep in mind the date of their publication, and whether or not they take into consideration certain information now available. Of course, the beginner will not be qualified to judge grammars, commentaries or lexicons in the manner suggested, but that ability will grow with experience. A knowledge of the history of Christian thought and of the history of exegetical science is very helpful here.

ANALYZING A SENTENCE

Since the sentence is really the unit in the expression of thought, it is necessary first to learn how to interpret single sentences. Every complete sentence has both a subject and a predicate. All of the thought of the sentence will revolve around the subject and the predicate as its two foci. As the shape of an ellipse is determined by the position of its two foci, so the meaning of a sentence is always shaped by its subject and predicate. Either may be indefinitely expanded by means of other

[2] A good example of this is seen in Calvin's commentary on the Epistle to the Romans and Karl Barth's commentary on the same Epistle. Calvin confronts the Roman Catholic Church and Barth is in revolt against extreme humanism, so the interpretation of each is colored by his situation. The task of the interpreter of Romans is to discover as completely as possible the situation which Paul faced as he wrote the Epistle and to attempt to understand how he dealt with it. The next step is to ask what bearing this has on Christian theology and Christian ethics for today.

words, phrases or clauses, as one desires to add more
thought-details. The first step in understanding a sentence is to take each word as it occurs in the sentence
and notice its grammatical form and meaning: if it is a
noun, its case-form and any preposition that may be
used with it; if it is a verb, its voice-, mode-, and tense-
signs. Then pick out the subject and predicate with the
descriptive materials that go with each. If the interpreter wishes to understand a sentence, it is absolutely
essential to keep these relations clearly in mind, for the
subject and predicate limit and control the meanings of
all their own modifiers. In the Greek language, sentences and even paragraphs are very closely bound
together by connective words. These conjunctions show
quite accurately the relation between the thoughts of
adjacent sentences and should be watched carefully. All
this, no doubt, sounds like a very elaborate and intricate
procedure, but when a student once forms the habit of
making a correct approach, the details of procedure
become more or less second nature.

The following is an eminently sensible statement of
the correct procedure in interpreting a sentence in
Greek: "In order to understand the meaning of a sentence in Greek one needs to know the original meaning
of each word, the development of these words in history,
the meaning of each form, the particular stage reached
at the time of writing, the context in the given instance.
Do not translate a Greek sentence until you understand
its meaning." [3]

---

[3] Robertson and Davis, *A New Short Grammar of the Greek New
Testament*, p. 199.

PART II

BUILDING A GREEK VOCABULARY

The most fundamental need of the student of any language is a working vocabulary. The acquisition of such a vocabulary is for many students a laborious task. This can be greatly lightened and enlivened by the right approach. In the Greek language, all words are built on primitive root-stocks which carry a constant basic meaning. There are only about four hundred of these roots in the entire vocabulary of all known Greek. Instead of developing a vocabulary by sheer mental drudgery, the student may learn certain principles of word formation which will enable him to achieve this end with pleasure.

There are only two classes of these root-stocks: one forms the basic element in all parts of speech but the pronouns; and the other forms the basic element of the pronouns. The kinship of roots is traced through the consonants. The vowels frequently change, as in λέγ-ω and λόγ-ος. This change in vowels is called vowel grada-tion. To illustrate, we may take the root λεγ- (λογ-) : on the weak stem, λεγ-, the verb λέγ-ω is formed, meaning 'I speak'; on the strong stem, λογ-, the noun λόγ-ος, 'word,' 'a thing spoken.' The primitive meaning of this root is 'collect.' Therefore, we have also the verb λέγω, 'I collect,' and the noun λόγος, 'a collecting,' 'an account.' Out of this noun form we have a verb λογίζομαι, 'I reckon.' The question naturally arises as to how two such diverse meanings as 'speak' and 'collect' are associated with the same root. This is easily understood when we recall that λέγω, 'I speak,' referred originally to considered speech, not mere chatter, as indicated in classical Greek by λαλέω: i. e., λέγω describes speech where one collected one's thoughts and uttered them coherently.

9

The pronominal roots, such as ἐγώ and σύ, have remained a separate and distinct class in all Indo-Germanic languages. They are never used in the formation of nouns, verbs or allied forms.

The great variety of words which can be formed on one basic root can be well illustrated by taking such a root as δικ-, which has in the Sanskrit the primary idea 'to show.' This root appears in the Greek verb δείκνυμι, 'I point out.' It is common in the present tense stem of the Greek verb to lengthen a root, as from δικ- to δεικ-. This had the effect of showing repeated action in the present tense form. Examine the following table as an illustration of the great number of words which may be built on a single root. Note also how the meaning of the root develops.

From δικ-, 'to show,' 'point out,' we get δίκ-η, 'the way pointed out,' i. e., 'the thing which is right,' 'justice.'

δίκ-η, 'right,' 'justice.'
δικ-άζω, 'I render justice.'
δικ-ασ-τής, 'a judge.'
δικ-ασ-μός, 'a giving of justice.'
δικ-άσ-ι-μος, 'judicial.'
δικ-ασ-τικός, 'pertaining to the courts,' 'the juror's fee.'
δίκ-αι-ος, 'one observant of the rules,' 'righteous.'
δικ-αι-όω, 'I declare righteous.'
δικ-αί-ω-μα, 'a righteous act,' 'an ordinance,' 'a decree.'
δικ-αί-ω-σις, 'the act of setting right,' 'doing justice.'
δικ-αι-ω-τής, 'a judge.'
δικ-ασ-τήριον, 'a place of justice,' 'a house of correction.'
Taking the longer root:
δείκ-νυ-μι, 'I show,' 'point out.'
δεῖγ-μα, 'a thing shown,' 'a pattern,' 'a sample.'
δειγ-ματ-ίζω, 'I make a show of.'
δειγ-ματ-ισ-μός, 'an exhibition,' 'a public show.'
δεικ-τήριον, 'a place for showing.'
δείκ-της, 'an exhibitor.'
δεικ-τικός, 'able to show.'
δεῖξ-ις, 'a showing,' 'displaying.'

This list could be indefinitely expanded by bringing in compound words where two nouns are united, διϰ-αι-ο-δό-της, 'one who gives justice,' and by compound verbs formed by prefixes. This list, however, will suffice to illustrate the principles of word building in Greek. The student should learn once and for all that every single letter added to a Greek root adds something to the idea expressed by the root. Before this table can benefit the student, it will be necessary to give the meanings of the various elements used in word building.

SUFFIXES

Noun Suffixes and Their Meanings

For the sake of convenience to the learner, the noun suffixes will be listed in the form in which they occur in the New Testament. The declension to which these nouns belong is indicated by the parentheses, (1), (2), (3).

1. Agent endings.

   a. -της, προ-φή-της, (1), 'one who speaks for another,' 'a prophet.' The corresponding feminine is προφῆτις, (3), 'a prophetess.'

   b. -τηρ, φωσ-τήρ, (3), 'a luminary.'

   c. -τωρ, ῥή-τωρ, (3), 'an orator.'

   d. -ευς (εϜ), γραμματ-εύς, 'a writer,' 'a scribe'; from γράφω, 'I write.'

   e. -ισσα, βασίλ-ισσα, (1), 'a queen'; the feminine of βασιλεύς, 'a king.'

2. Action endings.

   a. -σις, διϰαίω-σις, (3), 'an act of justifying.'

   b. -μος, ϰλαυθ-μός, (2), 'a weeping'; from ϰλαίω, 'I weep'; root ϰλαϜ.

3. Instrumental ending.

-τρον, λύ-τρον, (2), 'an instrument for loosing'; from the verb λύω, 'I loose.'
Compounded with ἀντι, we get ἀντί-λυ-τρον, 'a ransom,' 'something given instead of a person to loose (free) him.'

4. Result endings.

a. -μα, πράγ-μα, (3), 'a thing done,' 'a deed'; from πράσσω, 'I do.'

b. -εια, βασιλ-εία, (1), 'a thing ruled,' 'a kingdom'; from βασιλεύω, 'I rule.'

c. -ος, εἶδ-ος, (3), 'a thing seen,' 'appearance'; from εἶδον, 'I saw.'

5. Quality endings.

a. -οτης, ἁγι-ότης, (3), 'holiness'; from ἅγιος, 'holy.' This ending should not be confused with the agent ending, -της.

b. -ια, σοφ-ία, (1), 'wisdom'; from σόφος, 'wise.'

c. -συνη, σωφρο-σύνη, (1), 'soundmindedness,' 'good sense'; from σῶς, 'sound,' 'whole,' + φρήν, 'mind,' +συνη, 'ness.'

d. -ος, βάθ-ος, (2), 'depth'; from βαθύς, 'deep.'

6. Diminutive endings.

a. -ιον, παιδ-ίον, (2), 'a young boy'; from παῖς, 'a boy.'

b. -ισκος, νεαν-ίσκος, (2), 'a lad'; from νεανίας, 'a young man.'

c. -ισκη, παιδ-ίσκη, (1), 'a damsel'; see (a) above.

7. Place endings.

a. -τηριον, δικασ-τήριον, (2), 'a place where justice is dispensed'; from δικάζω, 'I judge.'

b. -ειον, μνημ-εῖον, (2), 'a place of memorial,' 'a tomb'; from the root μνη, 'to remember.'

8. Abundance, custom, chief characteristic.

-ολος, ἁμαρτ-ωλός, (2), 'a man completely given up to sin,' 'a sinner'; from ἁμαρτία, 'sin.'

εἴδ-ωλος, (2), 'something which is only appearance with no reality,' 'an idol'; from εἶδον, 'I saw.'

δοῦλος, (2), 'a bondman'; from δέω, 'I bind,' + ολος.

Adjective Suffixes and Their Meanings

1. Endings expressing the idea of:

a. Possession, belonging to:
-ιος, -ια, -ιον; οὐράν-ιος, 'belonging to the heavens,' 'heavenly'; from οὐρανός, 'heaven.'
The insertion of an iota often makes a substantive an adjective.

b. Ability, fitness:
(1) -ικος, -ικη, -ικον; κριτ-ικός, 'capable of judging'; from κρίνω, 'I judge.'
(2) -ιμος, -ιμη, -ιμον; (-σιμος, κ. τ. λ.); χρή-σιμος, 'useful'; from χράομαι, 'I use.'

c. Material:
(1) -ινος, -ινη, -ινον; ξύλ-ινος, 'made of wood,' 'wooden'; from ξύλον, 'wood.'
(2) -εος (contracted form, -ους), -εα, -εον; ἀργύρ-εος (ους), 'made of silver'; from ἄργυρος, 'silver.'

d. Complete possession of a quality, like the English -ful or -able:
-ρος, -ρα, -ρον; πονη-ρός, 'full of toil or pain,' 'in a sorry plight,' 'wicked,' 'evil'; from πόνος, 'toil.'

2. Endings correlative to nouns:
-ης, -ες (two terminations); ψευδ-ής, 'lying,' 'false'; from ψεῦδος, 'a lie.'

3. Endings from verbal stems, attributing the action of the verb to a person:
-μων, -μον; ἐλεή-μων, 'merciful'; from ἐλεέω, 'I show mercy.'

Verb Suffixes and Their Meanings

This list does not include those verbs built on primary stems, but those built on substantive, adjective, verb or even prepositional stems. They are usually called denominative verbs.

1. Endings in -αω,[4] -εω, -ευω usually denote action or state.

   a. ἀγαπάω, 'I love'; from ἀγάπη, 'love.'

   b. ξυρέω, 'I shave'; from ξύρον, 'a razor.'

   c. δουλεύω, 'I serve'; from δοῦλος, 'a slave.'

2. Endings in -οω, -αινω, -υνω generally express causation.[5]

   a. δουλόω, 'I enslave'; from δοῦλος, 'a slave.' Cf. δουλεύω, 'I serve' above.

   b. πικραίνω, 'I make bitter,' 'embitter'; from πικρός, 'sharp,' 'keen,' 'bitter.'

   c. πληθύνω may mean either 'I multiply' (transitive), or 'I abound' (intransitive); from πλῆθος, 'a throng.'

3. Endings in -αζω were originally built on stems in -αδ-, e. g., λιθάζω, 'I stone'; from λιθάς (λιθαδ-), 'a stone.' In the koine period they were formed on a great variety of stems.

   a. Originally such verb forms were either frequentative or intensive: στενάζω, 'I sigh (groan) often, or deeply'; from στένω, 'I sigh,' 'I groan.' In the New Testament, the frequentative or intensive force is usually lost: στενάζω (II Cor. 5:2,4) simply means 'to sigh.'

   b. The majority of the -αζω verbs in the New Testament are transitive: ὑπωπιάζω μου τὸ σῶμα (I Cor. 9:27), 'I strike my body under the eye,' 'I beat my body

---

[4] -αω verbs come from -α- stems, while -εω verbs come from -ο- stems. In modern Greek the -αω ending has displaced the -εω ending in many verbs.

[5] With verbs of mental action the idea of the -οω ending is 'to deem' or 'adjudge'; ἀξιόω, 'I deem worthy'; δικαιόω, 'I deem or adjudge righteous.' The latter verb is particularly important in the Pauline writings.

black and blue.'
A good lexicon must be consulted as well as the
context.

4. Endings in -ιζω, like those in -αζω, became very common in late Greek. Originally they were formed on
stems in -ις: ῥιπίζω, 'I fan into flame'; from ῥιπίς, 'a fan.'

a. In the New Testament, these endings usually have
the idea of becoming: Ἰουδαΐζω, 'I become a Jew,'
'I adopt Jewish manners.'

b. Occasionally these endings are causative: ἁγνίζει
ἑαυτόν (I Jn. 3:3), 'he purifies (makes pure) himself.'
In the New Testament, γνωρίζω should always be
given the causative force, even in Phil. 1:22.

c. Occasionally there is an instrumental force, as in
ῥαβδίζω, 'I beat with a rod'; from ῥάβδος, 'a rod.'

d. Often verbs in -ιζω express the simple idea of action,
the frequentative or iterative idea having been lost.
For example, in the New Testament ῥαντίζω, 'I
sprinkle,' has replaced ῥαίνω of earlier Greek.
The context and a good lexicon are the keys to
interpreting these verbs.

5. Endings in -υζω are usually onomatopoetic.

γογγύζω, 'to grumble.'

6. Endings in -σκω are usually inceptive, but sometimes
causative.

γηράσκω, 'I grow old.'
γαμίσκω, 'I give in marriage.'

PREFIXES

Besides suffixes a great number of prefixes are used
in forming compound words.

1. The prepositions are used in a great variety of ways
in forming compounds, both noun and verb. A fuller

discussion of this will be found in the section on prepositions.

2. Separate particles (adverbs) used in composition.

a. ἀ (from ἅμα, 'together') + πᾶς =ἅπας, 'all together.'

b. ἀρτι, 'lately,' forms only one compound in the New Testament: ἀρτιγέννητος (I Pet. 2:2), 'new born.'

c. εὖ, 'well,' forms a number of compounds, with the general idea of 'prosperously,' 'well disposed': εὐδοκία, 'good pleasure.'

d. πάλιν, 'again,' forms only one compound in the New Testament: παλινγενεσία (Mt. 19:28; Tit. 3:5), 'rebirth,' 'regeneration.'

e. παν from the neuter of πας (παντ-), forms a number of compounds, with the idea of 'all': πανδοχεύς, 'an innkeeper,' 'one who receives all comers'; from δέχομαι, 'I receive.'

f. τηλε, 'afar off,' forms only one compound in the New Testament: τηλαυγῶς (Mk. 8:25), 'seeing clearly at a distance.'

3. Inseparable particles in composition.

a. ἀ- (from the preposition ἀνά) has an intensive force: ἀτενίζω, 'to gaze steadfastly.'
   This is called alpha intensive.

b. ἀ-, ἀν- has the negative force like the English un-: ἀγνοέω, 'I am ignorant'; ἄσπιλος, 'unspotted.'
   This is called alpha privative.

c. ἀρχι-, 'chief': ἀρχιποίμην (I Pet. 5:4), 'chief shepherd; ἀρχιερεύς, 'chief priest.'

d. δυσ- has the sense of 'hardly,' 'with difficulty,' 'ill': δυσερμήνευτος, 'hard to explain'; δυσβάστακτος, 'difficult to carry.'

e. ἡμι- is equivalent to the Latin semi, 'half': ἡμιθανής, 'half dead'; ἡμίωρον, 'half an hour.'

4. Compounds of two or more noun or verb stems.

In these compounds the first part stands in a sort of case relation to the second part.

a. Accusative relation.

(1) κακό-εργος (κακοῦργος), 'one who does evil.'

(2) φωσ-φόρος, 'light bringing.'

b. Genitive relation.

(1) πατρι-άρχης, 'one who rules a clan.'

(2) οἴκο-δεσπότης, 'one who rules a house.'

c. Ablative relation.

(1) διο-πετής, 'a thing fallen from Zeus.'

(2) θεο-δίδακτος, 'taught from God.'

d. Dative relation.

(1) ἀνθρωπ-άρεσκος, 'a man pleaser.'

(2) εἰδωλό-θυτος, 'sacrificed to idols.'

e. Locative relation.

(1) γονυ-πετής, 'falling on the knees.'

(2) χείμαρ-ρος, 'flowing in winter.' (True of many streams in Palestine, because the rainy season is in winter.)

f. Instrumental relation.

(1) ποταμο-φόρητος, 'borne by river.'

(2) αἰχμ-άλωτος, 'captured by a spear.'

5. Descriptive compounds.

There are many other compounds where the first element describes the second.

μονο-γενής, 'only begotten.'

ἀγρι-έλαιος, 'wild olive.'

ACCENT

A word should be said about the general rules of accentuation in Greek.

1. There are in Greek three accents:

   a. The acute accent may occur on any one of the last three syllables, i. e., the antepenult, the penult, or the ultima: e. g., ἄγγελος, λόγος, αὐτός.
If the ultima is long, the antepenult can not take the accent: e. g., ἄγγελος, becomes ἀγγέλου, ἀγγέλῳ.

   b. The grave accent can occur only on the ultima and is used where another accented word follows immediately in the sentence: e. g., σαπρὸν δένδρον, or πολλοὶ ἐροῦσίν μοι. An unaccented word (an enclitic) like μοι does not change an acute accent to a grave, because it is pronounced with the preceding word.

   c. The circumflex can occur only on long vowels and only on the penult or the ultima.

     (1) If the ultima is long, the penult can not take the circumflex: e. g., δῶρον must become δώρῳ.

     (2) If the ultima is short, an accented, long penult must take the circumflex: e. g., δώρον would be incorrect, it must be δῶρον.

     (3) Since such combinations as ἐροῦσίν μοι are pronounced as one word, a secondary acute accent is placed over the final syllable of ἐροῦσιν to prevent the circumflex accent from occurring further from the end of the combination, ἐροῦσίν μοι, than convenient for pronunciation.

2. In general, the noun accent remains in the position it has in the nominative form, except as changes in the ultima necessitate changes in the accent: e. g., in ἄνθρωπος, the accent is forced to the penult by the long ultima, -ους. In such forms as δῶρον, changes occur analogous to those noted under 'c' above.
Certain exceptions will be noted as they occur.

3. In the verb, the accent is recessive, i. e., it occurs as far from the final syllable as the rules of accent allow.

Since the participle and the infinitive are verbal-nouns, they follow the rules of noun accent: e. g., λελυκώς, λελυμένος, ἀγαγεῖν, λιπεῖν.

For the convenience of the student, the vowels should be listed:

1. η and ω are always long; ε and ο are always short.

2. α, ι, υ are sometimes short and sometimes long. In the case of these vowels, each word-root must be observed.

3. The diphthongs, αι, ει, ευ, οι, ου, ηυ, υι (and the 'improper' diphthongs, ᾳ, ῃ, ῳ) are long, except where αι and οι are final. In the optative, αι and οι are regarded as long for purposes of accent.

PART III

THE PARTS OF SPEECH AND THEIR FUNCTION

THE NOUN

The term, noun, is used by most modern grammarians to designate both substantives and adjectives. This is due to the fact that originally no distinction was made between them. In the Sanskrit, for instance, they are treated together by all grammarians. The noun was used now as a substantive and then as an adjective. A survival of this is seen in our word 'ball,' both as a substantive and as an adjective: e. g., 'The ball is round,' and 'The ball game was lost.'

The word, noun, is derived from the Latin, *nomen* (Greek, ὄνομα, 'name'). This is because it named persons or things.

From this point on we shall divide our discussion of the noun under the two heads of substantives and adjectives.

The substantive performs many functions in the sentence. These various relations within the sentence are expressed by the cases.

The Cases

The name, case, is derived from the Latin, *casus*, 'falling.' The Greek term for case is πτῶσις, 'falling,' and the German is *der Fall*, a cognate of our English word, 'fall.' The substantive is conceived of as falling in a certain relationship to the rest of the sentence. One case, the nominative, is conceived of as falling in a direct or perpendicular relationship to the sentence; the others are regarded as falling in an oblique relation. This idea accounts for the origin of the term, oblique cases. It

21

should be observed here that the vocative, strictly speaking, is not a true case, but it is so treated by grammarians for the sake of convenience.

From the study of comparative grammar, it is quite evident that there were originally eight cases (including the vocative) in the Indo-Germanic family of languages. These were the nominative, genitive, ablative, dative, locative, instrumental (sometimes called the associative-instrumental), accusative and vocative. There were originally eight separate case-forms as well as eight separate case-ideas. This is clearly seen from the Sanskrit, the oldest member of the family. Gradually these separate case-forms began to coalesce until, in the Greek language, there were only five distinct case-forms, both in the classical Greek and in the *koine* of the New Testament. In modern Greek, there are only three left: the nominative, genitive and accusative. In English, there are only two case-forms in the substantive (there are three in the pronoun), whereas in the oldest existing Anglo-Saxon writings there were six. This tide, carrying away the case-forms, has run through the entire Indo-Germanic family of languages, until in the French, there is only one form of the substantive (three case-forms still remain in the pronoun); in the German, there are four. The development of the preposition is responsible for the retreat of the case-forms. This matter is discussed more fully under prepositions.

Declension of the Article

The article, historically, belongs with the pronouns, but for the sake of convenience its declension is given here.

	Singular			Plural		
	M.	F.	N.	M.	F.	N.
Nom.	ὁ [1]	ἡ	τό	οἱ	αἱ	τά
G. & Ab.	τοῦ	τῆς	τοῦ	τῶν	τῶν	τῶν
L. I. D.	τῷ	τῇ	τῷ	τοῖς	ταῖς	τοῖς
Acc.	τόν	τήν	τό	τούς	τάς	τά

[1] See Moulton and Howard, *A Grammar of New Testament Greek*, Vol. II, p. 117 for history of forms.

The Substantive

Paradigms of representative types follow. They fall
into three declensions.

I. THE FIRST (or a-stem) DECLENSION

1. Feminines.

ἡμέρα, 'day.' ἀλήθεια, 'truth.' δόξα, 'glory.' γραφή, 'writing.'

S i n g u l a r

Nom.	ἡ	ἡμέρα	ἀλήθεια	δόξα	γραφή
G. & Ab.	τῆς	ἡμέρας	ἀληθείας	δόξης [2]	γραφῆς
L. I. D.	τῇ	ἡμέρᾳ	ἀληθείᾳ	δόξῃ [2]	γραφῇ
Acc.	τὴν	ἡμέραν	ἀλήθειαν	δόξαν	γραφήν
Voc.		ἡμέρα	ἀλήθεια	δόξα	γραφή

P l u r a l

Nom.	αἱ	ἡμέραι	ἀλήθειαι	δόξαι	γραφαί
G. & Ab.	τῶν	ἡμερῶν	ἀληθειῶν	δοξῶν	γραφῶν
L. I. D.	ταῖς	ἡμέραις	ἀληθείαις	δόξαις	γραφαῖς
Acc.	τὰς	ἡμέρας	ἀληθείας	δόξας	γραφάς
Voc.		ἡμέραι	ἀλήθειαι	δόξαι	γραφαί

2. Masculines.

προφήτης, 'prophet.' μαθητής, 'disciple.' νεανίας, 'youth.'

S i n g u l a r

Nom.	ὁ	προφήτης	μαθητής	νεανίας
G. & Ab.	τοῦ	προφήτου	μαθητοῦ	νεανίου
L. I. D.	τῷ	προφήτῃ	μαθητῇ	νεανίᾳ
Acc.	τὸν	προφήτην	μαθητήν	νεανίαν
Voc.		προφῆτα	μαθητά	νεανία

[2] This change in the vowel of the genitive and dative forms (from
α to η) occurs to all nouns of this class where the α-vowel is short.

Plural

Nom.	οἱ προφῆται	μαθηταί	νεανίαι
G. & Ab.	τῶν προφητῶν	μαθητῶν	νεανιῶν
L. I. D.	τοῖς προφήταις	μαθηταῖς	νεανίαις
Acc.	τοὺς προφήτας	μαθητάς	νεανίας
Voc.	προφῆται	μαθηταί	νεανίαι

II. The Second (or o-stem) Declension

1. Masculines.[3]

φίλος, 'friend.' υἱός, 'son.' δοῦλος, 'slave.' ἄνθρωπος, 'man.'

Singular

Nom.	ὁ φίλος	υἱός	δοῦλος	ἄνθρωπος
G. & Ab.	τοῦ φίλου	υἱοῦ	δούλου	ἀνθρώπου
L. I. D.	τῷ φίλῳ	υἱῷ	δούλῳ	ἀνθρώπῳ
Acc.	τὸν φίλον	υἱόν	δοῦλον	ἄνθρωπον
Voc.	φίλε	υἱέ	δοῦλε	ἄνθρωπε

Plural

Nom.	οἱ φίλοι	υἱοί	δοῦλοι	ἄνθρωποι
G. & Ab.	τῶν φίλων	υἱῶν	δούλων	ἀνθρώπων
L. I. D.	τοῖς φίλοις	υἱοῖς	δούλοις	ἀνθρώποις
Acc.	τοὺς φίλους	υἱούς	δούλους	ἀνθρώπους
Voc.	φίλοι	υἱοί	δοῦλοι	ἄνθρωποι

2. Neuters.

τέκνον, 'child.' δῶρον, 'gift.'

Singular | Plural

Nom.	τὸ τέκνον	δῶρον	τὰ τέκνα	δῶρα
G. & Ab.	τοῦ τέκνου	δώρου	τῶν τέκνων	δώρων
L. I. D.	τῷ τέκνῳ	δώρῳ	τοῖς τέκνοις	δώροις
Acc.	τὸ τέκνον	δῶρον	τὰ τέκνα	δῶρα
Voc.	τέκνον	δῶρον	τέκνα	δῶρα

[3] There is a group of nouns in this declension having the same forms as the masculines which are accompanied by the feminine forms of the article. Some of the more common of these in the New Testament are: ἡ ὁδός, 'the way'; ἡ ἔρημος, 'the waste place'; ἡ τρίβος, 'the path'; ἡ νόσος, 'the sickness.' The first three occur in Mk. 1:3.

III.   THE THIRD (or Consonant-stem) DECLENSION

1.   Stems Ending in Mutes.

νύξ, 'night.' σάρξ, 'flesh.' ἐλπίς, 'hope.' χάρις, 'grace.'

Stem: νυκτ-   σαρκ-   ἐλπιδ-   χαριτ-

S i n g u l a r

Nom.	ἡ	νύξ	σάρξ	ἐλπίς	χάρις
G. & Ab.	τῆς	νυκτός ⁴	σαρκός ⁴	ἐλπίδος	χάριτος
L. I. D.	τῇ	νυκτί ⁴	σαρκί ⁴	ἐλπίδι	χάριτι
Acc.	τὴν	νύκτα	σάρκα	ἐλπίδα	χάριν ⁵
Voc.		νύξ	σάρξ	ἐλπί	χάρις

P l u r a l

Nom.	αἱ	νύκτες	σάρκες	ἐλπίδες	χάριτες
G. & Ab.	τῶν	νυκτῶν ⁴	σαρκῶν ⁴	ἐλπίδων	χαρίτων
L. I. D.	ταῖς	νυξί(ν) ⁴	σαρξί(ν)⁴	ἐλπίσι(ν)	χάρισι(ν)
Acc.	τὰς	νύκτας	σάρκας	ἐλπίδας	χάριτας
Voc.		νύκτες	σάρκες	ἐλπίδες	χάριτες

2.   Stems Ending in Nasals.

δαίμων, 'evil spirit.' ποιμήν, 'shepherd.' αἰών, 'age.'

Stem: δαιμον-   ποιμεν-   αἰων-

S i n g u l a r

Nom.	ὁ	δαίμων	ποιμήν	αἰών ⁶
G. & Ab.	τοῦ	δαίμονος	ποιμένος	αἰῶνος
L. I. D.	τῷ	δαίμονι	ποιμένι	αἰῶνι
Acc.	τὸν	δαίμονα	ποιμένα	αἰῶνα

P l u r a l

Nom.	οἱ	δαίμονες	ποιμένες	αἰῶνες
G. & Ab.	τῶν	δαιμόνων	ποιμένων	αἰώνων
L. I. D.	τοῖς	δαίμοσι(ν)	ποιμέσι(ν)	αἰῶσι(ν)
Acc.	τοὺς	δαίμονας	ποιμένας	αἰῶνας

There are no separate vocative forms in this type.

⁴ In monosyllables of this declension, the accent regularly falls in the ultima in the genitive and dative forms, both singular and plural.

⁵ In *koine* Greek, the form χάριτα, and even χάριταν, is found for the acc. sing., χάριν.

⁶ This word represents a class where there is no vowel change in the stem, such as occurs in ποιμήν, ποιμένος, κ.τ.λ. Those undergoing the vowel change are said to belong to the Strong Inflection.

3. Stems Ending in Liquids.

(ὁ) πατήρ, 'father.' (ἡ) μήτηρ, 'mother.' (ἡ) χείρ, 'hand.'
(ὁ) σωτήρ, 'saviour.'

Stem: πατερ-   μητερ-   χειρ-
      σωτηρ-

Singular

Nom.	πατήρ	μήτηρ	χείρ	σωτήρ
G. & Ab.	πατρός	μητρός	χειρός [7]	σωτῆρος
L. I. D.	πατρί	μητρί	χειρί [7]	σωτῆρι
Acc.	πατέρα	μητέρα	χεῖρα	σωτῆρα
Voc.	πάτερ			

Plural

Nom.	πατέρες	μητέρες	χεῖρες	σωτῆρες
G. & Ab.	πατέρων	μητέρων	χειρῶν	σωτήρων
L. I. D.	πατράσι(ν)	μητράσι(ν)	χερσί(ν)	σωτῆρσι(ν)
Acc.	πατέρας	μητέρας	χεῖρας	σωτῆρας

There are no vocative forms in the plural.

4. Stems Ending in -σ-.

(τὸ) τέλος, 'end.'   (ὁ) συγγενής, 'kinsman.'
Stem: τελεσ-   συγγενεσ-

Singular

Nom.	τέλος
G. & Ab.	τέλους = -ε(σ)ος
L. I. D.	τέλει = -ε(σ)ι
Acc.	τέλος

συγγενής
συγγενοῦς
συγγενεῖ
συγγενῆ = -ε(σ)α

Plural

Nom.	τέλη = -ε(σ)α
G. & Ab.	τελῶν = -ε(σ)ων
L. I. D.	τέλεσι = -εσ(σ)ι
Acc.	τέλη = -ε(σ)α

συγγενεῖς = -ε(σ)ες
συγγενῶν
συγγενέσι(ν)
συγγενεῖς

There are no vocative forms here.

[7] In monosyllables of this declension, the accent regularly falls in the ultima in the genitive and dative forms, both singular and plural.

5. Stems Ending in Semi-vowels.

(ἡ)πόλις, 'city.' (ἡ)ἰσχύς, 'strength.' (ὁ)βασιλεύς, 'king.'
Stem: πολει(ι)- ἰσχυ- βασιλευ-

S i n g u l a r

Nom.	πόλις	ἰσχύς	βασιλεύς
G. & Ab.	πόλεως [8]	ἰσχύος	βασιλέως
L. I. D.	πόλει	ἰσχύϊ	βασιλεῖ
Acc.	πόλιν	ἰσχύν	βασιλέα
Voc.	πόλι		βασιλεῦ

P l u r a l

Nom.	πόλεις	ἰσχύες	βασιλεῖς
G. & Ab.	πόλεων [8]	ἰσχύων	βασιλέων
L. I. D.	πόλεσι(ν)	ἰσχύσι(ν)	βασιλεῦσι(ν)
Acc.	πόλεις	ἰσχύας	βασιλεῖς

There are no vocative forms in the plural.

For a much fuller and more comprehensive treatment of the declensions see Moulton and Howard, *A Grammar of New Testament Greek*, Vol. II, pp. 117-155.

The Meaning of Cases

It is very important to approach the interpretation of a case from the viewpoint of the primary meaning of that particular case.

1. Nominative

The *nominative* is primarily the 'naming' case. The Greeks called it ἡ ὀνομαστικὴ πτῶσις. Its commonest use is as 'subject' of the sentence. As a matter of fact, originally the subject of the sentence was expressed by the personal ending of the verb: e. g., in the form λέγ-ει, the ending -ει is the real subject. But since the meaning of this ending was indefinite (he, she, or it), it was often felt to be necessary to name the subject

[8] Forms like πόλεως and πόλεων seem to be a breach of the rules of accent. This is due to the accent of such forms having become fixed when the genitive singular was πόληος. By metathesis of quantity, πόληος became πόλεως. The plural πόλεων followed the singular in accent.

more definitely, so a noun was used. This noun (substantive), used to name the subject, was in apposition with the subject expressed by the personal ending. As language became less and less inflected, the substantive came to be thought of as the subject of the sentence. There are a number of other uses of the nominative:

a. Nominative by apposition

A substantive in apposition with another in the nominative case is normally put in the nominative case. Sometimes, due to laxity in grammatical structure, the nominative may be in apposition with another case: e. g., Rev. 3:12, where the participle ἡ καταβαίνουσα is in apposition with τῆς καινῆς Ἰερουσαλήμ. This lax usage is a characteristic of Revelation.

b. Predicate nominative

The verbs εἰμί, γίνομαι, ὑπάρχω, require the nominative case after them as well as in their 'subjects.' Cf. Jn. 4:11; 1:14; Acts 16:3.

c. The 'hanging nominative' (nominativus pendens).[9]

This construction occurs occasionally: e. g., Rev. 3:21, Ὁ νικῶν δώσω αὐτῷ, 'The one overcoming, I will give to him.' Here the writer begins the sentence with a participle in the nominative case, which is later made to agree in sense with a pronoun in the dative case, but is left suspended with no grammatical agreement. This, like the nominative in apposition with another case, is a characteristic of the style of Revelation. Cf. Rev. 2:26; 3:12.

d. Nominative absolute

This is used in the titles of books: Ἀποκάλυψις Ἰωάνου (Rev. 1:1), 'The Revelation of John'; in the salutation of letters: Παῦλος δοῦλος ... κλῆτος ἀπόστολος (Rom. 1:1), 'Paul a bondservant . . . called as an apostle.'

In Mt. 15:32, ἡμέραι τρεῖς, 'for three days,' is used where the accusative for extent of time would have been expected.

[9] See Anacolouthon, p. 155a.

2. Genitive

The *genitive* case,[10] ἡ γεννητικὴ πτῶσις (Lat., *casus genitivus*), is primarily the 'describing' case. Its function is adjectival. In fact, comparative grammar shows that this usage is older than the adjective. The name is misleading, for it means 'generative,' 'productive.' A better name has been suggested, ἡ γενικὴ πτῶσις, i. e., the case which gives the genus or kind. Regardless of the name, it is the descriptive case.

A thing may be described from many viewpoints, so the genitive case will have a variety of meanings:

a. It may describe from the standpoint of ownership, then it is the genitive of possession: τὸν δοῦλον τοῦ ἀρχιερέως (Mt. 26:51), 'the slave belonging to the high priest.' This usage is about the only one left in popular English, so the notion is prevalent that possession is the primary meaning of this case. This is not true. It is the residuary usage in English, but only one of many in Greek.

b. It may describe from the standpoint of value, then it is called the genitive of price: Οὐχὶ δύο στρουθία ἀσσαρίου πωλεῖται; (Mt. 10:29), 'Are not two sparrows sold for a farthing?' Cf. Lk. 12:6; Rev. 6:6.

A similar genitive may express the penalty imposed: Mt. 26:66.

c. It may describe from the standpoint of source, then it is called the genitive of source: τρίχας καμήλου (Mk. 1:6), 'made of camel's hair.'

d. It may describe from the standpoint of quality: τὸ σῶμα τῆς ἁμαρτίας (Rom. 6:6), 'the body of sin.' This genitive of quality describes the body as characterized by or subject to sin.

---

[10] A word of caution should be expressed here. The interpreter must remember that the same form may express either the genitive or ablative idea. This question is the first one to be solved. Except with verbs and prepositions, the ablative case is not common in the New Testament. The presumption will be in favor of the form being genitive, if used with another noun. Cf. the Ablative, p. 32.

e. It may be used in apposition to another noun to further define it: τὸν ἀρραβῶνα τοῦ πνεύματος (II Cor. 1:22; 5:5). 'The earnest which is the spirit' is clearer than 'the earnest of the spirit.' Cf. II Cor. 5:1; II Pet. 2:6; Jn. 2:21; Rom. 4:11.

f. There is also a 'Hebraistic genitive'[11] which is primarily a genitive of definition. This construction is found in Sophocles,[12] and also in papyri where no Hebrew influence can be found. But it is very common in the LXX and the New Testament. This is due, no doubt in large part, to translation of the Hebrew idiom, the construct state of the noun. Cf. Mk. 2:26, οἱ ἄρτοι τῆς προθέσεως, 'the loaves of the setting forth,' 'the shew bread'; Lk. 4:22, οἱ λόγοι τῆς χάριτος, 'the words of grace.'

See also the many expressions using υἱός or τέκνον with a genitive as substitute for an adjective: Mk. 2:19; 3:17; Mt. 23:15; Lk. 10:6.

g. It may express the idea of time or place. In this sense, according to Robertson,[13] it means "this time and not that time," or "here not there." Both the locative and the accusative may express time or place. The locative answers the question 'when' or 'where,' while the accusative answers the question 'how long' or 'how far.' An example of the genitive expressing time is: χειμῶνος (Mt. 24:20), 'in winter.' It means 'winter' as contrasted with 'summer.' In the same verse, σαββάτῳ, 'on the Sabbath,' marks a point of time. Probably too sharp distinction should not be made between the genitive of time or place and the locative for these ideas. A writer might well have used them interchangeably with no consciousness of real difference.

h. The objective and the subjective genitive come in a special class. In these, the genitive case of one sub-

---

[11] Moulton and Howard, *A Grammar of New Testament Greek*, Vol. II, pp. 440, 441.
[12] See Jebb's *Notes on Antigone*, p. 114.
[13] *A Grammar of the Greek New Testament in the Light of Historical Research*, p. 522.

stantive is used with another substantive which expresses action. If the substantive in the genitive case is the agent of the action expressed by the other, it is called a subjective genitive.

If the substantive in the genitive case is the recipient of the action, it is called an objective genitive.

Moulton[14] states that the interpretation of this genitive is entirely a matter of exegesis and not of grammar. The immediate context and general usage must be called in to decide the point. In II Cor. 5:14, ἡ ἀγάπη τοῦ Χριστοῦ συνέχει ἡμᾶς ('the love of Christ constrains us') could mean 'the love which Christ has for us,' or 'the love which we have for Christ.' The immediate context does not solve this problem here, but general New Testament usage (cf. Gal. 2:20) makes it quite clear that Paul is speaking of Christ's love for him as the force which concentrates his energies on his task. This example, then, is a subjective genitive. In I Cor. 1:6, μαρτύριον τοῦ Χριστοῦ, 'testimony concerning Christ,' is objective genitive; while ὑπομονὴ τῆς ἐλπίδος (I Th. 1:3), 'the steadfastness which arises from hope,' is subjective genitive. Decisions in such cases must be made by the exegete, not the grammarian.

i. The genitive absolute consists of a substantive or pronoun in the genitive used with a participle in the same case: τοῦ Ἰησοῦ γεννηθέντος (Mt. 2:1), 'Jesus having been born'; καταβαινόντων αὐτῶν (Mt. 17:9), 'while they were coming down.' This has a very wide usage in Hellenistic Greek.

Sometimes, in the New Testament, we find the participle in the genitive case standing alone in the genitive absolute: ἐξελθόντων (Mt. 17:14), 'having gone out.' This usage is quite frequent in the papyri.[15]

Many other classifications of the genitive might be given, but that would not serve any good purpose

[14] Prolegomena, p. 72.
[15] Robertson, *A Grammar of the Greek New Testament in the Light of Historical Research*, p. 513.

here. The important thing to learn is that a genitive with another substantive is describing it in some way. The sense of the passage should, as a rule, tell you the exact meaning of the genitive. One should start with the idea that it is describing something, and then ask oneself just how it describes it. It is entirely wrong to start with the thought that the primary idea is possession or separation (as many of the older grammarians held).

j. The following classes of verbs take the genitive as their object:

(1) Verbs of sensation: seeing, hearing, tasting, etc.
(2) Verbs expressing mental attitudes: desiring, caring.
(3) Verbs of remembrance and forgetting.
(4) Verbs of sharing, filling, partaking, etc.
(5) Verbs of accusing, condemning, ruling, etc.

k. The genitive is common with adjectives of fulness, plenty, etc. Cf. Jn. 1:14.

The genitive after prepositions will be discussed under the preposition.

3. Ablative

The *ablative* case, ἡ ἀφαιρετικὴ πτῶσις, has no separate case-form in either classical or Hellenistic Greek. It was lost quite early. Originally, it had not only its own case-idea, but also its distinct case-form. It is the 'whence' case. The fact that the same form was used in classical Greek for both the genitive and the ablative led some of the older grammarians to call the genitive the 'whence' case, or case of separation. Winer, more than a century ago, showed the error of this position.

a. The ablative case modifying other substantives is not common in the New Testament. Where it does occur, the idea of origin, source, or separation is the fundamental notion. An example is probably found in τὴν ἔκβασιν τῆς ἀναστροφῆς (Heb. 13:7), 'the outcome from their life.' Possibly δικαιοσύνη θεοῦ (Rom. 1:17) supplies an example; if so, it means 'the right-eousness which comes from God as its source.' If it is genitive, it could mean the righteousness inherent in God's nature, or the righteousness which He imparts by grace to man. Both are true.

b. The ablative with verbs is fairly common. They fall into the following classes:

(1) Verbs of departure and removal: ἀποστήσονταί τινες τῆς πίστεως (I Tim. 4:1), 'some shall depart from the faith.'

(2) Verbs of ceasing or abstaining: πέπαυται ἁμαρτίας (I Pet. 4:1), 'he has ceased from sin'; ἀπέχεσθαι εἰδωλοθύτων (Acts 15:29), 'to abstain from sacrifices to idols.'

(3) Verbs of missing, lacking, or despairing: εἰ δέ τις λείπεται σοφίας (Jas. 1:5), 'but if anyone lacks wisdom.'

(4) Verbs of differing or excelling: πολλῶν στρουθίων διαφέρετε ὑμεῖς (Mt. 10:31), 'ye are better than many sparrows.'
Comparison is quite commonly expressed by the ablative.

(5) Verbs with the partitive idea: προσελάβοντο τροφῆς (Acts 27:36), 'they partook of food'; δώσω αὐτῷ τοῦ μάννα τοῦ κεκρυμμένου (Rev. 2:17), 'I will give to him from the hidden manna.' Cf. ἐσθίει ἀπὸ τῶν ψιχίων (Mt. 15:27), '(the dogs) eat from the crumbs.' The partitive idea is expressed by the preposition ἀπό.[16] Cf. the 'partitive genitive.'

c. The ablative with adjectives is not especially com-mon: ξένοι τῶν διαθηκῶν (Eph. 2:12), 'strangers from the covenants'; ἐν γεννητοῖς γυναικῶν (Mt. 11:11), 'among men born from women.'

One fundamental idea underlies the ablative: separa-tion. In determining whether a form is genitive or

[16] An interesting contrast is seen between this use of the ablative (Acts 27:36) and the accusative after a verb of eating: φαγεῖν εἰδωλόθυτα (Rev. 2:14), 'to eat sacrifices to idols.' When the whole is meant in the New Testament, the accusative is used.

ablative, one question should be asked: does it indicate kind or separation?

The ablative with prepositions will be discussed under prepositions.

4. Dative

The *dative* case, ἡ δοτικὴ πτῶσις, has as its primary idea that of personal interest. Throughout the history of the Greek language there has been quite a tendency for the dative case to die out. Moulton calls it the "decay of the dative." This is due to the fact that one form was impressed to express three ideas: locative, instrumental and dative. This produced a vagueness in meaning which ultimately led to substitutes being used for the dative. Two of these, εἰς and πρός with the accusative, already appear in the New Testament: εἰς ὑμᾶς (I Pet. 1:4), 'for you'; πρὸς τίνα (Heb. 1:8), used as a synonym for τίνι (Heb. 1:5). In modern Greek, as in English, the preposition with the accusative case has entirely displaced the dative form. In the New Testament however, it is still alive.

When the interpreter is confronted with a 'dative' form, he should remember that any one of three basic ideas may be expressed by this case-form:

1. The idea of place
2. The idea of the instrument
3. The true dative

A good passage upon which to test this is: τῇ γὰρ ἐλπίδι ἐσώθημεν (Rom. 8:24). Does Paul mean to say 'We are saved by hope' (instrumental), 'in hope' (locative), or 'to' (or 'for') 'hope' (dative)? If the case is dative, hope is, in a sense, personified and becomes the end of salvation rather than a means to that end. If the case is locative, hope is regarded as the sphere in which salvation occurs. If the case is instrumental, hope is considered as a means used in saving men. The only scientific way in which to decide this sort of question is to appeal to the Pauline viewpoint as reflected in the New Testament. Undoubtedly the instrumental is more consistent with that. The only objection is that Paul teaches salvation by faith elsewhere. But does faith as a means of salvation exclude hope? How do the two virtues differ? A glance at the context of Rom. 8:24 will reveal the propriety in using hope here rather than faith.

a. The dative is most commonly used to express the indirect object: Μὴ δῶτε τὸ ἅγιον τοῖς κυσίν (Mt. 7:6), 'Do not give that which is holy to the dogs.' This is probably the oldest use of the dative.

b. It may express advantage or disadvantage. In one case, the personal interest is affected favorably and in the other, unfavorably: καρπὸς . . . σπείρεται τοῖς ποιοῦσιν εἰρήνην (Jas. 3:18), 'fruit . . . sown for those making peace'; μαρτυρεῖτε ἑαυτοῖς (Mt. 23:31), 'ye testify against yourselves.'

c. It is often used as the direct object of transitive verbs which express personal relations, such as commanding, enjoying, pleasing, obeying, serving, worshipping, etc.: δουλεύω νόμῳ θεοῦ (Rom. 7:25), 'I serve the law of God.'

d. It may be used with intransitive verbs: τί ὑμῖν δοκεῖ; (Mt. 18:12), 'what seems to you?'

e. Once, the dative expresses agent: οὐδὲν ἄξιον θανάτου ἐστὶν πεπραγμένον αὐτῷ (Lk. 23:15), 'nothing worthy of death has been done by him.'

The dative with prepositions will be discussed under prepositions.

5. Locative

The *locative* case, ἡ τοπικὴ πτῶσις, has no form separate from the dative and instrumental in historical Greek, except for a few surviving adverbial forms: e. g., ἐκεῖ. The term 'dative of place,' as used by some grammarians instead of 'locative case,' is actually meaningless. The dative idea and the idea of place do not merge in this manner. Not only did they have a separate meaning historically, but also a separate form. The locative simply answers the question 'where.' It may locate both in time and in space.

a. Time: τῇ μιᾷ σαββάτων (Lk. 24:1), 'on the first (day) of the week.'

b. Space: τῷ θυσιαστηρίῳ παρεδρεύοντες (I Cor. 9:13), 'attending (sit beside) the altar.'

c. Figurative usage: πορευομένη τῷ φόβῳ (Acts 9:31), 'walking in fear.'

6. Instrumental

The *instrumental* case, ἡ χρηστικὴ πτῶσις, also called associative-instrumental, describes the means or instrument. Where a person is involved, the associative idea may come in. The older grammarians called this the 'instrumental dative.' There is no dative idea in it.

a. It may be used with expressions of time: χρόνοις αἰωνίοις (Rom. 16:25), 'by means of times eternal.' Here time is regarded as the medium through which a thing is accomplished.

b. The associative idea is found in such passages as: τίς μετοχὴ δικαιοσύνῃ καὶ ἀνομίᾳ; (II Cor. 6:14), 'what fellowship between righteousness and lawlessness?' Here righteousness and lawlessness are, so to speak, personified.

c. It may be used to express the idea of manner: δημοσίᾳ (Acts 16:37), 'publicly'; λάθρᾳ (Mt. 2:7), 'secretly.'

d. It may be used to express cause, motive or occasion: ἐγὼ δὲ λιμῷ ὧδε ἀπόλλυμαι (Lk. 15:17), 'I am perishing here because of famine.'

e. The commonest usage is to express means: οὐ φθαρτοῖς ἀργυρίῳ ἢ χρυσίῳ ἐλυτρώθητε . . . ἀλλὰ τιμίῳ αἵματι (I Pet. 1:18f), 'not with corruptible things, such as silver and gold, were ye ransomed . . . but with the precious blood.'

The instrumental with prepositions will be discussed under prepositions.

7. Accusative

The *accusative* case, ἡ αἰτιατικὴ πτῶσις, has as its primary meaning that of extension. This is the oldest case of all and has the most general usage. "The accusative measures an idea as to its content, scope, direction."[17]

a. It is the normal case to use after transitive verbs, unless there is a distinct reason for using some other case (see dative and genitive). Gradually the accusative displaced all other cases as objects of verbs.

(1) Where the verb and its object have the same root, it is called the cognate accusative: ἁμαρτά-νοντα ἁμαρτίαν (I Jn. 5:16), 'sinning a sin.'
Sometimes, the verb and its object will be from a totally different root, but the idea is the same: μὴ φοβούμεναι μηδεμίαν πτόησιν (I Pet. 3:6), 'fearing no fear at all.'
This is called an analogous cognate accusative.

(2) Many verbs take two accusatives:

(a) Verbs of saying often take two accusatives, the second being a predicate accusative, practically in apposition with the first: οὐκέτι ὑμᾶς λέγω δούλους (Jn. 15:15), 'no longer do I call you servants.'

There is a predicate accusative after εἰς in the New Testament which is usually found in passages quoted from the LXX: τέθεικά σε εἰς φῶς ἐθνῶν (Acts 13:47, quoted from Isa. 49:6), 'I have placed thee as a light for Gentiles.'

(b) Verbs of asking and teaching, clothing, unclothing and anointing usually have a double accusative of the person and the thing: ὑμᾶς διδάξει πάντα (Jn. 14:26), 'he will teach you all things'; ἐρωτήσω ὑμᾶς λόγον ἕνα (Mt. 21:24), 'I will ask you one word (question)'; ἐξέδυσαν αὐτὸν τὰ ἱμάτια αὐτοῦ (Mt. 27:31), 'they took off his

---

[17] Robertson, *A Grammar of the Greek New Testament in the Light of Historical Research*, p. 468.

garments'; ἔχρισέν σε ὁ θεὸς ἔλαιον (Heb. 1:9, quoted from Ps. 45:7), 'God anointed thee with oil.'

ἀλείφω, 'anoint,' is used with an accusative and an instrumental case in Mk. 6:13: καὶ ἤλειφον ἐλαίῳ πολλοὺς ἀρρώστους, 'and they were anointing with oil many sick people.'

(c) Verbs of swearing may take two accusatives: ὁρκίζω σε τὸν θεόν (Mk. 5:7), 'I adjure thee by God.'

(d) Verbs of doing good or evil may take a double accusative: Ἰουδαίους οὐδὲν ἠδίκηκα (Acts 25:10), 'I have wronged the Jews in no respect'; τί οὖν ποιήσω Ἰησοῦν; (Mt. 27:22), 'what then shall I do with Jesus?'

When these verbs are in the passive, the accusative of the person becomes the subject of the verb and in the nominative case. The other substantive remains in the accusative case.

b. The accusative is quite common as a means of expressing both extent of time and space. In these constructions it answers the question 'how long' or 'how far': τοσαῦτα ἔτη δουλεύω σοι (Lk. 15:29), 'I have served thee so many years'; προσελθὼν μικρόν (Mt. 26:39), 'having gone forward a little way.'

c. The adverbial accusative is fairly common in the New Testament. A good example is seen in: ἀνέπεσαν οἱ ἄνδρες τὸν ἀριθμὸν ὡς πεντακισχίλιοι (Jn. 6:10), where τὸν ἀριθμόν means 'in number.'

The most frequent usage is where the accusative case is used as a pure adverb. (See discussion on the adverb.)

(1) There are a few cases of the accusative absolute in the New Testament: γνώστην ὄντα σε (Acts 26:3), 'you being an expert.'
(2) The accusative of general reference with the infinitive will be discussed under the infinitive.
(3) The accusative with the preposition will be discussed under prepositions.

8. Vocative

The *vocative* (in reality, not truly a case), ἡ κλητικὴ πτῶσις, is used in direct address. The declensions should be consulted as to its case-form.

a. ὦ with the vocative is rare in the New Testament, occurring seventeen times. All but four of these instances are in Luke and Paul. It usually has a note of solemnity where it occurs.[18] Cf. ὦ γενεὰ ἄπιστος (Mk. 9:19), 'O faithless generation.'

b. In the New Testament, the article with the nominative case-form is often used for the vocative: ὁ πατήρ (Mk. 14:36), 'Father,' not 'the Father.' There are about sixty instances of this usage in the New Testament. Delbrück and Moulton find it quite in keeping with Indo-Germanic usage.

It should be noted, however, that the regular Aramaic idiom calls for the article with the vocative. See Ἀββᾶ (Mk. 14:36). The final alpha in ἀββᾶ represents the Aramaic article. So, Ἀββᾶ ὁ πατήρ (Mk. 14:36), literally translated, would be 'Father! Father!' Possibly here the Greek article, ὁ, is due to the literal translation of Ἀββᾶ, although it is good Greek.[19]

THE ADJECTIVE

Origin

The adjective began its career as a noun which might be used either as a substantive or as an adjective. This usage survives in English: e. g., in the sentences, 'This is a red apple' and 'This is an apple cart,' we have the word 'apple' serving first as a substantive and second as an adjective. Gradually a distinct class of words became specialized as adjectives. Their name, ὀνόματα ἐπίθετα, calls attention at once to their origin as nouns and to their function as descriptive words (cf. 'epithet').

[18] Moulton thinks that it does not have this emphasis in Luke. Proleg., p. 71.
[19] Cf. τὸ κοράσιον (Mk. 5:41), 'maid.'

Forms

The adjective is declined after the analogy of the substantive, and agrees in gender, number and case with the substantive it modifies.

1. Adjectives of three endings.

a. The majority of adjectives have three endings, i. e., a separate form for each gender.

Of these adjectives of three terminations, the majority belong to the second and first declensions: e. g., καλός, καλή, καλόν, 'good'; ἅγιος, ἁγία, ἅγιον, 'holy.'

	Singular			Plural		
	M.	F.	N.	M.	F.	N.
Nom.	καλός	καλή	καλόν	καλοί	καλαί	καλά
G. & Ab.	καλοῦ	καλῆς	καλοῦ	καλῶν	καλῶν	καλῶν
L. I. D.	καλῷ	καλῇ	καλῷ	καλοῖς	καλαῖς	καλοῖς
Acc.	καλόν	καλήν	καλόν	καλούς	καλάς	καλά
Voc.	καλέ					
Nom.	ἅγιος	ἁγία	ἅγιον	ἅγιοι	ἅγιαι	ἅγια
G. & Ab.	ἁγίου	ἁγίας	ἁγίου	ἁγίων	ἁγίων	ἁγίων
L. I. D.	ἁγίῳ	ἁγίᾳ	ἁγίῳ	ἁγίοις	ἁγίαις	ἁγίοις
Acc.	ἅγιον	ἁγίαν	ἅγιον	ἁγίους	ἁγίας	ἅγια
Voc.	ἅγιε					

It will be noted that the masculine and neuter forms belong to the second declension, while the feminine belongs to the first.

b. A considerable group of adjectives of three endings belong to the third and first declensions: e. g., πᾶς, πᾶσα, πᾶν, 'all.'

	Singular			Plural		
	M.	F.	N.	M.	F.	N.
Nom.	πᾶς	πᾶσα	πᾶν	πάντες	πᾶσαι	πάντα
G. & Ab.	παντός	πάσης	παντός	πάντων	πασῶν	πάντων
L. I. D.	παντί	πάσῃ	παντί	πᾶσι(ν)	πάσαις	πᾶσι(ν)
Acc.	πάντα	πᾶσαν	πᾶν	πάντας	πάσας	πάντα

2. Adjectives of two endings.

a. A group of adjectives belonging to the second declension have only two endings. The most of these are compounds: e. g., ἄπιστος, ἄπιστον, 'unfaithful.' These are declined just as the substantives of the second declension are.

b. Another group belonging to the third declension have two endings: e. g., ἀληθής, ἀληθές, 'true.'

	Singular		**Plural**	
	M. & F.	N.	M. & F.	N.
Nom.	ἀληθής	ἀληθές	ἀληθεῖς	ἀληθῆ
G. & Ab.	ἀληθοῦς	ἀληθοῦς	ἀληθῶν	ἀληθῶν
L. I. D.	ἀληθεῖ	ἀληθεῖ	ἀληθέσι(ν)	ἀληθέσι(ν)
Acc.	ἀληθῆ	ἀληθές	ἀληθεῖς	ἀληθῆ
Voc.	ἀληθές			

3. Adjectives of one ending.

A very small group have only one ending: e. g., ἀπάτωρ (masc.) and ἀμήτωρ (fem.), 'without father,' 'without mother.' They occur only once in the New Testament: Heb. 7:3.

Position in the Sentence

The adjective may have either of two positions in the sentence: attributive or predicative.

1. The attributive adjective can usually be recognized by the article which precedes it: τὸ ὕδωρ τὸ ζῶν (Jn. 4:11), 'the water the living.' The other normal position for the attributive adjective is: τὸ ζῶν ὕδωρ, 'the living water.' The meaning is essentially the same, although the idea in the adjective may be a little more emphatically expressed by the former position.

(1) It should be noted here that a phrase, ἡ κατ᾽ ἐκλογὴν πρόθεσις (Rom. 9:11), 'the according to election purpose'; an adverb, τῆς ἄνω κλήσεως (Phil. 3:14), 'of the upward calling'; or a pronoun or substantive, τὸ ἐμὸν ὄνομα (Mt. 18:20), 'my name,' can be used with the force of an attributive adjective.

(2) Occasionally, the attributive adjective is used without an article, as in ὕδωρ ζῶν (Jn. 4:10), 'living water.' It will be noted that in such constructions the substantive also does not have the article.

(3) The adjective πολύς often takes the predicative position, ὁ ὄχλος πολύς (Jn. 12:9), 'the great crowd,' even when attributive in meaning. This may be due to the fact that it forms a composite idea with ὄχλος.

2. The predicative adjective does not have the article: τὸ φρέαρ ἐστὶν βαθύ (Jn. 4:11), 'the well is deep'; ὁ ποιήσας με ὑγιῆ (Jn. 5:11), 'the one having made me well.' The copulative verb is quite frequently omitted in a Greek sentence. This does not affect the force of the predicative adjective.

The difference in meaning between the attributive and the predicative adjective consists in the fact that the predicative adjective makes a statement about the subject, as in τὸ φρέαρ ἐστὶν βαθύ (Jn. 4:11), which is the main point of the sentence. The attributive adjective simply supplies an incidental description of some substantive in the sentence, e. g., τὸ βαθὺ φρέαρ, 'the deep well.'

Comparison of Adjectives

There are two types of endings in the comparison of adjectives: -τερος, -τατος and -ιων, -ιστος.

The regular forms are:

Positive	Comparative	Superlative
μικρός [20] (small)	μικρότερος (smaller)	μικρότατος (smallest)
μακάριος (blessed)	μακαριώτερος (more blessed)	μακαριώτατος (most blessed)
ἀσθενής (weak)	ἀσθενέστερος (weaker)	ἀσθενέστατος (weakest)

[20] Both regular and irregular.

There are a group irregular in their comparison. Some of the more common of these follow:

Positive	Comparative	Superlative
ἀγαθός	βελτίων	
	κρείσσων	
	(κρείττων)	κράτιστος
κακός	ἥσσων	
	χείρων	
μέγας	μείζων [21]	μέγιστος
μικρός [20]	(μικρότερος)	(μικρότατος)
	ἐλάσσων	ἐλάχιστος [21]
πολύς	πλείων	πλεῖστος
	πλέων	

It is seldom that the superlative forms have the true superlative idea in the New Testament. The idea is usually elative, like our 'very.' See ὄχλος πλεῖστος (Mk. 4:1), 'a very great crowd,' not 'the greatest crowd' ever assembled.

An exception to this general rule is seen in ὕψιστος, 'highest,' which is always superlative in the New Testament: Mk. 5:7; Mt. 21:9. In each case the adjective refers to God. The elative sense would mean 'very high,' but God is regarded as the 'highest.'

There is a tendency in Hellenistic Greek for the comparative and the superlative to become confused. In I Cor. 13:13, μείζων δὲ τούτων ἡ ἀγάπη, 'the greater of these is love,' the comparative form is used with three objects, instead of the superlative. On the other hand, in Jn. 20:4, πρῶτος, 'first,' is used where πρότερον, 'former,' might have been expected. Only two disciples are running to the tomb, but πρῶτος is used of the 'first' arrival. From this, it is evident that the use of πρῶτον in Acts 1:1 should not be pressed as a proof that Luke planned a third volume.

Verbal adjectives will be discussed under the participle.

[21] A few odd forms are found: e. g., ἐλαχιστότερος (Eph. 3:8), where the comparative ending is added to a superlative stem. Cf. μειζοτέραν (III Jn. 4), where the comparative form has a second comparative ending attached. Such forms are due to the fading force of the endings and to desire for emphasis.

THE PRONOUN

The pronoun, as its name suggests, is used instead of the noun. It is a device to render unnecessary the repetition of the noun. It seems to be one of the oldest parts of speech. It has also been the most persistent in retaining its case-forms. In English, where only two case-forms have been retained by the substantive and one by the adjective, the pronoun has kept three.

The pronoun has a great variety of uses. In the Greek, a personal pronoun is not used as the subject of the verb, unless the author desires to be emphatic, for the simple reason that the personal endings make it unnecessary. The personal endings themselves seem to be of pronominal origin.

There are nine distinct classes of pronouns (ten, if one includes the negative pronouns).

1. The *personal pronouns* are:

   a. First person: ἐγώ (originally ἐγών), with which compare the Sanskrit *'aham,'* Lat. *ego*, Germ. *ich*, Ang.-Sax. *ic*, Eng. *I*.

	Singular	Plural
Nom.	ἐγώ	ἡμεῖς
G. & Ab.	ἐμοῦ (μου)	ἡμῶν
L. I. D.	ἐμοί (μοι)	ἡμῖν
Acc.	ἐμέ (με)	ἡμᾶς

   b. Second person: σύ (Doric τύ), with which compare the Sanskrit *tuam*, Lat. *tu*, Germ. *du*, Eng. *thou*.

	Singular	Plural
Nom.	σύ	ὑμεῖς
G. & Ab.	σοῦ	ὑμῶν
L. I. D.	σοί	ὑμῖν
Acc.	σέ	ὑμᾶς

c. Third person: αὐτός, αὐτή, αὐτό.

	Singular			Plural		
	M.	F.	N.	M.	F.	N.
Nom.	αὐτός	αὐτή	αὐτό	αὐτοί	αὐταί	αὐτά
G. & Ab.	αὐτοῦ	αὐτῆς	αὐτοῦ	αὐτῶν	αὐτῶν	αὐτῶν
L. I. D.	αὐτῷ	αὐτῇ	αὐτῷ	αὐτοῖς	αὐταῖς	αὐτοῖς
Acc.	αὐτόν	αὐτήν	αὐτό	αὐτούς	αὐτάς	αὐτά

When αὐτός is in the attributive position, it is an adjective, meaning 'same.'
When it is used in agreement with another substantive, it is an intensive pronoun, meaning 'himself,' etc.
Only when standing alone is it a personal pronoun.

2. The *possessive pronouns* are built on personal stems. They are:

a. First person: ἐμός, ἡμέτερος (plural).

b. Second person: σός, ὑμέτερος (plural).

These are declined like adjectives of the second and first declensions.

(1) There are other ways of expressing possession, such as the use of the article: ἐκτείνας τὴν χεῖρα (Mt. 8:3), 'having stretched forth his hand.' The context makes it clear to whom the article refers.
(2) Another way of expressing the idea of possession is with the genitive case of the personal pronoun.
(3) It will be noted that there is no possessive pronoun in the third person.

3. The *reflexive pronouns* are formed by combining the personal pronouns with the oblique cases of αὐτός. There are, it is obvious, no reflexive pronouns in the nominative.

	Singular			Plural
	1st per.	2nd per.	3rd per.	3rd per.
G. & Ab.	ἐμαυτοῦ	σεαυτοῦ	ἑαυτοῦ	ἑαυτῶν
L. I. D.	ἐμαυτῷ	σεαυτῷ	ἑαυτῷ	ἑαυτοῖς
Acc.	ἐμαυτόν	σεαυτόν	ἑαυτόν	ἑαυτούς

There are no forms of the first or second person plural reflexives in the New Testament, except in ὑμῶν αὐτῶν (I Cor. 5:13; 7:35), 'yourselves.' Sometimes, ἑαυτοῦ is shortened to αὐτοῦ, and in some manuscripts, ἐμαυτοῦ and σεαυτοῦ are shortened to ἐματοῦ and σαυτοῦ. See Jas. 2:8 in B. WH read the shortened form αὐτοῦ for ἑαυτοῦ in more than twenty places. The manuscripts bear them out in this reading.

4. The *intensive pronoun* αὐτός, appears in all persons, genders and numbers. It can be recognized by the presence of another substantive[22] or pronoun agreeing with it in case: αὐτὸς ἐγώ (Rom. 7:25), 'I myself'; αὐτὸς ὁ Ἰωάννης (Mt. 3:4), 'John himself.' The degree of emphasis in the intensive must be judged by the context.

The declension is the same as when used as a personal pronoun.

5. The *demonstrative pronouns* form a large class. All of the later grammarians, such as Robertson and Moulton, include the definite article, ὁ, ἡ, τό, under the demonstrative pronoun.[23] In fact, it was originally a demonstrative pronoun and was weakened to the article. One example of this original usage survives in the New Testament in Acts 17:28, where Luke quotes a line of poetry: τοῦ γὰρ καὶ γένος ἐσμέν, 'For of that one we are the offspring.'

Another line of development heightened the article to the relative ὅς (cf. ὁ ἦν, Rev. 1:4).

The demonstrative usage of the article in the New Testament is frequently resumptive, as in Mt. 2:5, where οἱ δέ refers to παρ' αὐτῶν (Mt. 2:4).

a. οὗτος, αὕτη, τοῦτο, 'this,' is the most common of all the demonstratives. It is a strong demonstrative. Sometimes, it has a note of contempt in it: οὗτος ἔφη

---

[22] Sometimes the substantive in agreement is represented in the personal ending of the verb: αὐτοὶ ἀκηκόαμεν (Jn. 4:42), 'we ourselves have heard.'

[23] See the Article, p. 53.

(Mt. 26:61), 'this one said.' Here the witnesses sneer at Jesus' claims. Sometimes, it has the resumptive or anaphoric force: in Mt. 27:58 it refers to Joseph (Mt. 27:57).

	Singular			Plural		
	M.	F.	N.	M.	F.	N.
Nom.	οὗτος	αὕτη	τοῦτο	οὗτοι	αὗται	ταῦτα
G. & Ab.	τούτου	ταύτης	τούτου	τούτων	τούτων	τούτων
L. I. D.	τούτῳ	ταύτῃ	τούτῳ	τούτοις	ταύταις	τούτοις
Acc.	τοῦτον	ταύτην	τοῦτο	τούτους	ταύτας	ταῦτα

b. ἐκεῖνος, ἐκείνη, ἐκεῖνο, 'that.' Οὗτος refers to the near object, while ἐκεῖνος refers to the more remote. This word may also have a contemptuous force: Jn. 9:28; or resumptive: Jn. 1:8.

	Singular			Plural		
	M.	F.	N.	M.	F.	N.
Nom.	ἐκεῖνος	ἐκείνη	ἐκεῖνο	ἐκεῖνοι	ἐκεῖναι	ἐκεῖνα
G. & Ab.	ἐκείνου	ἐκείνης	ἐκείνου	ἐκείνων	ἐκείνων	ἐκείνων
L. I. D.	ἐκείνῳ	ἐκείνῃ	ἐκείνῳ	ἐκείνοις	ἐκείναις	ἐκείνοις
Acc.	ἐκεῖνον	ἐκείνην	ἐκεῖνο	ἐκείνους	ἐκείνας	ἐκεῖνα

c. ὅδε, ἥδε, τόδε, 'this,' is simply the article plus the enclitic δε. There are only ten examples of this pronoun in the New Testament: Lk. 10:39; Acts 21:11; Jas. 4:13; Rev. 2:1, 8, 12, 18; 3:1, 7, 14.

	Singular			Plural		
	M.	F.	N.	M.	F.	N.
Nom.	ὅδε	ἥδε	τόδε	οἵδε	αἵδε	τάδε
G. & Ab.	τοῦδε	τῆσδε	τοῦδε	τῶνδε	τῶνδε	τῶνδε
L. I. D.	τῷδε	τῇδε	τῷδε	τοῖσδε	ταῖσδε	τοῖσδε
Acc.	τόνδε	τήνδε	τόδε	τούσδε	τάσδε	τάδε

d. τοιοῦτος, τοιαύτη, τοιοῦτο, is the usual correlative demonstrative in the New Testament. It means 'such.' The iota gives it the qualitative force. It

forms the antecedent for a variety of relatives: οἷος
(II Cor. 10:11); ὁποῖος (Acts 26:29); ὅς (Heb. 8:1);
ὅστις (I Cor. 5:1).
For declension, see οὗτος.

e. τοιόσδε, τοιάδε, τοιόνδε, is a correlative demonstrative.
It also means 'such.' The iota gives it the qualitative force. It occurs only once in the New Testament: II Pet. 1:17. It is simply τοιός + δε (the
enclitic). It is used without the article.

f. τοσοῦτος, τοσαύτη, τοσοῦτο, is a correlative demonstrative, 'so much.' Note that only one letter, sigma
instead of iota, distinguishes it from τοιοῦτος. It is
formed from τόσος and οὗτος. It expresses size:
τοσαύτην πίστιν (Mt. 8:10), 'so great faith'; or quantity: ἄρτοι τοσοῦτοι (Mt. 15:33), 'so many loaves.'
It is used as a correlative with ὅσος: Heb. 1:4;
7:20-22.

g. τηλικοῦτος, τηλικαύτη, τηλικοῦτο, is a correlative demonstrative, 'so great.' In classical Greek, it was a
correlative of age, but in the New Testament, it
always refers to size.
It occurs once as a predicate: τηλικαῦτα ὄντα (Jas.
3:4), 'being so great.'
Elsewhere, it is always attributive: Heb. 2:3.
Once, it is used redundantly with οὕτως μέγας:
Rev. 16:18.

h. A miscellaneous group with slight demonstrative
force should be mentioned briefly:

(1) ἄλλος, ἄλλη, ἄλλο, 'other.'
(2) ἕτερος, ἑτέρα, ἕτερον, 'different.' Sometimes, this
means 'other of two,' but should be differentiated
from ἄλλος. See Gal. 1:6.
(3) ὁ δεῖνα, 'so and so,' occurs only once in the New
Testament, and then in the accusative case: Mt.
26:18.
(4) ἕκαστος, ἑκάστη, ἕκαστον, 'each.'

6. The *relative pronoun* has the specialized function of relating clauses to clauses. The name is descriptive of the function. The relative usually agrees with its antecedent in gender and number. Sometimes, the relative is attracted to the case of its antecedent, e. g., Acts 3:25, where the accusative ἥν is attracted to the genitive ἧς by the antecedent, διαθήκης; but attraction does not always occur: τῷ λόγῳ ὅν εἶπεν (Jn. 2:22).

a. ὅς is the common relative. It is used more frequently than all others together.

Occasionally, the relative does not agree with the grammatical gender of its antecedent, but with its natural gender: παιδάριον ὅς ἔχει (Jn. 6:9), 'a small boy who has.' In I Cor. 15:10, εἰμὶ ὃ εἰμί, 'I am what I am,' is not a grammatical slip. Paul wants to bring out a qualitative note by referring to himself with the neuter relative. Εἰμὶ ὅς εἰμί, 'I am who I am,' would have given quite a different turn to Paul's thought.

In I Tim. 3:16, τὸ . . . μυστήριον, is followed by ὅς because Christ is the 'mystery.' A very interesting textual change grew out of this lack of agreement.[24] Another example is found in Eph. 1:14, where πνεῦμα (neuter) is the antecedent followed by ὅς (masculine). This probably indicates that Paul was thinking of the Holy Spirit as a person.

	S i n g u l a r			**P l u r a l**		
	M.	F.	N.	M.	F.	N.
Nom.	ὅς	ἥ	ὅ	οἵ	αἵ	ἅ
G. & Ab.	οὗ	ἧς	οὗ	ὧν	ὧν	ὧν
L. I. D.	ᾧ	ᾗ	ᾧ	οἷς	αἷς	οἷς
Acc.	ὅν	ἥν	ὅ	οὕς	ἅς	ἅ

b. ὅσγε and ὅσπερ are the simple relative plus the intensive enclitics γέ and πέρ.

They are declined like ὅς with the enclitic added.

---

[24] Robertson, *An Introduction to the Textual Criticism of the New Testament*, pp. 151, 158, 160, 213, 214.

c. ὅστις, ὅτι, is commonly called the indefinite relative. In this usage it means 'whoever.' In the New Testament, it is practically confined to the nominative case. There are a few instances of the neuter accusative.

	Singular			**Plural**		
	M.	F.	N.	M.	F.	N.
Nom.	ὅστις	ἥτις	ὅτι	οἵτινες	αἵτινες	ἅτινα
Acc.			ὅτι			ἅτινα

There is also a definite usage, confined largely to causal clauses. A few are merely descriptive. An example of the causative usage is found in Jn. 8:53, ᾽Αβραὰμ ὅστις ἀπέθανεν, 'Abraham seeing that he died.' Cf. Acts 10:47. An example of the descriptive use is found in Mt. 7:15, τῶν ψευδοπροφητῶν οἵτινες ἔρχονται, 'false prophets who come.' Often no real difference can be detected between ὅς and ὅστις.

d. οἷος, οἵα, οἷον, is a correlative qualitative, 'of which kind,' 'such as.' Its antecedent is properly τοιοῦτος, but in the New Testament it is often not expressed. Cf. Mt. 24:21. Sometimes, the antecedent follows: I Cor. 15:48.

e. ὁποῖος, ὁποία, ὁποῖον, is a qualitative relative, corresponding to the interrogative ποῖος. Note the effect of the iota in expressing the qualitative idea, as usual. The meaning is 'such as.'
Only one instance is correlative: Acts 26:29.

f. ὅσος, ὅση, ὅσον, is the quantitative, correlative pronoun, 'as many as,' 'as much as.' It occurs more than a hundred times in the New Testament. Cf. Mk. 6:30, 56.

g. ἡλίκος, ἡλίκη, ἡλίκον, as a relative, may express either age, 'as old as,' or size, 'as tall as.' There are only four examples in the New Testament, all of which are indirect interrogatives. In Col. 2:1, it means 'how great.' In Jas. 3:5, once it means 'how small' and once 'how great': ἰδοὺ ἡλίκον πῦρ ἡλίκην ὕλην ἀνάπτει. 'Behold what sized fire (how small a fire)

kindles what sized forest (how large a forest).'[25]
The basic ambiguity in ἡλίκος (either age or size)
leads to ambiguity in the substantive ἡλικία which
is derived from it. In Jn. 9:21, ἡλικία refers to age;
in Mt. 6:27, it is translated 'stature' in the AV.
The ARV is no doubt more correct in translating it
'the measure of his life.'

7. The *Interrogative pronouns.*

a. τίς, τί, 'who,' is the usual interrogative. It may be
used as an adjective: τίνα μισθὸν ἔχετε; (Mt. 5:46),
'what reward have ye?'; or as a substantive: τίς
ὑπέδειξεν ὑμῖν; (Mt. 3:7),'who warned you?'

	Singular		Plural	
	M. & F.	N.	M. & F.	N.
Nom.	τίς	τί	τίνες	τίνα
G. & Ab.	τίνος	τίνος	τίνων	τίνων
L. I. D.	τίνι	τίνι	τίσι(ν)	τίσι(ν)
Acc.	τίνα	τί	τίνας	τίνα

Occasionally, the interrogative τίς is used where a relative would be
expected.

b. ποῖος, ποία, ποῖον, 'of what sort,' is a qualitative
interrogative. It occurs in the New Testament
sixteen times in indirect questions. Generally, the
qualitative force is present: ποίῳ θανάτῳ; (Jn. 12:33),
'by what sort of death?'; but sometimes, it seems
to be merely equivalent to τίς: ποίᾳ ἡμέρᾳ (Mt. 24:42),
'on what day.' Cf. I Pet. 1:11, where many commentators think a distinction is drawn between τίνα
and ποῖον; others think not.

In modern Greek, it is used as the equivalent of
τίς, and is the usual interrogative.[26]

c. πηλίκος, πηλίκη, πηλίκον, 'how great,' is the quantita-

---

[25] Some manuscripts read ἡλίκος in Gal. 6:11. WH read πηλίκος.
See note on πηλίκος, p. 52.
[26] Robertson, *A Grammar of the Greek New Testament in the Light
of Historical Research,* p. 740.

tive interrogative of size. It occurs only twice in the New Testament: Gal. 6:11;[27] Heb. 7:4.

d. πόσος, πόση, πόσον, 'how many,' 'how much,' is the quantitative interrogative of number or quantity. It occurs chiefly in the Synoptic Gospels: in a direct question, Mt. 15:34; and in an indirect question, Mt. 27:13.

e. ποταπός, ποταπή, ποταπόν, is a late form of ποδαπός. Originally, it meant 'from what country.' In the New Testament, it means 'of what sort,' and is equivalent to ποῖος: ἴδετε ποταπὴν ἀγάπην δέδωκεν ἡμῖν ὁ πατήρ (I Jn. 3:1), 'Behold what manner of love the Father hath bestowed upon us!' It is interesting to consider the effect of the original meaning of the pronoun here: 'Behold what other-worldly love the Father hath bestowed upon us!'

8. The *indefinite pronoun*, τις, τι.

This pronoun, τις, should be distinguished from τίς, the interrogative. It is always an enclitic. It may mean 'any one,' 'anybody': Mt. 11:27; or 'somebody in particular': Acts 5:34. Except for the accent, it is declined like τίς, τί.

Sometimes, it is used as an adjective, meaning 'a kind of': Jas. 1:18; or 'a certain': Lk. 1:5.

Sometimes, πᾶς seems to be used as a virtual equivalent of τις: Mt. 5:22; 13:19.

9. The *reciprocal pronoun*, ἀλλήλων, 'one another,' is a reduplication of ἄλλος, and occurs only in the oblique cases: ἀγαπῶμεν ἀλλήλους (I Jn. 4:7), 'let us love one another.'

Sometimes, ἴδιος is used with virtually a reciprocal force.

The reflexive ἑαυτῶν is sometimes used as a reciprocal. Cf. νουθε-τοῦντες ἑαυτούς (Col. 3:16), 'admonishing one another,' not 'admon-ishing yourselves.' Eph. 5:19 offers another example: λαλοῦντες ἑαυτοῖς, 'speaking to one another,' not 'speaking to yourselves.'

[27] ἡλίκος is read by P⁴⁶B; πηλίκος byℵ ACDFGS. See note on ἡλίκος, p. 51.

10. Another class might be mentioned, i. e., *negative pronouns*, such as οὐδείς and μηδείς, 'no one.'

	M.	F.	N.
Nom.	οὐδείς	οὐδεμία	οὐδέν
G. & Ab.	οὐδενός	οὐδεμιᾶς	οὐδενός
L. I. D.	οὐδενί	οὐδεμιᾷ	οὐδενί
Acc.	οὐδένα	οὐδεμίαν	οὐδέν

μηδείς is declined like οὐδείς. They differ in meaning as οὐ and μή differ.

An alternate spelling of these words was popular in the first century A. D., οὐδείς being spelled οὐθείς and μηδείς rendered μηθείς. The New Testament verb ἐξουθενέω (cf. I Cor. 16:11), 'to make nothing of,' 'to belittle,' was evidently formed on the stem οὐθείς while that spelling was popular.[28]

The Article

Origin

The definite article, ὁ, ἡ, τό, was originally a demonstrative pronoun.[29] The demonstrative use was, along one line, weakened to the article, and, along another, heightened to the relative, ὅς, ἥ, ὅ.

In the Sanskrit, the demonstrative ('sa,' 'sa,' 'tad,' the same as the Greek, ὁ, ἡ, τό) never developed the use as an article.[30] In fact, like the Latin, the Sanskrit never developed either the definite or the indefinite article.[31]

From Homer through Herodotus there was in Greek a distinct development in the use of the definite article.

The indefinite article was never developed in the Greek. The modern European languages have developed an indefinite article out of the numeral 'one.' Cf. the English, *a (one)* ; German, *ein*; French, *un*. There are traces in the Greek of the beginning of the development

---

[28] Moulton and Howard, *A Grammar of New Testament Greek*, Vol. II, p. 111.
[29] See Demonstrative Pronoun, p. 46.
[30] Whitney, *A Sanskrit Grammar*, pp. 171-176.
[31] Robertson, *A Grammar of the Greek New Testament in the Light of Historical Research*, pp. 754, 755.

of an indefinite article: εἷς γραμματεύς (Mt. 8:19), 'a scribe'; νομικός τις (Lk. 10:25), 'a lawyer.' It would not give quite the correct idea to translate these 'one scribe,' and 'a certain lawyer.' This usage of an indefinite article never advanced beyond a few scattered examples. Cf. ἑνός, Rev. 8:13; μίαν, Rev. 9:13.

Function

1. The article points out (*Deictic use*) objects. The Greek grammarians called it ὁριστική (from ὁρίζω, 'I mark off'). It is not so emphatic as the demonstrative pronoun and it does not tell whether the object is near (οὗτος) or distant (ἐκεῖνος).

The article distinguishes:

a. Individuals from individuals
In Mt. 5:1, τὸ ὄρος points to 'the mountain' close at hand. The English versions often miss the flavor which the article gives to the sentence, e. g., τῷ ἁμαρτωλῷ (Lk. 18:13) is rendered 'a sinner.' But the publican was thinking of a particular sinner when he prayed. The article calls attention to this fact. In Jn. 4:27, the AV translates μετὰ γυναικός, 'with the woman.' But the disciples were surprised that their Master would talk with any woman in public.

b. Classes from classes
This' generic' article is rather common: ὁ ἐθνικὸς . . . ὁ τελώνης (Mt. 18:17). Here, gentiles and publicans are set off from other men, as well as from each other.

c. Qualities from qualities
In English, we do not use the article with abstract qualities unless they have been previously mentioned. The Greek may use it: τὰς ὀφειλὰς . . . τὸν φόρον τὸν φόρον . . . τὸ τέλος τὸ τέλος . . . τὸν φόβον τὸν φόβον . . . τὴν τιμὴν τὴν τιμήν (Rom. 13:7); or may omit it: χαρίσματα ἰαμάτων. . .ἐνεργήματα δυνάμεων. . .προφητεία. . .διακρίσεις πνευμάτων . . . γένη γλωσσῶν . . . ἑρμηνεία γλωσσῶν (I Cor. 12:9, 10). The difference in meaning is that in one list a *definite* list of obligations is under con-

sideration, while in the other the *general* endowments of the Holy Spirit are considered.

In the songs in the Apocalypse, usually each of the attributes of God has an article: λαβεῖν τὴν δόξαν καὶ τὴν τιμὴν καὶ τὴν δύναμιν (Rev. 4:11); ἡ εὐλογία καὶ ἡ τιμὴ καὶ ἡ δόξα καὶ τὸ κράτος (Rev. 5:13). But in Rev. 5:12, one article is used with the whole list: τὴν δύναμιν καὶ πλοῦτον καὶ σοφίαν καὶ ἰσχὺν καὶ τιμὴν καὶ δόξαν καὶ εὐλογίαν. In the former examples, each attribute is looked at separately; in the latter, they are looked at as a harmonious whole.[32]

2. The article often refers to something just mentioned.

This is called the *'Anaphoric use.'* In Jn. 4:10, Jesus speaks of living water, ὕδωρ ζῶν; the woman replies in Jn. 4:11, with τὸ ὕδωρ τὸ ζῶν. The article takes up Jesus' mention of living water. Cf. μάγοι (Mt. 2:1); τοὺς μάγους (Mt. 2:7).

3. *Miscellaneous* uses of the article.

a. It may be used as the equivalent of a possessive pronoun: ἀπενίψατο τὰς χεῖρας (Mt. 27:24), 'he washed off his hands.' It is Pilate's own hands that he washed.

b. It may be used with any variety of:

(1) Words: ὁ ἀμήν (Rev. 3:14); τὸ Ἅγαρ (Gal. 4:25); τὸ ἀνέβη (Eph. 4:9); ἀπὸ τοῦ νῦν (Lk. 5:10). In the first two examples, the article points to nouns; in the third, to a verb; and in the fourth, to an adverb. It serves to single each out and make it definite.

---

[32] Other examples of a single article with several nouns are:

(1) ὅ τε Πέτρος καὶ Ἰωάνης καὶ Ἰάκωβος καὶ Ἀνδρέας κ. τ. λ. (Acts 1:13). The eleven disciples are looked at as a group, rather than as separate individuals.

(2) κατανοήσατε τὸν ἀπόστολον καὶ ἀρχιερέα τῆς ὁμολογίας ἡμῶν Ἰησοῦν (Heb. 3:1), 'consider the apostle and high priest of our confession, namely Jesus.' The one article with 'apostle' and 'high priest' calls attention to the fact that both offices are bound up in one personality. 'Jesus' is in explanatory apposition to make clear who that personality is.

(2) Phrases: τῆς ἐν Χριστῷ Ἰησοῦ (Rom. 3:24). The article, τῆς, points to the phrase as an attributive adjective, modifier of the noun, ἀπολυτρώσεως. Without the article, the above phrase would be adverbial, as in κατέκρινε τὴν ἁμαρτίαν ἐν τῇ σαρκί (Rom. 8:3). The insertion of the article, τήν, before ἐν τῇ σαρκί would have located the sin in Jesus' flesh. As the sentence stands, the phrase modifies the verb, κατέκρινε, so it is the *condemnation* of sin which is placed in Jesus' flesh, not the *sin* itself.

(3) Clauses: τό εἰ δύνῃ (Mk. 9:23), the article singles out the conditional clause, 'if thou art able,' in the distressed father's request. It centers the attention on the question as to Jesus' ability to heal the epileptic son.

4. The *non-use* of the article.

a. There are several constructions in which the Greek does not use the article, but in translating into English it must be used.

(1) Prepositional phrases frequently do not use the article even though their meaning is definite: ἐν ἀγορᾷ (Lk. 7:32) does not mean 'in a market-place,' but 'in the market-place.' On the other hand, the article may be used: ἐν τῷ οἴκῳ (Jn. 11:20), 'in the house,' i. e., 'at home.' The latter example illustrates how the English has started along the same road travelled by the Greek, but has not gone so far.

(2) A noun with the genitive may be anarthrous but definite: πύλαι Ἅιδου (Mt. 16:18), 'the gates of Hades'; υἱὲ διαβόλου (Acts 13:10), 'son of the devil'; ποτήριον κυρίου (I Cor. 10:21), 'the cup of the Lord.' The context must decide whether such examples are definite and hence whether or not they require the article in English.

(3) Titles of books or headings frequently do not

use the article, but English idiom calls for it in translation: 'Αποκάλυψις 'Ιησοῦ Χριστοῦ (Rev. 1:1), 'The revelation of Jesus Christ'; 'Αρχὴ τοῦ εὐαγγελίου 'Ιησοῦ Χριστοῦ (Mk. 1:1), 'The beginning of the Gospel of Jesus Christ'; Βίβλος γενέσεως 'Ιησοῦ Χριστοῦ (Mt. 1:1), 'The book of the generation of Jesus Christ.' Cf. I Pet. 1:1, 2.

(4) Frequently ordinal numbers do not have the article but English idiom calls for it: ἕως τρίτου οὐρανοῦ (II Cor. 12:2), 'unto the third heaven.'

b. With proper names usage is not uniform. The purpose of the writer is decisive at this point. A proper name was sufficiently definite in itself to make the article unnecessary, but if it was desirable to call particular attention to a person, it could be used quite effectively: τὸν 'Ιησοῦν ὃν Παῦλος κηρύσσει (Acts 19:13), 'the Jesus whom Paul preaches.'

c. Closely related to this use with proper names is that referring to objects where there is only one of a kind: ἡλίου ἀνατείλαντος (Mt. 13:6), 'the sun having risen'; τὸ ἔργον κυρίου (I Cor. 16:10), 'the work of the Lord.' Such words may also take the article: οὕτως γὰρ ἠγάπησεν ὁ θεὸς τὸν κόσμον (Jn. 3:16), 'for God so loved the world.'

d. A qualitative force is often expressed by the absence of the article: ἐν τοῖς προφήταις (Heb. 1:1), 'in the prophets,' calls attention to a particular group, while ἐν υἱῷ (Heb. 1:2), 'in son,' calls attention to the rank of the Son as a 'spokesman' for God. The ARV in trying to bring out the force of this phrase translates it, 'in his Son,' italicizing 'his.'

e. The predicate of a sentence may be recognized by the absence of the article: θεὸς ἦν ὁ λόγος (Jn. 1:1), 'the Word was God'; καὶ ὁ λόγος σὰρξ ἐγένετο (Jn. 1:14), 'And the Word became flesh'; ἔσονται οἱ ἔσχατοι πρῶτοι (Mt. 20:16), 'the last shall be first.' The article with each of these predicate nouns would equate them and make them interchangeable, e. g., ὁ θεὸς ἦν ὁ λόγος would make God and the Word identical. The effect of this can be seen in ὁ θεὸς ἀγάπη ἐστίν (I Jn. 4:8), 'God is love.' As the sentence now stands 'love' describes a primary quality of God; the article ἡ with ἀγάπη would make God and love equivalents, e. g., God would possess no qualities not subsumed under love.

Summary

The primary function of the article is to make something definite. It may point out something new to the discussion, or something already mentioned.

For the article with the vocative case, see the discussion of the vocative case.

THE VERB

No other part of speech is so important in exegesis as the verb. The verb has two functions: it expresses action (or state), and makes affirmations. Other parts of speech, e. g., the noun, the infinitive, and the participle, may express action, but the finite verb alone can make assertions. It is by means of the personal ending that the verb makes assertions (or affirmations).

There are three ways of making assertions:

1. An assertion may be positive and clearcut. This manner of making an assertion is called the indicative mode (manner).

2. An assertion may be doubtful or hesitant. Either the subjunctive or optative mode is used for these assertions.

3. An assertion may take the form of a command. The imperative mode is then the normal one to use.

Remember that the term mode (mood refers to the frame of mind in which the statement is made) refers to the manner in which a statement is made, not necessarily to the truth or falsity of the statement.

There are two phases of action to be expressed by a verb:

1. The verb tells what kind of action is asserted. This is done by the tense form.
2. The verb tells how that action is related to the subject of the sentence. This is done by the voice.

It is absolutely essential that the student master the conjugation of the verb before he proceeds to do exegesis. He may read commentaries and repeat other men's interpretations without such mastery, but it is utterly impossible for him to do a piece of independent exegesis—the ideal goal of every true expositor and teacher of the New Testament. Nothing adds more freshness of insight and vigor of thought to one's preaching than this. It is not an impossible goal to attain. There are a few basic principles to be kept in mind and some basic facts to learn. Then one may turn to his New Testament for a life of adventure and discovery. To aid the student in mastering the conjugations, the following tables are given, primarily to illustrate principles.

The Conjugation of λύω, *'I loose'* (*a regular verb*)

Stem λυ-

Principal Parts

Pres. Ac.	Fut. Ac.	Aor. Ac.
λύω	λύσω	ἔλυσα
Per. Ac.	Per. M. & P.	Aor. Pass.
λέλυκα	λέλυμαι	ἐλύθην

Before proceeding further, the student should fix in mind the following basic facts of the principal parts, for all forms of λύω will be built on them.

1. The stem of the verb should be isolated in the student's mind.

2. The sign of the future tense, in the regular verb, is sigma attached to the stem and preceding the personal endings.

3. There are three earmarks of the aorist active:
   a. The augment ε- preceding the stem;
   b. The sigma attached to the end of the stem;[33]
   c. The personal ending, alpha.

4. There are two signs for the perfect active:[34]
   a. The syllable λε- (reduplication of the first syllable of the stem);
   b. The ending -κα attached to the stem.

5. The earmarks of the perfect middle and passive are three:
   a. Reduplication, as in the active;
   b. The personal ending -μαι, which in the perfect (as in the present) may be either middle or passive;
   c. The absence of the thematic vowel ο/ε between the stem and the personal ending. There is no need to confuse the present λύ-ο-μαι with the perfect λέ-λυ-μαι.

6. The distinguishing features of the aorist passive are two:
   a. The augment ε-, as in the aorist active;
   b. The ending θη- (θε-) attached to the stem.

These things are basic to the mastery of the Greek verb.

---

[33] There can be no reason for confusing the future forms and the sigmatic aorist. For, while they have the sigma in common, the aorist has two other signs which the future does not have.

[34] See the discussion of the perfect, p. 66f.

The Present Tense

	Indicative		Subjunctive [35]	
	Act.	**M. & P.**	**Act.**	**M. & P.**
S. 1.	λύω	λύομαι [36]	λύω	λύωμαι
2.	λύεις	λύῃ=λυ-ε(σ)αι	λύῃς	λύῃ
3.	λύει	λύεται	λύῃ	λύηται
P. 1.	λύομεν	λυόμεθα	λύωμεν	λυώμεθα
2.	λύετε	λύεσθε	λύητε	λύησθε
3.	λύουσι	λύονται	λύωσι	λύωνται

Imperative

	Act.	**M. & P.**
S. 2.	λῦε	λύου
3.	λυέτω	λυέσθω
P. 2.	λύετε	λύεσθε
3.	λυέτωσαν	λυέσθωσαν

Optative

Paradigms for the optative are not given here because the optative has almost faded out of the picture in the New Testament. The few which do occur will be discussed later under the optative mode.

The Imperfect Tense

Indicative

	Act.	**M. & P.**
S. 1.	ἔλυον	ἐλυόμην
2.	ἔλυες	ἐλύου=ελυ-ε(σ)ο
3.	ἔλυε(ν)	ἐλύετο
P. 1.	ἐλύομεν	ἐλυόμεθα
2.	ἐλύετε	ἐλύεσθε
3.	ἔλυον	ἐλύοντο

[35] The student has just one new thing to learn in passing from the indicative to the subjunctive: the thematic vowel o/ε lengthens to ω/η. In the indicative, -o- occurs before personal endings beginning with μ or ν; elsewhere the -ε- is used.

[36] The personal endings should be thoroughly mastered. These endings, -μαι, -σαι, -ται, -μεθα, -σθε, -ονται, are the same for all the primary tenses (present, future and perfect).

It should be noted:

1. That the imperfect is always built on the present tense stem. In this particular verb, the present and aorist stems are the same; but in verbs like λαμβάνω, the imperfect is ἐλάμβανον, whereas the aorist is ἔλαβον. More will be said about this under the aorist tense.

2. That there is a different set of personal endings for the imperfect: -ον, -ες, -ε(ν), -ομεν, -ετε, -ον, and -μην, -σο, -το, -μεθα, -σθε, -ντο. These, with their variations from the present, should be learned thoroughly, once and for all. They will also occur in the second aorist forms.

The Future Tense

Indicative

	Act.	Mid.	Pass.
S. 1.	λύσω [37]	λύσομαι [37]	λυθήσομαι [38]
2.	λύσεις	λύσῃ=ε(σ)αι	λυθήσῃ=ε(σ)αι
3.	λύσει	λύσεται	λυθήσεται
P. 1.	λύσομεν	λυσόμεθα	λυθησόμεθα
2.	λύσετε	λύσεσθε	λυθήσεσθε
3.	λύσουσι(ν)	λύσονται	λυθήσονται

Departures from the Norm in the Formation of the Future

There are certain 'irregularities' in the formation of the future.

1. When sigma is added to a verb whose stem ends in a palatal mute, κ, γ, χ, the future stem ends in ξ.

[37] It should be noted that the only difference between both the future active and middle forms and the corresponding present forms is the sigma inserted between the thematic vowel ο/ε and the verb stem.

[38] The future passive has as its distinguishing marks the -θη- from the aorist passive, the sigma of the future, the thematic ο/ε and the personal endings -μαι, -σαι, κ. τ. λ.

Most of these stems are disguised in the present tense: e. g., κηρυκ-, 'act as a herald,' appears in the *koine* as κηρύσσω (in the Attic, κηρύττω) ; future, κηρύξω. The future of all present stems in -σσ- take this form: e. g., πράσσω, 'practice,' πράξω.

2. Stems ending in labials, π, β, φ, give ψ in the future: e. g., βλέπω, 'see,' future βλέψω; γράφω, 'write,' future γράψω.

3. Stems ending in dentals, τ, δ, ϑ, drop the dental before the sigma: e. g., πείϑω, 'persuade,' future πείσω.

4. Stems ending in ζ behave in the same manner as '3': e. g., σώζω, 'save,' future σώσω; καϑαρίζω, 'make clean,' future καϑαρίσω. The Attic future, καϑαριῶ, occurs in Heb. 9:14. Cf. also Mt. 3:12.

5. Stems ending in liquids or nasals shift the accent to the ultima; the accent becomes a circumflex: e. g., κρίνω, 'judge,' becomes κρινῶ, 'I will judge,' in the future; αἴρω, 'raise,' becomes ἀρῶ; ἀγγέλλω, 'announce,' becomes ἀγγελῶ. It will be noted that in the last two verbs the stem changes. This shortening is quite common in verbs of this type. A stem containing a diphthong, such as -ει, usually drops the iota: ἐγείρω, 'raise,' future ἐγερῶ. A stem ending in double lambda drops one: βάλλω, 'throw,' βαλῶ. Moulton explains these as coming from futures in -ε(σ)ω instead of -σω.[39] Contraction of -εω gives -ῶ: e. g., βαλέ(σ)ω would yield βαλῶ.

6. The contract verb should give no trouble to the student. There are three types of stems, each type ending in a short vowel, which is lengthened before the tense sign is added:

  a. ἀγαπάω, 'love,' future ἀγαπήσω.
  b. ποιέω, 'do,' future ποιήσω.
  c. δουλόω, 'enslave,' future δουλώσω.

[39] *A Grammar of New Testament Greek*, Vol. II, p. 187.

The First Aorist Tense

Indicative

		Act.	Mid.	Pass.
S.	1.	ἔλυσα	ἐλυσάμην	ἐλύθην
	2.	ἔλυσας	ἐλύσω=σα(σ)ο	ἐλύθης
	3.	ἔλυσε(ν)	ἐλύσατο	ἐλύθη
P.	1.	ἐλύσαμεν	ἐλυσάμεθα	ἐλύθημεν
	2.	ἐλύσατε	ἐλύσασθε	ἐλύθητε
	3.	ἔλυσαν	ἐλύσαντο	ἐλύθησαν

(1) When the sigma is attached to the various types of consonantal stems and to contract verbs, they behave as in the future tense. On the liquid and nasal stems the sigma is not used. The following will serve to illustrate how these verbs form the aorist:

   (a) ἀγγέλλω (present), 'announce,' ἤγγειλα (aorist).

   (b) σπείρω (present), 'sow,' ἔσπειρα (aorist).

   (c) κρίνω (present), 'judge,' ἔκρινα (aorist).

(2) The personal endings should be mastered. The aorist middle uses the secondary tense endings, as does the imperfect.

(3) When the verb stem begins with a consonant, the syllabic augment ε- is regular; when with a vowel, contraction between the ε- and the initial vowel of the stem forms the 'temporal' augment: e. g., ἀκούω, 'hear,' aorist ε + ακουσα = ἤκουσα.

(4) Such verbs as ἔχω, 'have,' imperfect εἶχον, aorist ἔσχον, call for separate discussion.

(5) Many verbs do not have a 'first' aorist form, but employ the 'second' aorist (a few have both). In form, the second aorist differs from the imperfect only in that it is built on the 'shortened' primitive stem:

   (a) λείπω, 'leave,' imp. ἔλειπον, 2nd aor. ἔλιπον.

   (b) μανθάνω, 'teach,' imp. ἐμάνθανον, 2nd aor. ἔμαθον.

   (c) βάλλω, 'throw,' imp. ἔβαλλον, 2nd aor. ἔβαλον.

(6) Actually, the 'second' aorist is a much older form than the 'first' aorist. This will be explained in discussing Aktionsart p. 69.

(7) In koine Greek, many verbs with the second aorist stems took on first aorist endings: e. g., εἶπον, 'I said,' became εἶπα; εἶδον, 'I saw,' became εἶδα. Many such forms occur in the New Testament.

(8) In later Greek, there was a strong tendency for certain 'first' aorist passives to give way to what are called 'second aorist passives,' e. g., the first aorist passive ὑπετάχθην (from ὑποτάσσω, 'subject') becomes ὑπετάγην (cf. Rom. 10:3). This statement does not apply to such primitive second aorist passive forms as ἐχάρην (from χαίρω, 'rejoice') and ἐφάνην (from φαίνω, 'show').[40]

Subjunctive

The aorist subjunctive should give no trouble at all. There is one thing to remember: drop the augment and personal endings of the aorist indicative forms and add the subjunctive endings of the present: e. g.

1. ἔ-λυσ-α gives

    S. 1. λύσω
       2. λύσῃς
       3. λύσῃ
    P. 1. λύσωμεν
       2. λύσητε
       3. λύσωσι(ν)

2. ἐ-λυσ-άμην gives

    S. 1. λύσωμαι
       2. λύσῃ=ε(σ)αι
       3. λύσηται
    P. 1. λυσώμεθα
       2. λύσησθε
       3. λύσωνται

3. ἐ-λύθη-ν (λυθε) gives

    S. 1. λυθέω—λυθῶ
       2. λυθέῃς—λυθῇς
       3. λυθέῃ—λυθῇ
    P. 1. λυθέωμεν—λυθῶμεν
       2. λυθέητε—λυθῆτε
       3. λυθέωσι(ν)—λυθῶσι(ν)

---

[40] Robertson, *A Grammar of the Greek New Testament in the Light of Historical Research*, p. 347.

Imperative

Act.	Mid.	Pass.
S. 2. λῦσον	λῦσαι	λύθητι
3. λυσάτω	λυσάσθω	λυθήτω
P. 2. λύσατε	λύσασθε	λύθητε
3. λυσάτωσαν	λυσάσθωσαν	λυθήτωσαν

The aorist imperatives are built on the aorist indicative stems after the augment and personal endings are dropped. The imperative endings should be mastered.

The Perfect Tense

Indicative

Act.	M. & P.
S. 1. λέλυκα	λέλυμαι
2. λέλυκας	λέλυσαι
3. λέλυκε	λέλυται
P. 1. λελύκαμεν	λελύμεθα
2. λελύκατε	λέλυσθε
3. λελύκασι(ν) or -καν	λέλυνται

1. The first sign to notice in the perfect is the reduplication of the first syllable, λε-λυ.

   a. When a verb stem begins with a vowel, reduplication may have the appearance of the temporal augment: e. g., ἀγαπάω, 'love,' perfect ἠγάπηκα.

   b. When a verb stem begins with a group of consonants which would produce a harsh sound when repeated in successive syllables, e. g., στέλλω, 'send,' στε-σταλκα, reduplication often looks like a syllabic augment, ἔσταλκα (the correct perfect form of στέλλω). Forms like ἵστημι give ἔστηκα.

2. The next sign to notice in the perfect active is the ending -κα. This will occur in most of the perfect forms in the New Testament. There are, however, a

few 'second' perfects (actually much older than -κα
forms) which should be noted:

a. λέλοιπα, from λείπω, 'leave.'
b. πέποιθα, from πείθω, 'persuade.'
c. γέγονα, from γίνομαι, 'become.'
d. ἐνήνοχα, used with φέρω, 'bear.'
e. πέπονθα, from πάσχω, 'suffer.'
f. οἶδα, 'know' (present form not used). κ. τ. λ.

3. In the perfect middle and passive the primary tense
endings of the middle occur as in the present and the
future. The absence of the thematic o/ε should be
noted as a distinguishing mark (in addition to reduplication) of the perfect middle and passive.

All of these tense signs should be fixed indelibly in
the mind. It will save much time and many errors.

Tense

The student should disabuse his mind at once of the
notion that the primary idea of tense in the Greek verb
is time. The fundamental idea is the kind of action stated.[41]

1. Action may be regarded as in progress, going on. The
common term for this sort of action is linear or durative action.

2. Action may be regarded as simple, undefined (aoristic,
α-οριστος, from ἀορίζω, 'I do not define') action. The
common term for this is punctiliar action.

3. Action may be regarded as completed. When so
regarded, it is called perfect action, i. e., action in a
state of completion.

Remember that the same act may be looked at from
any of these three viewpoints.

There is a time element in the Greek tense, but it is
decidedly secondary to the kind of action described. The
time element appears directly only in the indicative mode.
In the subjunctive, optative and imperative modes and in

---

[41] See, Moulton, *Prolegomena*, pp. 108-110; Robertson, *A Grammar
of the Greek New Testament in the Light of Historical Research*,
pp. 820-826.

the infinitive and participle, it is only relative, if it appears at all. This is why the indicative uses all of the tense forms and the other modes are confined largely to the present and the aorist.

There are three periods of time in which an action may be considered: past, present and future. Any one of the three kinds of action may be placed in any one of these three periods of time. But, as said above, this is true only for the indicative mode. Hence, in the indicative mode, the completed tense system would have nine differ-ent tense forms. As a matter of fact, a separate form was not developed in the Greek verb for both linear and punctiliar action in the present and future time. So, we find one form in the present used for both ideas. But normally, a present tense form will express linear action. When a present tense form does express punctiliar action (usually called aoristic-present), the context will make clear that it does. As in the present, so in the future, one form must do double duty, but the future tense forms usually express punctiliar action.

Diagrammatically the tense system in the indicative might be expressed as follows:

	In present time	In past time	In future time
Linear Action.	Present tense.	Imperfect tense.	Occasionally by the future tense.
Punctiliar Action.	Occasionally by the present tense. [42]	Aorist tense.	Future tense.
Completed Action.	Present perfect tense.	Pluperfect tense.	Future perfect tense.

[42] The historical present (punctiliar) is quite common in Mk. and Jn., but it refers to action in past time. It is used to give a narrative vividness. See historical present, p. 71.

In the subjunctive, optative and imperative modes, and in the infinitive and participle, a present tense form is timeless and durative, and an aorist is timeless and punctiliar.

Aktionsart

There is another way in which the kind of action expressed by the verb may come in for consideration. The verb root itself may express linear action, punctiliar (either ingressive or effective), or completed. This kind of action expressed by the verb root is called Aktionsart.[43] The verb ἐσθίω expressed the linear idea, 'I eat,' while the root φαγ- expressed the idea from a punctiliar point of view. Consequently, ἔφαγον is used in the aorist and ἐσθίω in the present and imperfect. Since the future is usually punctiliar, the future, φάγομαι, is built on the root φαγ-. (In classical Greek, there was a future ἔδομαι, but this form does not occur in the New Testament.) This explains the existence of many of the so-called irregular verbs. The linear idea was so persistent in some roots that they never were used in the aorist, and a good synonym from a punctiliar root made it unnecessary. Many other verbs like βλέπω, 'see,' with a basically linear idea, in later Greek added the sigmatic aorist endings, e. g., ἔβλεψα, to express the punctiliar idea. (The 'second' aorist is much older than the first aorist. The second aorist of the -μι verbs are our most primitive forms.[44]) On the other hand, εἶδον, 'saw,' was never used to express the linear idea, and ὁράω, 'see,' never developed the aoristic (punctiliar) form, except an occasional form in the passive. This explains why such principal parts as the following may be given:

ὁράω, ὄψομαι, εἶδον, ἑώρακα . . . ὤφθην.

There are three verb stems here: ὁρα-, ἰδ-, ὀπ-; not one irregular verb.

[43] Moulton, *Prolegomena*, p. 108; Robertson, *A Grammar of the Greek New Testament in the Light of Historical Research*, pp. 823f.
[44] Robertson, *A Grammar of the Greek New Testament in the Light of Historical Research*, pp. 345-350.

Interpreting the Tenses

"The translators of our English version have failed more frequently from their partial knowledge of the tenses than from any other cause."[45] Most of these errors have grown out of 'the habit of trying to equate the Greek tenses with Latin, English or German tenses.

Action in Present Time

1. The exegete should remember that the *present tense* normally expresses continued action going on at the time of writing, or speaking. There are, however, several phases to this meaning. The context should make clear the exact shade of meaning.

   a. The force may be primarily descriptive, called the 'descriptive present': σβέννυνται (Mt. 25:8), 'are going out.' Here the AV obscures the meaning and gives an entirely wrong picture by rendering: 'our lamps are gone out.' The present tense tells you that the lamps are still burning but getting very dim and, no doubt, smoking badly.

   b. The force may be to 'gather up the past and the present time into one phrase': ἰδοὺ τρία ἔτη ἀφ' οὗ ἔρχομαι (Lk. 13:7). The vinedresser has not been on a three-year journey to reach the figtree in the vineyard, but annually he has come seeking figs and has been disappointed. In English, we would express this idea by a present perfect: 'Behold for three years I have been coming.' This is called the 'progressive present.'

   c. It may express iterative or customary action, called the 'iterative present': νηστεύω δὶς τοῦ σαββάτου (Lk. 18:12). This does not mean that I am fasting now, but that it is my custom to fast twice a week. Cf. Mk. 2:18, where ἦσαν . . . νηστεύοντες tells us that John's disciples and the Pharisees were fasting at that time.[46]

[45] Farrar, *Greek Syntax*, p. 123.
[46] See the periphrastic imperfect, p. 75.

d. Sometimes, it describes an act which was attempted or begun but not carried out, called 'conative' or 'inchoative present': λιθάζετε (Jn. 10:32), 'ye try to stone,' or 'begin to stone.'

e. It is often used of a past act as though it were going on. This is called the 'historical present,' and is characteristic of Mark (cf. ἔρχονται καὶ θεωροῦσιν, 5:15, 'they came and they saw'), and John. Jn. 20:1-18 supplies an excellent example of weaving together historical presents, imperfects, aorists, perfects and pluperfects with great dramatic effect. There are eighteen historical presents here, nine simple presents and one futuristic present (ἀναβαίνω, Jn. 20:17).[47] Luke evidently does not like this idiom, for, in following Mark's narrative, he changes all of these historical presents but one: ἔρχεται (Lk. 8:49). Both Mark and John write with dramatic effect, while Luke writes with more polish and elegance of style. These presents are nearly all aoristic or punctiliar.

f. It is also used to express general truths, 'gnomic present,' i. e., something that is true of all times: ἐκ τῆς Γαλιλαίας προφήτης οὐκ ἐγείρεται (Jn. 7:52), 'no prophet arises out of Galilee.'
The gnomic present is also an aoristic (punctiliar) present.

g. A few forms have the perfect force: ὁ ἀδελφὸς ἥκει (Lk. 15:27), 'thy brother has come and is here.' This is due to the *aktionsart* of the verb root.

h. A few present forms are used of future events: ἀναβαίνομεν (Mk. 10:33), 'we go up.' This futuristic present adds vividness to the narrative, as does the historic present. It is possible that Jesus may regard the journey to Jerusalem as already begun. In that case, this would be a descriptive present. A clear example of the futuristic present is: ἀναβαίνω πρὸς τὸν πατέρα μου (Jn. 20:17), 'I go to my Father.'
These futuristic presents are usually aoristic.

---

[47] See the futuristic present, 'h'.

i. A few perfect forms have lost their perfect force and are used just like a present tense: οἶδεν (Mt. 6:8), 'he knows.' That is because οἶδα, 'I know,' is a state resulting from εἶδον, 'I have seen.'

j. The periphrastic present is always durative. It is limited in the New Testament almost entirely to the imperative: ἴσθι εὐνοῶν (Mt. 5:25), 'be habitually well disposed.'

2. The *present perfect tense* describes an action as completed at the time of writing or speaking. Moulton calls the perfect tense the most important exegetically of all Greek tenses.[48] There are two major types of thought expressed by the perfect tense.

   a. It may describe an act completed after effort: ἠγώνισμαι . . . τετέλεκα . . . τετήρηκα (II Tim. 4:7), 'I have fought . . . I have finished . . . I have kept.' The life effort of Paul has gone into winning his contest, finishing his course, and guarding the faith. His task then is done. This is called the 'intensive perfect.'[49]

   b. It may describe an act that has abiding results: ἐγήγερται (I Cor. 15:4), 'he has risen and still is risen.' This perfect does not describe the completion of prolonged effort (as in 'a'); it describes a completed act which has abiding consequences. This is called the 'extensive perfect.' Note that this perfect tense comes in a group of aorists: ἀπέθανον, ἐτάφη, ὤφθη, κ. τ. λ. The perfect tense of these verbs would make Paul say that Jesus was still dead, still buried, and that Peter still saw Him. The aorist simply calls attention to an incident that occurred in past history. The perfect tells you that the event occurred and still has significant results.

The difference in the meaning of the intensive and extensive perfect grows out of the aktionsart of the verb root. If the action of the verb root is linear, the intensive meaning is natural; if punctiliar, the extensive is natural.

[48] Moulton, *Prolegomena*, p. 140.
[49] Robertson, *A Grammar of the Greek New Testament in the Light of Historical Research*, p. 893.

c. There are a few less common usages of the perfect which should be mentioned.

(1) The 'perfect of broken continuity': ἀπέσταλκα (II Cor. 12:17). Here Paul refers to the sending of several missions to the Corinthians.[50]

(2) The 'dramatic historical present perfect' is sometimes used to bring a past event vividly into the present. John is particularly fond of this idiom: τεθέαμαι (Jn. 1:32), 'I have seen'; εὑρήκαμεν (Jn. 1:41), 'we have found.' Paul uses it in II Cor. 2:13, οὐκ ἔσχηκα ἄνεσιν, 'I got no relief.'[51] The memory is still vivid and dreadful to Paul.

(3) The 'gnomic present perfect.' "A few examples of this idiom seem to appear in the New Testament. The present was always the more usual tense for customary truths, though the aorist and the perfect both occur."[52] A good example is δέδεται (I Cor. 7:39), '(she) is bound.' This perfect describes a custom of society.

(4) Sometimes, it is used with futuristic force: δεδόξασμαι ἐν αὐτοῖς (Jn. 17:10), 'I am glorified in them.' Jesus is looking forward to his disciples' glorifying his name. It can hardly be said that they had already glorified Him. Sometimes, this is called the 'perfect of prophecy.'

(5) The periphrastic perfect consists of the perfect participle with an auxiliary verb. The common auxiliary is εἰμί (about forty times in the New Testament).

There are a few instances with γίνομαι: ἐγένετο ἐσκοτωμένη (Rev. 16:10), 'became darkened.'

The use of ἔχω in periphrastic constructions has begun in the New Testament: ἔχε με παρῃτημένον

---

[50] Moulton, *Prolegomena*, p. 144; Robertson, *A Grammar of the Greek New Testament in the Light of Historical Research*, p. 896.

[51] Moulton thinks this may be an aoristic perfect. *Prolegomena*, p. 145.

[52] Robertson, *A Grammar of the Greek New Testament in the Light of Historical Research*, p. 897.

(Lk. 14:19), 'hold me excused.' Another good example is τῶν διὰ τὴν ἕξιν τὰ αἰσθητήρια γεγυμνασμένα ἐχόντων πρὸς διάκρισιν καλοῦ τε καὶ κακοῦ (Heb. 5:14), 'of those who because of use have their faculties exercised for the discernment of good and evil.' In modern Greek, this use of ἔχω, 'have,' with the perfect participle is the usual idiom. See the English, German and Latin idiom.

Action in Past Time

The tense forms for the past time are better developed than for either the present or future, there being a separate form for each kind of action in past time.

1. The *imperfect* expresses continuous action in past time. In historical narrative, the imperfect is the proper tense to use for descriptive purposes. "The aorist tells the simple story. The imperfect draws the picture. It helps you to see the course of the act. It passes before the eye the flowing streams of history."[53]

There are a variety of ways in which it may do this.

a. It may express the iterative idea: ἐπορεύοντο κατ' ἔτος (Lk. 2:41), tells that it was the custom of Jesus' family to go to Jerusalem yearly. Another example of the iterative force of the imperfect is seen in ἐβαστάζετο . . . ἐτίθουν καθ' ἡμέραν (Acts 3:2). The verbs are both in the imperfect tense, expressing a continued carrying and a continued placing of the lame man at the door of the temple. καθ' ἡμέραν defines the action further as one repeated daily.

b. It may express the progressive idea: τί ὅτι ἐζητεῖτε; (Lk. 2:49), 'why were you seeking?'

c. It may be used to accent the beginning of an action (inchoative imperfect), or to tell of an action attempted but interrupted (conative imperfect). In

[53] Ibid., p. 883.

English, we have to say 'began' for the one, and 'tried' for the other. This must be kept in mind to get the right idea from a good many passages. In Mt. 5:2, ἐδίδασκε tells us that Jesus 'began' to teach. In Mt. 3:14, διεκώλυεν brings out the idea of action interrupted ('tried'), for John did go on and baptize Jesus, although he (John) had tried to 'hinder' it.

d. It may be used to refer to present time. It is used to express a wish politely or hesitantly. In Acts 25:22, ἐβουλόμην enables Agrippa to say that he would like to hear Paul preach without seeming too eager about it. The present tense, βούλομαι, would have given away his interest too much to be becoming to his position. In Rom. 9:3, ηὐχόμην enables Paul to express a great yearning to win his people to Christ without expressing a moral wrong. The present tense, εὔχομαι, would have expressed the desire for spiritual suicide in order to win the Jew to Christ. This is called the 'potential imperfect.' The name is not satisfactory.

e. The periphrastic imperfect is very common in the New Testament. It stresses the durative idea in the participle: ἦσαν . . . νηστεύοντες (Mk. 2:18). This tells us that the disciples of John and of the Pharisees were actually fasting at that time. The same verb occurs twice in this verse in the present tense: νηστεύουσιν . . . νηστεύουσιν. These two examples tell us that it was the custom (the present of customary action) for the disciples of John and of the Pharisees to fast, but not for Jesus' disciples. Here is a good place to note the difference in force between the periphrastic and the simple verbal construction.[54]

2. The *aorist tense* expresses punctiliar action in past time. The term aorist (from α + ὁριστος) means undefined.[55] The action is stated without describing it.

[54] See the present of iterative action, p. 70.
[55] See p. 67.

The so-called 'second' aorist is the oldest form of the verb, the present tense forms developing later to express repeated or continued action.[56] The so-called 'first' aorist is a still later development. It grew out of the need to make linear verb roots (see aktionsart) express punctiliar action. So far as the meanings of the first and second aorist are concerned, they are the same, except in the verb ἵστημι, where the first aorist, ἔστησα, is transitive ('I placed'), and the second aorist, ἔστην ('I stood'), is intransitive.

Very few verbs have both forms of the aorist.

a. The phases of emphasis of the aorist

A given aorist tense form may have any one of three phases of emphasis: it may accent the beginning of the act, ingressive aorist; it may accent the conclusion of the act, effective aorist; or it may look at the whole act without particular emphasis upon its beginning or conclusion, constative aorist. The key to this problem of interpretation lies in the *aktionsart* of the verb.[57]

(1) Ingressive aorist.

A verb which stresses the idea of beginning will have the ingressive force: ἐγένετο (Jn. 1:14), '(he) became.' Other good examples may be seen in: ἐπτώχευσεν (II Cor. 8:9), 'he became poor'; ἐδάκρυσεν (Jn. 11:35), 'he burst out weeping.'

(2) Effective aorist.

Other names for this are the 'upshot aorist' (Gildersleeve), and aorist of the 'culminating point' (Munro). All of these terms are attempts to say that the emphasis is on the end of the action, rather than its beginning. When Paul says, ἐγὼ γὰρ ἔμαθον ἐν οἷς εἰμι αὐτάρκης εἶναι (Phil. 4:11), he is talking about a lesson already learned, not one just begun. ἐνίκησεν (Rev. 5:5) does not mean that the Lion of the tribe of Judah has begun to

[56] See p. 65.
[57] See p. 69.

conquer, but that his victory is won. Another good example is ἐκώλυσεν (Acts 27:43), where the centurion prevented the soldiers from putting Paul to death along with the other prisoners.

There is another use of the effective aorist which Moulton calls the "aorist for the thing just happened." This often had a very dramatic effect, e. g., ἔγνων τί ποιήσω (Lk. 16:4), 'I know what I shall do,' i. e., 'I have the solution for my problem.' In popular English, one might say, 'I've got it.'

(3) Constative aorist.

This aorist can be recognized by the fact that the verb root has the idea of a continued act: ἐβασίλευσεν (Rom. 5:14), covers the period from Adam to Moses in which death reigned; ἐκρύβη (Heb. 11:23), covers a period of three months in which Moses was hidden; οἰκοδομήθη (Jn. 2:20), covers a period of forty-six years during which the Temple was built. The difference between this aorist and the imperfect is that the aorist views the whole period of time involved at a glance, whereas the imperfect would describe the process as going on.

The commonest of these three emphases is the ingressive. The constative can always be recognized by a context which makes it clear that a period of time of some length is covered.

b. **The uses of the aorist.**

(1) It is the normal tense to use in narrative. The historian uses it, unless he wants to picture some act recorded. The Gospels and Acts are full of narrative aorists. In Acts 28:11-15, a part of the account of the storm in which Paul was shipwrecked, there are fifteen aorists and one perfect.

(2) The gnomic aorist is used to express a 'universal' or 'timeless' truth. The difference between this aorist and the gnomic present is that the present may be durative, and the aorist is punctiliar. Good

examples of gnomic aorists are: ἐβλήθη and ἐξηράνθη (Jn. 15:6); ἐξηράνθη and ἐξέπεσεν (I Pet. 1:24).
The verbs in Jn. 15:6 state a universal truth: any
man who does not abide in Christ 'is cast forth'
and 'is withered'; those in I Pet. 1:24 mean that
the grass 'withers' and its flower 'drops off' as a
part of the natural process. These truths could
have been expressed by the gnomic present
(linear), but the aorist seems to state the truth
more abruptly and startlingly.

(3) The epistolary aorist is used by a writer when
he puts himself in the position of his reader and
looks back on the time of writing as a past event.
Examples are: ἔπεμψα (Acts 23:30; Eph. 6:22;
Phil. 2:28; Col. 4:8), 'I send'; ἔγραψα (Philem. 19;
I Pet. 5:12; I Jn. 5:13), 'I write.' A New Testament writer may see fit to use the present, γράφω.
In fact, this is more common in the New Testament. Cf. I Cor. 4:14; 14:37; II Cor. 13:10; etc.

The English past tense will often translate the Greek
aorist. But the aorist covers much more ground than
the past tense in English. Sometimes, it should be translated by the perfect, and sometimes, by the pluperfect.
The epistolary aorist should be translated by the present.
The context must decide each translation.

3. The pluperfect.

This has been called a "luxury in Greek." The aorist
tense could be used for all narrative purposes, unless
the durative idea is to be expressed. Then, the imperfect was available. One must remember this when
interpreting an aorist tense. Often it must be translated into English by a pluperfect.

The Greeks, as a rule, did not feel the need of the
pluperfect because they cared little or nothing about
relative time. It was never widely used. But when
used, it expressed an action completed at a specified
point of time in the past: δέδωκει (Mk. 14:44), 'he had
given,' tells the reader that Judas had made a previous

agreement to betray Jesus. Cf. τεθεμελίωτο (Mt. 7:25), 'it had been founded,' i. e., the foundation of the house had been laid before the flood struck.

The pluperfect in the New Testament does not have the augment to express past time, as it did in classical Greek.

Action in Future Time

1. The future tense is usually punctiliar, just as the present tense is usually linear. The future active and middle forms seem to have been derived from the aorist subjunctive. This would give them associations with the punctiliar idea. Then, in the nature of the case, it is more natural to look at a future act as punctiliar rather than as linear.

There are three shades of meaning in the future tense: the volitive, the deliberative, and the futuristic. There is no difference in the form. Only the context can reveal which meaning is appropriate in each instance. There are, for example, in τέξεται δὲ υἱόν, καὶ καλέσεις τὸ ὄνομα αὐτοῦ Ἰησοῦν· αὐτὸς γὰρ σώσει τὸν λαὸν αὐτοῦ ἀπὸ τῶν ἁμαρτιῶν αὐτῶν (Mt. 1:21), three verbs in the future tense: τέξεται, καλέσεις, σώσει. The first expresses mere futurity: Mary will bear a son; the second expresses a command: Joseph is commanded to name the child, Jesus; the third expresses a simple future fact (mere futurity) that this son shall save his people from their sins.

a. The most frequent use is the merely futuristic: φαινήσεται (Mt. 24:30), 'it will appear.' It is simply a statement of fact that in the future, under given conditions, the sign of the Son of Man will appear. Another example is: βαπτίσει (Mt. 3:11), 'he shall baptize.'

b. It may express determination (or give a command for the future) as well as futurity: οὐ φονεύσεις (Mt. 5:21), 'thou shalt not kill'; ἀγαπήσεις (Mt. 5:43), 'thou shalt love.' This is called the volitive future.

c. It may be used to consult the judgment of another person: ποσάκις ἁμαρτήσει; (Mt. 18:21), 'how often shall (he) sin?'; ζήσομεν; (Rom. 6:2), 'shall we live (in sin)?' This is called the deliberative future.

When confronting a future form, the most natural meaning to look for is simple futurity. If that does not fit the context, look for one of the other meanings. Sometimes, the deliberative, as in the example from Rom. 6:2, is used argumentatively.

It should be noted here that both subjunctive and optative modes have all three usages: futuristic, volitive and deliberative.

2. The future perfect was never widely used and is almost extinct in the New Testament. Heb. 8:11, εἰδήσουσιν (from οἶδα, 'I know'), is the only sure instance in the New Testament, and it has lost the perfect force. It means 'they shall know.'

There are a few future perfect periphrastics: ἔσται δεδεμένον and ἔσται λελυμένον (Mt. 16:19). This is wrongly translated 'shall be bound' and 'shall be loosed,' seeming to make Jesus teach that the apostles' acts will determine the policies of heaven.[58] They should be translated 'shall have been bound' and 'shall have been loosed.' This makes the apostles' acts a matter of inspiration or heavenly guidance. Cf. Mt. 18:18. This incorrect translation has given expositors and theologians a great deal of trouble.

Voice[59]

The verb also tells how the action is related to the subject of the sentence. This is done by the voice.

1. When the subject is represented as acting, it is called the *active voice.*

2. When the subject is represented as acting with reference to itself, it is called the *middle voice.* This action may be reflexive,[60] or it may affect the subject in a

[58] Moulton, *Prolegomena*, pp. 149f.
[59] Cf. Ibid., pp. 152-163.
[60] Moulton considers ἀπήγξατο (Mt. 27:5), 'he strangled himself,' the clearest example of a reflexive middle in the New Testament. *Prolegomena*, p. 155.

less direct way. The middle voice calls especial attention to the subject, but it does not indicate the particular thing about the subject which is emphasized. The context must do that. As the dative case is the case which expresses personal interest, so the middle voice is the voice of personal interest.

Commentators and translators often make unnecessary difficulty for themselves by assuming that the primary meaning of the middle voice is reflexive. A classic example of this is ἀπεκδυσάμενος (Col. 2:15). Such an excellent translation of the New Testament as Weymouth confuses the figures in this sentence. He, influenced by Lightfoot's interpretation, has Jesus stripping off from himself (as a garment) the demonic agencies and then displaying them in his triumph. This mars the force and clarity of Paul's figure which seems to represent Jesus as stripping the demonic powers (as defeated foes) [61] and then leading them in his triumph as did the victorious generals or emperors of that day. This latter interpretation reflects the primary meaning of the middle voice: personal interest. The instrument by which Jesus achieved his victory was the cross.

3. When the subject is represented as the recipient of the action of the verb, it is said to be in the *passive voice*.

The passive voice is a much later development than the middle or active. In all tenses but the aorist and the future, the passive borrowed its forms from the middle. Gradually, the passive crowded the middle voice out of usage. In modern Greek, the middle voice is gone. This had happened to all European languages, except Greek, before they developed a literature. To express the middle idea, they use a reflexive pronoun with the active voice, or some preposition with the accusative case, e. g., 'for himself.'

In the New Testament, there are a good many passive forms which clearly have a middle force. One must watch these in interpreting: ἀπεκρίθησαν (Mt. 25:9), 'they answered.' This form always has the middle idea

----

[61] Mk. 3:27.

in the New Testament. Cf. δεήθητι (Acts 8:22), 'pray thou'; δεήθητε (Acts 8:24), 'pray ye'; κολλήθητι (Acts 8:29), 'join thyself.' Forms like σταθῆναι (Mk. 3:24), used parallel with στῆναι (Mk. 3:25, 26), have lost, apparently, their passive force. Probably no distinction in meaning should be sought between these two infinitive forms.

The sign of the passive voice, θη (lengthened from θε), is thought by some grammarians to be from an old adverb, θεν (cf. Eng. 'thence'). That is, the action of the verb is conceived of as coming from without the subject.[62]

Mode

The mode has to do with the *manner* in which the statement is made. It does not refer to the *truth* of the statement. As A. T. Robertson has said, "Most untruths are told in the indicative mode."[63]

1. The *indicative mode* is used whenever a positive assertion is made, or a positive question is asked.

2. The *subjunctive mode* is used for doubtful assertions. The name suggests that it is used primarily for subjoined (subordinate) clauses. That is not true. It is used in hesitant statements; in exhortations (hortatory or volitive); in deliberative questions; and in prohibitions (negative commands with μή); as well as in certain types of subordinate clauses to be discussed later.

   The subjunctive has the same three turns of thought as the future tense: futuristic, ὃ προσενέγκη (Heb. 8:3), 'which he may offer'; deliberative, δῶμεν ἢ μὴ δῶμεν; (Mk. 12:15), 'shall we give or shall we not give?'; hortatory, ἔχωμεν (Rom. 5:1), 'let us have'; and a negative command, μὴ νομίσητε (Mt. 5:17), 'don't begin[64] to think.'

[62] Cf. Moulton, *Prolegomena*, p. 161.
[63] *A Grammar of the Greek New Testament in the Light of Historical Research*, p. 915.
[64] It is the aorist tense which gives the verb its ingressive force. The AV misses this point.

The *deliberative subjunctive* expresses perplexity on the part of the speaker: ποιήσωμεν; (Acts 4:16), 'what shall we do?' Cf. ποιοῦμεν; (Jn. 11:47), 'what are we doing?' In the latter example, the present indicative does not register doubt, it is a rebuke for inactivity. The hortatory (volitive) subjunctive is used to urge some one to unite with the speaker in a course of action upon which he has already decided: προσερχώμεθα (Heb. 4:16), 'let us draw near.'

3. The *optative mode* has a name that suggests that it is used for wishes. That is true of wishes about the future.[65] The optative is a weaker mode than the subjunctive. The latter may be said to carry the idea of probability, while the former carries the idea of possibility. It is used in Luke and Acts in an indirect question, when the direct question had the subjunctive. It is also used in fourth class (future less vivid) conditions.

The optative, not being a necessity, was gradually crowded out of Greek as it was in Latin. In Sanskrit, it was the subjunctive that had to give way.

The optative forms can be recognized with little difficulty in the New Testament, for this mode is almost extinct in the New Testament. There are only sixty-five (or sixty-seven, depending on the text followed) examples in the New Testament. The characteristic vowels used before the personal endings are: -αι, -οι, -ιη.

Like the subjunctive, it has the futuristic, volitive and deliberative forces.

a. The volitive optative.

(1) There are fifteen examples of μὴ γένοιτο, 'let it not happen.' Fourteen of these occur in Paul (ten in Romans, one in I Corinthians, and three in Galatians). One occurs in Lk. 20:16.

(2) There are fifteen examples of the volitive optative in Paul, exclusive of μὴ γένοιτο:

[65] P. 211.

(a) ἁγιάσαι (I Th. 5:23), 'may he (the God of peace) sanctify you.'

(b) δῴη (Rom. 15:5; II Th. 3:16; II Tim. 1:16, 18), 'may he give.'[66]

(c) κατευθύναι (I Th. 3:11; II Th. 3:5), 'may he direct.'

(d) λογισθείη (II Tim. 4:16), 'may it (not) be reckoned (to them).'

(e) ὀναίμην (Philem. 20), 'may I be profited.'[67]

(f) παρακαλέσαι (II Th. 2:17), 'may he comfort.'

(g) περισσεύσαι (I Th. 3:12), 'may he make you overflow.'

(h) πλεονάσαι (I Th. 3:12), 'may he make you increase.'

(i) πληρώσαι (Rom. 15:13), 'may he make full.'

(j) στηρίξαι (II Th. 2:17), 'may he strengthen.'

(k) τηρηθείη (I Th. 5:23), 'may he guard.'

(3) Other examples are:

(a) εἴη (Acts 8:20), 'may it be.'

(b) ἐπιτιμήσαι (Jude 9), 'may he rebuke.'

(c) καταρτίσαι (Heb. 13:21), 'may he make perfect.'

(d) πληθυνθείη (I Pet. 1:2; II Pet. 1:2; Jude 2), 'may (it) be multiplied.'

(e) φάγοι (Mk. 11:14), 'may (he) eat.'

The volitive use of the optative has persisted longer than any other and is most frequent in the New Testament (thirty-eight times).[68]

b. The deliberative optative.

(1) There are nine examples of εἴη (present third singular optative of εἰμί) in indirect questions. All occur in Luke or Acts.

[66] T. R. reads δῴη Eph. 1:17. B, 63, Cyr. read δῴ. P46 reads δώῃ. Other manuscripts read δῴη, the subjunctive.

[67] This is the only New Testament example of the volitive optative in the first person. The others are all third person singular.

[68] Moulton, *Prolegomena*, pp. 194f.

(2) There are five examples with εἰ (not in the protasis of a condition) where hesitation or uncertainty seems implied:

(a) εἰ εἴη (Acts 20:16), 'if (he) might be.'

(b) εἰ βούλοιτο (Acts 25:20), 'if he might wish.'

(c) εἰ δύναιντο (Acts 27:39), 'if they might be able.'

(d) εἰ ψηλαφήσαιεν . . . εὕροιεν (Acts 17:27), 'if they might feel after . . . and find.'

c. The futuristic optative.

There are six examples with ἄν (exclusive of εἴη):

(1) τί ἄν γένοιτο (Acts 5:24), 'what (this) might become.'

(2) πῶς ἄν δυναίμην; (Acts 8:31), 'how should I be able?'

(3) εὐξαίμην ἄν (Acts 26:29), 'I could pray.'

(4) τί ἄν θέλοι (Lk. 1:62), 'what he might wish'; also Acts 17:18.

(5) τί ἄν ποιήσαιεν (Lk. 6:11), 'what they might do.'

These are the potential optative, practically the apodosis of an unexpressed protasis.

d. Other uses.

(1) There are two examples after πρὶν ἤ: ἔχοι and λάβοι (Acts 25:16). By means of these optatives, Festus courteously reminds the Jewish leaders at Jerusalem that it is not in keeping with Roman custom to condemn a man before he is faced by his accusers, κατὰ πρόσωπον ἔχοι τοὺς κατηγόρους, and has opportunity to make his defense, τόπον τε ἀπολογίας λάβοι.

(2) There are five examples in fragmentary conditional sentences of the fourth class (future less vivid):

(a) εἰ ἔχοιεν (Acts 24:19), 'if they should have.'

(b) εἰ θέλοι (I Pet. 3:17), 'if he should wish.'

(c) εἰ πάσχοιτε (I Pet. 3:14), 'if ye should suffer.'

(d) εἰ τύχοι (I Cor. 14:10; 15:37), 'if it should chance, perchance.'

The latter two examples seem to have become stereotyped expressions.

4. The *imperative mode* has various uses.[69] The context must determine the force of each imperative.

   a. It may issue a direct command: ἀγαπᾶτε τοὺς ἐχθροὺς ὑμῶν (Mt. 5:44), 'love your enemies.'

   b. It may be primarily hortatory: ποιησάτω (Rev. 22: 11), 'let him do.'

   c. It may express an entreaty: βοήθησον ὑμῖν (Mk. 9:22), 'Help us.'

   d. It may grant a permission: καθεύδετε λοιπὸν καὶ ἀναπαύεσθε (Mt. 26:45), 'Sleep on now, and refresh yourselves.'

   e. It may express a condition: λύσατε τὸν ναὸν τοῦτον καὶ ἐν τρισὶν ἡμέραις ἐγερῶ αὐτόν (Jn. 2:19), 'Destroy (If you destroy) this temple and in three days I will raise it up.' Cf. Eph. 4:26.

   f. It may issue a prohibition (a negative command): μὴ θησαυρίζετε (Mt. 6:19), 'Quit laying up treasures.'
   The difference between μή with the present imperative and with the aorist subjunctive can be illustrated here: μὴ θησαυρίσητε would mean 'Don't begin to lay up treasures.' The point of Jesus' command is that men are already laying up treasures on earth instead of in heaven, and he would have them quit. This difference is lost in the English versions.

The present imperative may have any of the characteristic ideas of linear action. The aorist imperative usually has a note of urgency in it. The Lord's Prayer, for instance, has seven imperatives, all of them aorists. Moulton[70] points out that in the petitions to human beings, recorded in the papyri, the imperative is seldom

⁶⁹ Moulton, *Prolegomena*, pp. 171-179.
⁷⁰ *Prolegomena*, p. 173.

used. But Jesus set the example of using the imperative in its most urgent form in our prayer.

In the subjunctive, optative and imperative modes, the present tense is timeless and durative; the aorist is timeless and punctiliar. The perfect imperative is a negligible quantity in the New Testament: πεφίμωσο (Mk. 4:39) is a command that the muzzling be decisive and final; ἔρρωσθε (Acts 15:29) is an epistolary formula, the verb having the force of the present.

Verb Building by Means of Conjugations

The verb not only makes assertions about the subject (mode); tells how the action is related to the subject (voice); tells of what sort the action is (tense); but it also tells the person and number of the subject. All of these ideas are usually built into one word. It is a marvelously intricate, compact and effective way of expressing ideas. In spite of its intricacy, remarkable clarity of thought is easily attained. The student should learn to pick out unhesitatingly and unerringly the mode-, tense-, voice-, person-, and number-signs. All five of these will occur in every verb and can be easily recognized. The best method for studying these is to take a table of conjugations and fix in one's mind the sign of each mode, tense, voice, person and number. Remember that there is never a wasted letter in a Greek word. Every one adds something to the total meaning.

Classes of Verbs

In the large, there are two kinds of verbs: those whose 'simple form' ends in -μι, as ἵστημι; and those ending in -ω, as λέγω. They are called μι-verbs and ω-verbs. The μι-verbs are the older. There was a gradual process throughout the history of the Greek language of replacing them with ω-verbs. In the New Testament, only five μι-verbs are used at all frequently. They are: ἵστημι, δίδωμι, τίθημι, ἵημι and εἰμί. In modern Greek, only εἰμί is left. The student should be prepared to find many forms such as ἱστάνω, ἱστάω, στήκω, all late forms of ἵστημι. In modern Greek, all of these are gone, being replaced by στέκω.

The conjugation of the regular ω-verb has been given, pp. 59f. It is necessary now to give the conjugation of the μι-verbs, in so far as they differ in formation from the regular ω-verb, and also to discuss the contract-verb, the most important variation from the regular ω-verb.

The Conjugation of the μι -verb

1. δίδωμι, 'I give.' Present tense stem διδο-[71], root δο-[71].

Principal Parts

Pres. Ac.	Fut. Ac.	Aor. Ac.
δίδωμι	δώσω	ἔδωκα
Perf. Ac.	Perf. M. & P.	Aor. Pass.
δέδωκα	δέδομαι	ἐδόθην

Indicative

	Pres. Ac.	Pres. M. & P.	Imperf. Ac.	Imperf. M. & P.
S. 1.	δίδωμι	δίδομαι	ἐδίδουν [71]	ἐδιδόμην
2.	δίδως	δίδοσαι	ἐδίδους	ἐδίδοσο
3.	δίδωσι(ν)	δίδοται	ἐδίδου	ἐδίδοτο
P. 1.	δίδομεν	διδόμεθα	ἐδίδομεν	ἐδιδόμεθα
2.	δίδοτε	δίδοσθε	ἐδίδοτε	ἐδίδοσθε
3.	διδόασι(ν)	δίδονται	ἐδίδοσαν	ἐδίδοντο

Subjunctive

	Pres. Ac.	Pres. M. & P.
S. 1.	διδῶ	διδῶμαι
2.	διδῷς	διδῷ
3.	διδῷ	διδῶται
P. 1.	διδῶμεν	διδώμεθα
2.	διδῶτε	διδῶσθε
3.	διδῶσι(ν)	διδῶνται

[71] The important thing to remember about this verb is the stem and the root. This will explain many seeming irregularities. In the imperfect, it behaves like a contract verb in -οω.

Imperative

S.	2. δίδου		δίδοσο
	3. διδότω		διδόσθω
P.	2. δίδοτε		δίδοσθε
	3. διδότωσαν		διδόσθωσαν

Infinitive

διδόναι   δίδοσθαι

Participle

διδούς, διδοῦσα, διδόν.   διδόμενος, διδομένη, διδόμενον.

In the aorist system, the irregularities seem many, but if one recalls the verb root, δο-, they are not so bad.

The aorist indicative active, ἔδωκα, is one of the three kappa-aorists (δίδωμι, τίθημι, -ιημι) in the New Testament. Otherwise, it is conjugated like the first aorist.

The aorist indicative middle and passive are regular.

The Aorist Indicative

		Mid.	Pass.
S.	1.	ἐδόμην	ἐδόθην
	2.	ἔδου=ο(σ)ο	ἐδόθης
	3.	ἔδοτο	ἐδόθη
P.	1.	ἐδόμεθα	ἐδόθημεν
	2.	ἔδοσθε	ἐδόθητε
	3.	ἔδοντο	ἐδόθησαν

The Aorist Subjunctive

		Ac.	Mid.
S.	1.	δῶ	Not in New Testament
	2.	δῷς	
	3.	δῷ	
P.	1.	δῶμεν	
	2.	δῶτε	
	3.	δῶσι(ν)	

The Aorist Imperative

S. 2. δός   Not in New Testament
3. δότω
P. 2. δότε
3. δότωσαν

Infinitive

δοῦναι   Not in New Testament

Participle

δούς, δοῦσα, δόν.   Not in New Testament

2. τίθημι, 'I place.' Present tense stem τιθε-, root θε-.

Principal Parts

Pres. Ac.	Fut. Ac.	Aor. Ac.
τίθημι	θήσω	ἔθηκα
Perf. Ac.	Perf. M. & P.	Aor. Pass.
-τέθεικα	τέθειμαι	ἐτέθην

Indicative

	Pres. Ac.	Pres. M. & P.	Imperf. Ac.	Imperf. M. & P.
S. 1.	τίθημι	τίθεμαι	ἐτίθην	ἐτιθέμην
2.	τίθης	τίθεσαι	ἐτίθεις	ἐτίθεσο
3.	τίθησι	τίθεται	ἐτίθει	ἐτίθετο
P. 1.	τίθεμεν	τιθέμεθα	ἐτίθεμεν	ἐτιθέμεθα
2.	τίθετε	τίθεσθε	ἐτίθετε	ἐτίθετε
3.	τιθέασι(ν)	τίθενται	ἐτίθεσαν	ἐτίθεντο

The other forms are sufficiently regular to be easily identified.

It should be kept in mind that the aorist active is another kappa-aorist.

3. ἵστημι, 'I stand.' Present tense stem ἱστα-, root στα-.

Principal Parts

Pr. Ac.	F. Ac.	Aor. Ac.	Per. Ac.	Per. M. & P.	Aor. Pass.
ἵστημι	στήσω	ἔστην	ἔστηκα		ἐστάθην
		ἔστησα			

Indicative

Pres. Ac.	Pres. M. & P.	Imperf. Ac.	Imperf. M. & P.
S. 1. ἵστημι	ἵσταμαι	ἵστην	ἱστάμην
2. ἵστης	ἵστασαι	ἵστης	ἵστασο
3. ἵστησι(ν)	ἵσταται	ἵστη	ἵστατο
P. 1. ἵσταμεν	ἱστάμεθα	ἵσταμεν	ἱστάμεθα
2. ἵστατε	ἵστασθε	ἵστατε	ἵστασθε
3. ἱστᾶσι(ν)	ἵστανται	ἵστασαν	ἵσταντο

No comment should be needed on the other forms, except in the aorist active. Here, there are two forms:

The second aorist (always intransitive)	The first aorist (always transitive)

Indicative

S. 1. ἔστην, 'I stood.'   ἔστησα, 'I placed.'
   2. ἔστης   (like ἔλυσα)
   3. ἔστη
P. 1. ἔστημεν
   2. ἔστητε
   3. ἔστησαν

4. εἰμί, 'I am.'

Indicative

	Pres.	Imperf.	Fut.
S. 1.	εἰμί	ἤμην	ἔσομαι
2.	εἶ	ἦς	ἔσῃ
3.	ἐστί(ν)	ἦν	ἔσται
P. 1.	ἐσμέν	ἦμεν	ἐσόμεθα
2.	ἐστέ	ἦτε	ἔσεσθε
3.	εἰσί(ν)	ἦσαν	ἔσονται

Subjunctive

S. 1. ὦ
   2. ᾖς
   3. ᾖ
P. 1. ὦμεν
   2. ἦτε
   3. ὦσι(ν)

Imperative

S. 2. ἴσθι
   3. ἔστω
P. 2. ἔστε
   3. ἔστωσαν

Infinitive

εἶναι

Participle

ὤν, οὖσα, ὄν

The Conjugation of the Contract-verb

The contract-verb introduces little that is new to the student who has mastered the regular ω-verb. There are three types of stems, each of which ends in one of the following short vowels: α, ε, ο. Examples of each type are: ἀγαπάω, 'I love'; φιλέω, 'I love'; δηλόω, 'I make plain.' There are two important new facts to learn about these verbs:

1. In the present and imperfect tenses, when the personal endings are added, contraction takes place between the short vowel of the stem and the vowels of the personal endings.

   a. ἀγαπάω, 'I love.' Present tense stem ἀγαπα-.

Indicative

		Pres. Ac.			M. & P.	
S.	1.	ἀγαπά+ω	= ἀγαπῶ	ἀγαπά+ομαι	= -ῶμαι
	2.	ἀγαπά+εις	= ἀγαπᾷς	ἀγαπά+ῃ	= -ᾷ
	3.	ἀγαπά+ει	= ἀγαπᾷ	ἀγαπά+εται	= -ᾶται
P.	1.	ἀγαπά+ομεν	= ἀγαπῶμεν	ἀγαπα+όμεθα	= -ώμεθα
	2.	ἀγαπά+ετε	= ἀγαπᾶτε	ἀγαπά+εσθε	= -ᾶσθε
	3.	ἀγαπά+ουσι	= ἀγαπῶσι(ν)	ἀγαπά+ονται	= -ῶνται

Subjunctive

The present subjunctive forms are exactly like the present indicative forms in the contract-verbs in -αω. This is due to the fact that contraction of the stem vowel with the personal endings gives forms identical with the lengthened stem vowel.

PARTS OF SPEECH 93

Imperative

Pres. Ac.

S. 2. ἀγάπα+ε   = ἀγάπα
   3. ἀγαπα+έτω   = ἀγαπάτω
P. 2. ἀγαπά+ετε   = ἀγαπᾶτε
   3. ἀγαπα+έτωσαν = ἀγαπάτωσαν

M. & P.

S. 2. ἀγαπά+ου   = -ῶ
   3. ἀγαπα+έσθω   = -άσθω
P. 2. ἀγαπά+εσθε   = -ᾶσθε
   3. ἀγαπα+έσθωσαν= -άσθωσαν

Infinitive

Pres. Ac.	Pres. M. & P.
ἀγαπά+ειν = ἀγαπᾶν	ἀγαπά+εσθαι = ἀγαπᾶσθαι
Sometimes, ἀγαπᾷν	

Participle

ἀγαπά+ων   = ἀγαπῶν   ἀγαπα+όμενος = -ώμενος
ἀγαπά+ουσα = ἀγαπῶσα   ἀγαπα+ομένη = -ωμένη
ἀγαπά+ον   = ἀγαπῶν   ἀγαπα+όμενον = -ώμενον

The imperfect is formed in the same manner.

	Ac.		M. & P.	
S. 1. ἠγάπα+ον	= ἠγάπων	ἠγαπα+όμην	= -ώμην
2. ἠγάπα+ες	= ἠγάπας	ἠγαπά+ου	= -ῶ
3. ἠγάπα+ε	= ἠγάπα	ἠγαπά+ετο	= -ᾶτο
P. 1. ἠγαπά+ομεν	= ἠγαπῶμεν	ἠγαπα+όμεθα	= -ώμεθα
2. ἠγαπά+ετε	= ἠγαπᾶτε	ἠγαπά+εσθε	= -ᾶσθε
3. ἠγάπα+ον	= ἠγάπων	ἠγαπά+οντο	= -ῶντο

b. φιλέω, 'I love.'[72] Present tense stem φιλε-.

[72] See a good lexicon for the difference in meaning between ἀγαπάω and φιλέω.

Indicative

	Pres. Ac.		M. & P.	
S.	1. φιλέ+ω	= φιλῶ	φιλέ+ομαι	= -οῦμαι
	2. φιλέ+εις	= φιλεῖς	φιλέ+η	= -ῇ
	3. φιλέ+ει	= φιλεῖ	φιλέ+εται	= -εῖται
P.	1. φιλέ+ομεν	= φιλοῦμεν	φιλε+όμεθα	= -ούμεθα
	2. φιλέ+ετε	= φιλεῖτε	φιλέ+εσθε	= -εῖσθε
	3. φιλέ+ουσι(ν)	= φιλοῦσι(ν)	φιλέ+ονται	= -οῦνται

Subjunctive[73]

S.	1. φιλέ+ω	= φιλῶ	φιλέ+ωμαι	= -ῶμαι
	2. φιλέ+ῃς	= φιλῇς	φιλέ+η	= -ῇ
	3. φιλέ+η	= φιλῇ	φιλέ+ηται	= -ῆται
P.	1. φιλέ+ωμεν	= φιλῶμεν	φιλε+ώμεθα	= -ώμεθα
	2. φιλέ+ητε	= φιλῆτε	φιλέ+ησθε	= -ῆσθε
	3. φιλέ+ωσι(ν)	= φιλῶσι(ν)	φιλέ+ωνται	= -ῶνται

Imperative

S.	2. φίλε+ε	= φίλει	φιλέ+ου	= -οῦ
	3. φιλε+έτω	= φιλείτω	φιλε+έσθω	= -είσθω
P.	2. φιλέ+ετε	= φιλεῖτε	φιλέ+εσθε	= -εῖσθε
	3. φιλε+έτωσαν	= φιλείτωσαν	φιλε+έσθωσαν	= -είσθωσαν

Infinitive

φιλέ+ειν = φιλεῖν   φιλέ+εσθαι=-εῖσθαι

Participle

φιλέ+ων	= φιλῶν	φιλε+όμενος	= -ούμενος
φιλέ+ουσα	= φιλοῦσα	φιλε+ομένη	= -ουμένη
φιλέ+ον	= φιλοῦν	φιλε+όμενον	= -ούμενον

[73] The present subjunctive forms differ from the present indicative forms in the contract-verbs in -εω, because contraction of the stem vowel -ε- with the personal endings in the indicative gives the diphthongs ει and ου, whereas in the subjunctive, the lengthened vowel of the personal ending dominates the resultant form, giving the resultant long vowels η and ω.

The imperfect is formed in the same manner.

		Ac.		M. & P.	
S.	1.	ἐφίλε+ον = ἐφίλουν		ἐφιλε+όμην = -ούμην
	2.	ἐφίλε+ες = ἐφίλεις		ἐφιλέ+ου = -οῦ
	3.	ἐφίλε+ε = ἐφίλει		ἐφιλέ+ετο = -εῖτο
P.	1.	ἐφιλέ+ομεν = ἐφιλοῦμεν		ἐφιλε+όμεθα = -ούμεθα
	2.	ἐφιλέ+ετε = ἐφιλεῖτε		ἐφιλέ+εσθε = -εῖσθε
	3.	ἐφίλε+ον = ἐφίλουν		ἐφιλέ+οντο = -οῦντο

c. δηλόω, 'I make plain.' Present tense stem δηλο-.

Indicative

		Pres. Ac.		M. & P.
S.	1.	δηλό+ω = δηλῶ		δηλό+ομαι = -οῦμαι
	2.	δηλό+εις = δηλοῖς [74]		δηλό+ῃ = -οῖ [74]
	3.	δηλό+ει = δηλοῖ [74]		δηλό+εται = -οῦται
P.	1.	δηλό+ομεν = δηλοῦμεν		δηλο+όμεθα = -ούμεθα
	2.	δηλό+ετε = δηλοῦτε		δηλό+εσθε = -οῦσθε
	3.	δηλό+ουσι(ν) = δηλοῦσι(ν)		δηλό+ονται = -οῦνται

Subjunctive

S.	1.	δηλό+ω = δηλῶ		δηλό+ωμαι = -ῶμαι
	2.	δηλό+ῃς = δηλοῖς [74]		δηλό+ῃ = -οῖ [74]
	3.	δηλό+ῃ = δηλοῖ [74]		δηλό+ηται = -ῶται
P.	1.	δηλό+ωμεν = δηλῶμεν		δηλο+ώμεθα = -ώμεθα
	2.	δηλό+ητε = δηλῶτε		δηλό+ησθε = -ῶσθε
	3.	δηλό+ωσι(ν) = δηλῶσι(ν)		δηλό+ωνται = -ῶνται

Imperative
Pres. Ac.

S.	2.	δήλο+ε = δήλου
	3.	δηλο+έτω = δηλούτω
P.	2.	δηλό+ετε = δηλοῦτε
	3.	δηλο+έτωσαν = δηλούτωσαν

M. & P.

S.	2.	δηλό+ου = -οῦ
	3.	δηλο+έσθω = -ούσθω
P.	2.	δηλό+εσθε = -οῦσθε
	3.	δηλο+έσθωσαν = -ούσθωσαν

[74] In these forms with the diphthong -οι-, contraction occurs between the stem vowel and the iota of the personal ending, rather than between the ε or the η and the stem vowel.

Infinitive

Pres. Ac.	M. & P.
δηλό+ειν = δηλοῦν	δηλό+εσθαι = -οῦσθαι
Sometimes, δηλοῖν	

Participle

δηλό+ων	= δηλῶν	δηλο+όμενος	= -ούμενος
δηλό+ουσα	= δηλοῦσα	δηλο+ομένη	= -ουμένη
δηλό+ον	= δηλοῦν	δηλο+όμενον	= -ούμενον

Imperfect

	Ac.		M. & P.	
S. 1.	ἐδήλο+ον = ἐδήλουν		ἐδηλο+όμην = -ούμην	
2.	ἐδήλο+ες = ἐδήλους		ἐδηλό+ου = -οῦ	
3.	ἐδήλο+ε = ἐδήλου		ἐδηλό+ετο = -οῦτο	
P. 1.	ἐδήλό+ομεν = ἐδηλοῦμεν		ἐδηλο+όμεθα = -ούμεθα	
2.	ἐδήλό+ετε = ἐδηλοῦτε		ἐδηλό+εσθε = -οῦσθε	
3.	ἐδήλό+ον = ἐδήλουν		ἐδηλό+οντο = -οῦντο	

2. The second important fact to learn about these contract-verbs is that when the tense signs are added, the short vowels are lengthened.

a. ἀγαπάω, ἀγαπήσω, ἠγάπησα, ἠγάπηκα, κ. τ. λ.

b. φιλέω,[75] φιλήσω, ἐφίλησα, πεφίληκα, κ. τ. λ.

c. δηλόω, δηλώσω, ἐδήλωσα, κ. τ. λ.

The personal endings are regular.

The Participle

The participle is a verbal adjective, i. e., it has both a verbal and an adjectival force.

As a verb, it has voice and tense. It may also be either transitive or intransitive, i. e., it can take a direct object or not.

[75] Verbs like τελέω, τελέσω, ἐτέλεσα, τετέλεκα, τετέλεσμαι, ἐτελέσθην, seem to be exceptions to this rule. Such verbs are not true contract-verbs, i. e., the stem did not end originally in a short vowel but in a consonant which has been lost. The original form of τελέω seems to have been τελέϜω.

As an adjective, it is declined in all genders and both numbers. It may also be in either the predicative or the attributive position. Sometimes, like other adjectives, the participle with the article may be used as a substantive: πώλησόν σου τὰ ὑπάρχοντα (Mt. 19:21), 'sell what belongs to you.' Here, the participle is the direct object of the verb.

The forms of the participle should be mastered before proceeding further.

The Forms of the Participle

1. From the regular verb:

Pres. Ac.	M. & P.
λύων, λύουσα, λῦον [76]	λυόμενος, -μένη, -μενον[77]
Aor. [78] Ac.	M.
λύσας, λύσασα, λῦσαν [76]	λυσάμενος, -μένη, -μενον[77]
	P.
	λυθείς, λυθεῖσα, λυθέν[76]
Perf. [79] Ac.	M. & P.
λελυκώς, λελυκυῖα, λελυκός[76]	λελυμένος, -μένη, -μένον [77]

Fut. Ac. (very rare in New Testament).
λύσων, λύσουσα, λῦσον[76]

2. From the μι-verb:

a. δίδωμι

Pres. Ac.	M. & P.
διδούς, διδοῦσα, διδόν	διδόμενος, -μένη, -μενον
Aor. Ac.	M.
δούς, δοῦσα, δόν	δόμενος, -μένη, -μενον

[76] These are declined in the masculine and neuter genders like nouns of the third declension; the feminine, like nouns of the first declension.

[77] These are declined in the masculine and neuter like nouns of the second declension; in the feminine, like the first declension.

[78] Verbs, which have second aorist forms, have their participles as follows: λαβών, λαβοῦσα, λαβόν (from λαμβάνω, 'I take'). The accent in these forms is not recessive, as in the present participle.

[79] The second perfect participles, e. g., from οἶδα, are like εἰδώς, εἰδυῖα, εἰδός.

b. τίθημι

Pres. Ac.	M.
τιθείς, τιθεῖσα, τιθέν	τιθέμενος, -μένη, -μενον
Aor. Ac.	M.
θείς, θεῖσα, θέν	θέμενος, -μένη, -μενον

c. ἴστημι

Pres. Ac.	M. & P.
ἱστάς, ἱστᾶσα, ἱστάν	ἱστάμενος, -μένη, -μενον
Aor. Ac.	M.
στάς, στᾶσα, στάν	στάμενος, -μένη, -μενον

The Participle as an Adjective

The participle, like other adjectives, will be either attributive or predicative. The attributive participle describes a substantive in some way; the predicative makes a statement about the subject of the sentence.[80] This description of some noun in the sentence is incidental to the sentence, but the statement about the subject is the main point of the sentence.

Attributive Participle

There are three positions of the attributive participle, corresponding exactly to other adjectives.

1. The article may precede the participle which is followed by the substantive: τῇ ὑγιαινούσῃ διδασκαλίᾳ (Tit. 2:1), 'the wholesome teaching.'

2. The common order is article-substantive, article-participle: ὁ ἄρτος ὁ ἐκ τοῦ οὐρανοῦ καταβαίνων (Jn. 6:50), 'the bread, the coming-down-out-of-heaven (bread).' It should be noted that the phrase ἐκ τοῦ οὐρανοῦ is an adverbial phrase which modifies the participle, καταβαίνων.

   In some cases, the substantive will not have the article. In such cases, it is regarded as sufficiently definite without the article: σοφίαν θεοῦ . . . τὴν ἀποκε-

---

[80] This statement is not true of the genitive absolute, which usually does not refer to the subject of the sentence.

κρυμμένην (I Cor 2:7), 'a wisdom of God . . . the hidden wisdom.' The participle, however, is still attributive.

3. The construction least usual is where the article is not used with either the substantive or the participle: ὕδωρ ζῶν (Jn. 4:10), 'living water.' Had the article been used with the substantive and not with the participle, τὸ ὕδωρ ζῶν, the meaning would have been, 'the water is living.' Here is a good place to note the difference in the effect of the predicative and attributive adjectives in the sentence.

Often the attributive participle should be translated into English by a relative clause: κατὰ δύναμιν θεοῦ, τοῦ σώσαντος ὑμᾶς καὶ καλέσαντος κλήσει ἁγίᾳ (II Tim. 1:8,9), 'according to the power of God, who saved us and called us with a holy calling.'

The future participle with the article always expresses futurity. It expresses time subsequent to that of the main verb: τῶν λαληθησομένων (Heb. 3:5), 'of the things which shall be spoken.'[81]

All of the anarthrous (i. e., without the article) examples in the New Testament are used to express aim or purpose: εἰ ἔρχεται . . . σώσων (Mt. 27:49), 'if he will come (futuristic present) to save'; ἐληλύθει προσκυνήσων (Acts 8:27), 'he had come to worship.' Cf. also Acts 22:5; 24:11,17; Heb. 13:17.[82]

Predicative Participle

There are two kinds of predicative participle: the complementary and the circumstantial.

1. The complementary, or supplementary, participle is fairly common in the New Testament. It is the verbal aspect of the participle that is emphasized, for it fills out the verbal notion: ἦν ἐκβάλλων δαιμόνιον (Lk. 11:14), 'he was casting out a demon.'

[81] Robertson, *A Grammar of the Greek New Testament in the Light of Historical Research*, p. 1119.
[82] Moulton, *Prolegomena*, p. 151; Moulton and Howard, *A Grammar of New Testament Greek*, Vol. II, p. 220.

a. The periphrastic construction is the commonest usage of the complementary participle in the New Testament. Many scholars think that the frequency of this construction in the New Testament is due to Semitic influence. It does occur in those books most subject to Aramaic influence, but it is found as early as Pindar.[83] There is a steady decrease in the use of this construction after New Testament times. This is partly due to the use of the infinitive with such verbs as ἄρχομαι, δοκέω, λανθάνω, τυγχάνω, φαίνομαι, κ. τ. λ., and to the use of the ὅτι clause.

Types of periphrastics:

(1) Present periphrastic consists of the present tense of a copulative verb and the present tense of a participle.

(2) Imperfect periphrastic: imperfect tense of a copulative verb with the present participle.

(3) Present perfect periphrastic: present tense of a copulative verb with the perfect participle.

(4) Future periphrastic: future tense of a copulative verb with the present tense of the participle.

(5) Future perfect periphrastic: future tense of a copulative verb with the perfect tense of the participle.

b. The complementary participle is also used in indirect discourse after verbs of mental action, such as οἶδα, μανθάνω, γινώσκω, ὁμολογέω. Cf. ἔγνων δύναμιν ἐξεληλυθυῖαν ἀπ' ἐμοῦ (Lk. 8:46), 'I perceive power gone out from me.' In this usage, the participle takes the place of the verb in direct discourse.

The difference in meaning between the participle and the infinitive in indirect discourse is that the participle describes an actual experience, while the infinitive and the ὅτι clause tell only of an intellectual apprehension. The suggestion of the participle in Lk. 8:46 is that Jesus experienced a sense of exhaustion in healing the woman.

[83] Robertson, *A Grammar of the Greek New Testament in the Light of Historical Research*, pp. 887f; Moulton, *Prolegomena*, p. 226.

PARTS OF SPEECH   101

2. The circumstantial participle can always be recognized
by the fact that it stands in the predicative position,
i. e., not in the attributive position.[84] It can be distinguished from the complementary participle by the fact
that the complementary is required to complete the idea
of the speaker, while the circumstantial is not. "The
circumstantial participle may be removed and the sentence will not bleed."[85]

It is practically an additional clause, really adverbial
in force. But the additional idea stated has a loose
relation to the rest of the sentence.

Clauses added by means of conjunctions have their
exact meaning rather sharply defined by means of the
conjunction itself: ἐὰν τὰς ἐντολάς μου τηρήσητε, μενεῖτε
ἐν τῇ ἀγάπῃ μου (Jn. 15:10), 'If you guard my command-
ments, ye shall abide in my love.' Here the condition
is stated by the if-clause. But the conditional idea can
be implied by a circumstantial participle: τὸν νόμον
τελοῦσα (Rom. 2:27), 'keeping (if they keep) the law.'
Here Paul is saying with a participle what he might
have said with a conditional clause. It is the context
that gives the participle its conditional force here.

The circumstantial participle may have quite a wide
range of meanings. The context alone can clarify the
meaning of these participles. They may suggest:

a. Time, equivalent to a temporal clause: ταῦτα δὲ αὐτῶν
λαλούντων αὐτὸς ἔστη ἐν μέσῳ αὐτῶν (Lk. 24:36), 'while
they were saying these things, he himself stood in
their midst'; καὶ ἐλθὼν ἐκεῖνος ἐλέγξει τὸν κόσμον (Jn.
16:8), 'and that one, after he has come, will convict
the world.'

b. Conditions: πῶς ἡμεῖς ἐκφευξόμεθα τηλικαύτης ἀμελήσαντες σωτηρίας; (Heb. 2:3), 'how shall we escape, if
we neglect so great salvation?' Cf. I Tim. 4:4; I Cor.
11:29; Gal. 6:9; Rom. 2:27.

c. Concession, equivalent to our 'though,' 'although':
καὶ μηδεμίαν αἰτίαν θανάτου εὑρόντες ᾐτήσαντο Πειλᾶτον

[84] See Attributive participle, p. 98.
[85] Robertson, *A Grammar of the Greek New Testament in the Light
of Historical Research*, p. 1124.

ἀναιρεθῆναι αὐτόν (Acts 13:28), 'and although they found no capital offense in him yet they asked Pilate that he should be put to death.' Cf. Mt. 14:9; Mk. 4:31.

Sometimes, καίπερ (Heb. 5:8), καί γε (Acts 17:27), and καίτοι (Heb. 4:3), are used to emphasize the concessive force of the participle.

A concessive participle is used when attention is called to something having been done in spite of unfavorable circumstances: καίπερ ὢν υἱὸς ἔμαθεν ἀφ' ὧν ἔπαθεν τὴν ὑπακοήν (Heb. 5:8), 'Although being a Son he learned obedience through the things he suffered'; ἔργων...γενηθέντων (Heb. 4:3) (genitive absolute, concessive), 'although the works were completed,' before the foundation of the world, we are in danger of not benefitting thereby, because of unbelief. καίτοι calls attention to the concessive force of the participle here.

d. Cause: ἐχάρησαν οὖν οἱ μαθηταὶ ἰδόντες τὸν κύριον (Jn. 20:20), 'the disciples rejoiced, having seen the Lord.' The participle gives the reason for the joy of the disciples. Another example: συνκεκρασμένους (-νος)[86] (Heb. 4:2) gives the reason for the failure of the truth to benefit men. It was not mingled with faith in them. The same idea could have been expressed by a ὅτι clause or διά. Cf. Mt. 2:3, 10; Acts 9:26.

Sometimes, ὡς is prefixed to the causal participle to call attention to the fact that the participle gives the alleged reason for the act: I Cor. 4:18.

e. Purpose or design, usually in the future tense: ἐληλύθει προσκυνήσων εἰς Ἰερουσαλήμ (Acts 8:27), 'He had come to Jerusalem to worship.' This was a common classic idiom, but in the koine it is being crowded out by ἵνα clauses and the infinitive constructions.

In Acts 3:26, εὐλογοῦντα, a present participle, expresses purpose. God sent his Son 'to bless.'

[86] There is an uncertainty about the text here.

f. **Means:** τίς . . . μεριμνῶν δύναται προσθεῖναι (Mt. 6:27), 'who by means of worry is able to add . . . '. Cf. Acts 16:16; Heb. 2:18.

g. **Manner:** ἑαυτὸν ἐκένωσεν μορφὴν δούλου λαβών (Phil. 2:7), 'He emptied himself (by) taking the form of a servant.' The participle, λαβών, describes how Jesus emptied himself. The assumption of the form of a servant (the incarnation) was the method by which he laid aside the 'trappings of deity.' Sometimes, ὡς is used with the participle to make the point plainer: ὡς ἐξουσίαν ἔχων (Mk. 1:22), 'as one having authority.' Here ὡς calls attention to the force of the participle. Cf. Acts 2:13.

h. **Attendant circumstance:** ἐκεῖνοι δὲ ἐξελθόντες ἐκήρυξαν πανταχοῦ, τοῦ κυρίου συνεργοῦντος καὶ τὸν λόγον βεβαιοῦντος (Mk. 16:20), 'and they went forth and preached everywhere, the Lord working with them and confirming the word.' The participles, συνεργοῦντος and βεβαιοῦντος, call attention to the circumstances under which the apostles preached: the Lord co-operating with them. The participle, ἐξελθόντες, is a temporal participle: they went out and then preached.

The genitive absolute is a circumstantial participle. It consists of a participle and a substantive (noun or pronoun), which may at times be omitted. Generally, the substantive refers to a person or thing which would not otherwise be mentioned in the sentence: Γαλλίωνος ἀνθυπάτου ὄντος (Acts 18:12), 'Gallio being proconsul.'

The genitive absolute may express any of the eight ideas that any other circumstantial participle may express.

The Participle as a Verb

The participle retains enough of its verbal consciousness to 'govern' cases: ἐπικαλεσάμενος τὸ ὄνομα (Acts 22: 16), 'having called upon the name.'

The participle will be followed by the same case as its corresponding finite verb.

1. Participles from verbs of sensation will generally take the genitive case: ἀκούων αὐτοῦ (Jn. 3:29), 'hearing him.'

2. Participles from verbs expressing the idea of personal interest will generally take the dative case: οὐχ ὡς ἀνθρώποις ἀρέσκοντες (I Th. 2:4), 'not as pleasing men.'

3. Participles from verbs that take the accusative case will be followed by the accusative: ὁ ἔχων τὴν νύμφην (Jn. 3:29), 'the one having the bride.'

The Verbal Adjectives in -τος and -τεος

These verbals are, strictly speaking, not participles. They do not partake of the verbal nature to the extent of having voice and tense, nor do they take objects. They are simply adjectives formed on verb stems: ἀγαπάω, 'I love,' yields ἀγαπητός, 'beloved'; ἐκλέγω, 'I choose,' gives ἐκλεκτός, 'chosen,' 'elect.'

The verbal in -τος is very common. Most of these have the passive force, as does ἀγαπητός (Mt. 3:17), 'beloved'; but ζεστός (Rev. 3:15), 'boiling,' is active. ἀδύνατος may be either active (Acts 14:8; Rom. 15:1), 'incapable'; or passive (Mt. 19:26; Mk. 10:27), 'impossible.' Sometimes, as in Rom. 8:3, there is room for doubt as to whether ἀδύνατος is active or passive. The context must decide such examples.

The verbal in -τεος has the idea of necessity. It is really a gerundive. There is only one example in the New Testament: βλητέον (from βάλλω, 'I throw') (Lk. 5:38), 'one must put.' Several manuscripts add βλητέον in Mk. 2:22. The AV translates a text reading the verbal in Mark.

THE INFINITIVE

The Nature of the Infinitive

Like the participle, the infinitive is a hybrid: it is a verbal substantive. In some examples the verbal force will be uppermost, and in some the substantive.

1. As a substantive, it may be used in any case but the vocative, always in the singular number and in the neuter gender. It is always indeclinable. It may be used with or without the article. The article, when used, is always declined and is helpful in recognizing the case relation of the infinitive: τὸ θέλειν (Rom. 7:18) is in the nominative case, subject of the verb, παράκειται, 'to will is present'; τὸ εἶναι (Phil 2:6) is in the accusative case, object of ἡγήσατο, 'he did (not) reckon being' on an equality with God; τοῦ ζῆν (Heb. 2:15) is in the genitive case after διά. The verbal noun, ζῆν (or verbal substantive), is further modified by the adjective, παντός, 'through all the living'; the AV renders, 'through all their life-time.'

2. As a verb, the infinitive may have voice and tense, but not mode. The force of the voice may not be as prominent as in the finite verb, but it is always present. The tense will always be timeless; and if present, durative; if aorist, punctiliar; and if perfect, completed.

   As a verb, the infinitive may also 'govern cases,' as a finite verb does. In general, the infinitive will be followed by the same case as the finite verb:

   a. Verbs of personal interest will take the dative case: δοθῆναι αὐτῇ (Mk. 5:43), 'to be given to her.'

   b. Verbs of sensation will take the genitive: ἐπιλαθέσθαι τοῦ ἔργου ὑμῶν (Heb. 6:10), 'to forget your work.'

   c. Verbs with the idea of separation are followed by the ablative: τοῦ ἀπέχεσθαι τῶν ἀλισγημάτων (Acts 15:20), 'to hold back (abstain) from the pollutions.'

   d. Copulative verbs will take the predicate nominative: καταγγελεὺς εἶναι (Acts 17:18), 'to be a proclaimer'; τὸ εἶναι ἴσα (Phil. 2:6), 'to be equal.'

   e. Verbs that take the accusative, will take the accusative.

   Both the verbal and the substantival force should be watched in interpreting. Sometimes one will predominate and sometimes the other, but both will be present. A good example to study is Phil. 2:6. This is a relative clause (introduced by ὅς) with the force of an adjective. The subject (with its modifiers) of the clause is ὅς ἐν μορφῇ θεοῦ ὑπάρχων. The predicate is οὐχ ἁρπαγμὸν ἡγήσατο τὸ εἶναι ἴσα θεῷ κ. τ. λ. The verb, ἡγήσατο, takes a double accusative: τὸ εἶναι ἴσα θεῷ is the direct object of ἡγήσατο, and ἁρπαγμόν is the predicate accusative. The direct accusative analyzes itself further: τὸ εἶναι, the simplest form of the direct object, is followed by the predicate nominative adjective, ἴσα, which in turn governs the instrumental case, θεῷ (after a word expressing likeness or identity). A word on the participle, ὑπάρχων, may be said here: it is a circumstantial participle, expressing concession. The idea of the clause then is: 'Although Jesus existed (from the beginning) in the form of God, He did not reckon the being on an equality with God a prize to be clutched to Himself.' Before you know what the clause means, you must go to a good lexicon for the exact meaning of μορφή. Contrast it with σχῆμα.

The Uses of the Infinitive

The uses of the infinitive are quite varied.

1. It may be used as the subject of the verb: ἐμοὶ γὰρ τὸ ζῆν Χριστός (the copulative, ἐστί, is omitted, but that makes no real difference) (Phil. 1:21), 'living is Christ, so far as I am concerned.'

   It may also be the direct object of a verb.[87]

2. It may be used to explain another word in the sentence.

   a. When it explains a verb, it is called the 'epexegetical infinitive': ποιεῖν (τὰ μὴ καθήκοντα) (Rom. 1:28), 'to do' (the things that are unseemly), explains what Paul means by παρέδωκεν αὐτοὺς ὁ θεὸς εἰς ἀδόκιμον νοῦν, 'God gave them up to a reprobate mind.' The list of unseemly acts follows. The example just cited does not have the article with the infinitive. The presence or absence of the article makes no real difference in the meaning of the construction.

[87] See Phil. 2:6, above.

b. When it explains a noun, it is called the 'appositional infinitive': θρησκεία καθαρὰ καὶ ἀμίαντος . . . ἐπισκέπτεσθαι ὀρφανοὺς καὶ χήρας (Jas. 1:27), 'pure religion and undefiled is . . . to visit orphans and widows.' Here the infinitive further defines 'religion.'

c. There is another construction, τοῦ with the infinitive, which is often epexegetical: τοῦ κατὰ σάρκα ζῆν (Rom. 8:12), 'to live according to the flesh.' This infinitive explains what it means to 'be a debtor to the flesh': to be a debtor to the flesh is to live by a fleshly pattern.

Just as any other substantive, sometimes, this construction, τοῦ with the infinitive, is in the genitive case: ἔχει πίστιν τοῦ σωθῆναι (Acts 14:9), 'he has faith to be saved,' i. e., he has saving faith; and sometimes, ablative: ἐνεκοπτόμην . . . τοῦ ἐλθεῖν (Rom. 15:22), 'I was hindered from coming.' These usages are not epexegetical.

Sometimes, the ἵνα clause is used with the epexegetical force: πόθεν μοι τοῦτο ἵνα ἔλθῃ; (Lk. 1:43), 'whence is this to me, that (she) should come?' The ἵνα clause with epexegetical force is a characteristic of the Johannine writings. It is found elsewhere occasionally.

3. The infinitive may be used to express purpose or result.

a. The simple infinitive: ἦλθον καταλῦσαι (Mt. 5:17), 'I have come to destroy.'

b. τοῦ with the infinitive. This is the normal usage of this construction in Attic Greek, but in the New Testament the epexegetic use is the more frequent.

Luke uses τοῦ with the infinitive more often than any other New Testament writer: Gospel, twenty-three times; Acts, twenty-one. About half of his express purpose. Paul uses it thirteen times, and only two of his (Rom. 6:6; Phil. 3:10) definitely express purpose, and both of these come within a ἵνα clause of purpose. When Paul desired to express purpose he did not, as a rule, use this idiom. Matthew has it six times; Hebrews, four; Revelation, one;

James, one; I Peter, one. In Lk. 17:1 and Acts 10:
25, τοῦ with the infinitive is used in the nominative
case. The expression had become more or less
crystallized.

c. εἰς τό and the infinitive will usually express purpose:
εἰς τὸ στηριχθῆναι (Rom. 1:11), 'to be strengthened.'
It is almost exclusively a Pauline idiom (fifty
times). There are eight instances in Hebrews; one
each in Mark, Acts and Luke; two each in James
and I Peter (cf. Jas. 1:19); and three in Matthew.
Westcott, on Heb. 5:1, thinks that ἵνα refers to
immediate purpose, whereas εἰς τό refers to more
remote purpose. Sometimes, εἰς τό seems to express
result: εἰς τὸ εἶναι (Rom. 1:20), 'so as to be.'
The interpretation of εἰς τό with the infinitive is
often quite important theologically, e. g., was the
revelation in nature (Rom. 1:20) designed to make
men inexcusable when they sinned; or, did it reveal
God clearly enough that, as a result, men were
inexcusable when they sinned? A similar theological
issue is raised by the ἵνα clause: μὴ ἔπταισαν ἵνα
πέσωσιν (Rom. 11:11). Did they stumble in order
that they might fall, or, did they stumble (so
seriously) that they did fall? For a long time some
commentators would not admit that these two constructions could express result, but in the light of
the papyri such a position can not be maintained
any longer.

d. πρὸς τό with the infinitive also is used to express
purpose. It occurs five times in Matthew, and once
in Mark, in this sense. It occurs only once
in Luke (18:1) and once in Acts (3:19), but it does
not seem to express purpose in these instances. It
occurs four times in Paul to express 'subjective
purpose' in the 'agent's' mind.

4. Other uses of the infinitive.

a.   διὰ τό with the infinitive expresses cause, as with
any other substantive: διὰ τὸ μὴ ἔχειν (Mt. 13:5),
'on account of not having.'

b. ἐν τῷ with the infinitive is a very common usage. It occurs fifty-five times in the New Testament. About three-fourths of these instances are in Luke. Apparently, Luke was influenced by the style of the LXX, as it translated the Hebrew preposition ‎ב.

Ordinarily, the infinitive is in the present tense, and generally means 'while,' 'during': ἐν τῷ σπείρειν (Lk. 8:5), 'while sowing.' It occurs twelve times with the aorist infinitive. In these cases, it presents the simple action of the verb, leaving the precise time relation to be defined by the context, like the aorist participle of simultaneous action. In Heb. 8:13, ἐν τῷ λέγειν, the idea is rather causal.

c. The infinitive may be used with other prepositions, just as any other substantive: ἀντὶ τοῦ λέγειν (Jas. 4:15), 'instead of saying.'

d. The infinitive may be used absolutely, as in the greetings of letters: χαίρειν (Jas. 1:1; Acts 15:23), 'greeting.' Another absolute use of the infinitive is found in στοίχειν (Phil. 3:16), 'walk'; κλαίειν (Rom. 12:15), 'weep.' The context gives these the imperative force.

THE ADVERB

Some grammarians include under the term 'adverb,' not only the true adverbs, but conjunctions, prepositions, intensive particles, and interjections. There is evidence in historical grammar for this, but for practical purposes we shall confine our discussion to the pure adverb.

The Origin of the Adverb

Originally, all adverbs had just as clearcut case-forms as the nouns. Traces of these case endings are found in nearly all adverbs. So, it need not surprise the student to find any case-form of a noun, pronoun, or participle used adverbially.

1. By far the commonest adverbial ending in the New Testament is -ως, a survival of an old ablative case

ending. Moulton[88] calls attention to the fact that there
are about a hundred of these in the New Testament,
fully a third of the total. By attaching this ending to
a participle, ὁμολογουμένως (I Tim. 3:16), 'confessedly';
to an adjective in the positive degree, κακῶς (Mt. 14:
35), 'badly'; in the comparative degree, σπουδαιοτέρως
(Phil. 2:28), 'more zealously'; in the superlative degree,
ἐσχάτως (Mk. 5:23), 'extremely'; to a pronoun, οὕτως
(I Cor. 7:25), 'thus'; etc., an adverb may be made.

2. The genitive case is represented by such forms as:
ὅπου (Mt. 6:19), 'where.'

3. The locative case is represented by such forms as:
ἐκεῖ (Jn. 18:13), 'there'; κύκλῳ (Mk. 3:34), 'in a circle.'

4. The instrumental is represented by such forms as:
τάχα (Rom. 5:7), 'perhaps'; λάθρα (Mt. 1:19), 'secretly.'

5. The dative survives in such forms as χαμαί (Jn. 9:6),
'on the ground.'

6. The accusative is quite frequent: δωρεάν (Mt. 10:8),
'freely'; ταχύ (Mt. 5:25), 'quickly.'

7. The nominative survives in one word: ἅπαξ (II
Cor. 11:25), 'once'; and its compound, ἐφάπαξ (Heb.
7:27), 'once for all.'

Adverbial Phrases

A great variety of phrases are used with adverbial
force.[89] These are too numerous to be listed. They should
be easily recognized.

The Uses of the Adverb

1. The commonest use is with verbs: σπουδαίως (Lk. 7:
4), 'eagerly.' Here, the adverb describes the manner
in which a request is made.

The adverb may be used as the predicate after the
verbs γίνομαι (I Th. 2:10), and εἰμί (Mt. 1:18). In I Th.
2:10, three adverbs, ὁσίως, δικαίως, ἀμέμπτως, are used
in the predicative position.

---

[88] *A Grammar of New Testament Greek*, Vol. II, p. 163.
[89] Robertson, *A Grammar of the Greek New Testament in the Light
of Historical Research*, pp. 550f.

There is a peculiar use with ἔχω: τοὺς κακῶς ἔχοντας (Mt. 14:35), 'those having (holding) badly'; ἐσχάτως ἔχει (Mk. 5:23), 'he has (holds) in the last stages,' i. e., 'he is extremely ill.'

2. Another frequent use is with adjectives: ὁμολογουμένως μέγα (I Tim. 3:16), 'confessedly great.'

3. The adverb may modify another adverb: μᾶλλον περισσότερον (Mk. 7:36), 'more exceedingly.'

4. It may be used with a substantive, as an adjective: ἐν τῷ νῦν καιρῷ (Rom. 3:26), 'in the present (now) time.'

Sometimes, an adjective will be used where the English reader would expect an adverb: δευτεραῖοι ἤλθομεν (Acts 28:13), 'we came, second day men (on the second day).' See also αὐτομάτη ἡ γῆ καρποφορεῖ (Mk. 4:28), 'the earth bears fruit of herself (automatically).'

5. It may be treated as a substantive: ἀπὸ τὸ νῦν (Lk. 1: 48), 'from the present.'

The common word for 'neighbor' is simply the adverb πλησίον, 'near.'

Adverbial Suffixes

There are a few adverbial suffixes that it is quite useful to know.

1. -θεν is a locative ending, meaning 'from there': μακρόθεν (Mt. 27:55), 'from afar.' Cf. ὄπισθεν, 'from behind'; πάντοθεν, 'from everywhere (all around)'; ἔξωθεν, 'from without'; κύκλοθεν, 'from around.'

2. -κις is a multiplicative and answers the question 'how often': ἑβδομηκοντάκις ἑπτά (Mt. 18:22), 'seventy times seven'; πολλάκις (Mt. 17:15), 'frequently.'

3. -ιστι answers the question 'in what language': Ἑλληνιστί (Jn. 19:20); Ῥωμαϊστί (Jn. 19:20); Ἑβραϊστί (Jn. 19:20); Λυκαονιστί (Acts 14:11).

Adverbs Distinguished from Adjectives

The interpreter must be on his guard to note the difference between the adverb and the adjective. Two examples will suffice here: ἦν πρῶτος (Jn. 20:4) means that 'the other disciple' came before Peter (to the tomb) ; ζητεῖτε πρῶτον (Mt. 6:33) means 'the first thing you do seek (the kingdom of God . . .).' The test to apply here is the agreement in case between the adjective and the subject of the verb: πρῶτος, being nominative, can be an adjective, whereas πρῶτον can not in this sentence.

THE PREPOSITION

Origin

The preposition started its career as an adverb. Originally, the case-form of the noun was sufficient to express the relation between words in the sentence. As language grew more complex, it was felt to be necessary to make these case-ideas clearer, so adverbs began to be used.

Nearly all of these adverbs had a local force, and so their value in further defining the case-idea can best be illustrated with the locative case: Δαμασκῷ (Acts 9:10) might mean 'in,' 'near,' 'beside,' or even 'upon' Damascus. So the 'local adverb' was called into service to clear up such ambiguities. The preposition ἐν tells us that Ananias dwelt within the city of Damascus. The preposition πρός would have meant that he dwelt 'near'; παρά, 'beside' Damascus. So it becomes clear that prepositions were the interpreters of the case-forms. They do not 'govern' cases, as many grammarians have taught. This function of the preposition gradually made the case-forms unnecessary for the expressing of the relation between nouns within the sentence.[90]

The name 'preposition' grew out of the belief that the original usage of this part of speech was with verbs to form compounds, e.g., προσ-έρχομαι, ἐπι-καλέω. There are differences of opinion among the authorities on this point, and we shall not attempt to settle the dispute.

[90] Cf. The Cases, p. 20.

However, it is worth noting that this idea of the original usage of prepositions led to the common twofold classification: 'proper prepositions,' those that form compounds with verbs; and 'improper prepositions,' those that do not. This theory of the original use of the preposition led the older grammarians to speak of 'tmesis' (cutting or separation), whenever Homer 'separated' the preposition from the verb, as he very often did. It should be kept in mind that Homer represents the oldest considerable volume of Greek literature that we have. His procedure is regarded as abnormal, because Attic Greek is taken as the norm. But Homer is a better criterion for original usages than Attic writers who followed him by some five hundred years or more.

Once, even in the New Testament, a preposition is used as a simple adverb: ὑπὲρ ἐγώ (II Cor. 11:13), 'I more.'

The 'Improper Prepositions'

We shall deal with the so-called 'improper prepositions' first, because their usage is much simpler, since they are not used in compounds. There are forty-two of these.

1. ἅμα, 'together with,' with the associative-instrumental: Mt. 13:29.
2. ἄνευ, 'without,' with the ablative: Mt. 10:29.
3. ἄντικρυς, 'over against,' with the genitive: Acts 20:15.
4. ἀντίπερα, 'opposite,' with the ablative: Lk. 8:26.
5. ἀπέναντι, 'before,' with the ablative: Mt. 27:24.
6. ἄτερ, 'without,' with the ablative: Lk. 22:35.
7. ἄχρι, 'until,' with the genitive: Acts 1:22.
8. ἐγγύς, 'near,' with the genitive: Jn. 3:23; dative: Acts 9:38.
9. ἐκτός, 'outside of,' with the ablative: II Cor. 12:2.
10. ἔμπροσθεν, 'in front of,' with the ablative: Mk. 9:2.
11. ἔναντι, 'before,' with the genitive: Acts 7:10.
12. ἐναντίον, 'in the presence of,' with the genitive: Lk. 20:26.

114 AN EXEGETICAL GRAMMAR

13. ἕνεκα (-εν, εἵνεκεν), 'on account of,' with the genitive: Mt. 10:18.

14. ἐντός,⁹¹ 'within,' with the genitive: Mt. 23:36; Lk. 17:21.

15. ἐνώπιον, 'in the sight of,' with the genitive: Lk. 1:19.

16. ἔξω, 'outside of,' with the ablative: Mt. 10:14.

17. ἔξωθεν, 'from without,' with the ablative: Rev. 14:20.

18. ἐπάνω, 'above,' with the genitive: Mk. 14:5.

19. ἐπέκεινα, 'beyond,' with the ablative: Acts 7:43.

20. ἔσω, 'within,' with the genitive: Mk. 15:13.

21. ἕως, 'as far as,' with the genitive: Lk. 10:15.

22. κατέναντι, 'over against,' with the genitive: Mk. 11:2.

23. κατενώπιον, 'before the face of,' with the genitive: Col. 1:22.

24. κυκλόθεν, 'from all sides,' 'around,' with the genitive: Rev. 4:3, 4, 8.

25. κύκλῳ, 'in a circle,' with the genitive: Rev. 4:6.

26. μέσον, 'in the midst of,' with the genitive: Phil. 2:15.

27. μεταξύ, 'between,' with the ablative: Mt. 23:35.

28. μέχρι, 'as far as,' 'until,' with the genitive: Mt. 13:30.

29. ὄπισθεν, 'from behind,' with the ablative: Mt. 15:23.

30. ὀπίσω, 'behind,' with the ablative: Mt. 10:38.

31. ὀψέ, 'after,' with the ablative: Mt. 28:1.

32. παραπλήσιον, 'near to,' with the genitive: Phil. 2:27.

33. παρεκτός, 'except,' with the ablative: Acts 26:29.

34. πέραν, 'on the other side,' with the ablative: Mk. 3:8.

35. πλήν, 'besides,' with the ablative: Acts 8:1.

36. πλησίον, 'near,' with the genitive: Jn. 4:5.

⁹¹ In Lk. 17:21, many New Testament students think that ἐντός must mean 'among,' for the reason that Jesus could hardly say to the Pharisees, his enemies, 'the kingdom of God is within you.' Allen (*Expository Times*, July, 1938) suggests that ὑμῶν should be "taken impersonally, as often in our Lord's teaching." Taken in this sense, he feels that the difficulty disappears. The late Professor Sledd of Emory University suggested that ἐντός should be taken in the sense of "the group within the group," i. e., out of the Pharisaic group and those they represent will come the (nucleus of) kingdom of God.

37. ὑπεράνω, 'above,' with the ablative: Eph. 4:10.

38. ὑπερέκεινα, 'beyond,' with the ablative: II Cor. 10:16.

39. ὑπερεκπερισσοῦ, 'far more than,' with the ablative: Eph. 3:20.

40. ὑποκάτω, 'underneath, with the ablative: Mk. 6:11.

41. χάριν,⁹² 'for the sake of,' with the genitive: Gal. 3:19.

42. χωρίς, 'without,' with the ablative: Rom. 3:21.

The 'Proper Prepositions'

These prepositions are much more complex, because they are not only used with cases, but also in a great variety of compounds. There are eighteen of these 'proper prepositions.' We shall deal first with their usage with the cases.

1. ἀμφί, 'on both sides,' is obsolete in Hellenistic Greek as a preposition, so it will be found in the New Testament only in compound words.

2. ἀνά, 'upwards,' is akin to the English 'on,' German 'an.' It occurs thirteen times (Nestle's text) in the New Testament. WH omit it in Lk. 9:3, but Nestle retains it.

   It is always used with the accusative, except in Rev. 21:21, where we read ἀνὰ εἷς. Here, the word is merely an adverb (cf. Homer), not a preposition.

   There are six examples of ἀνὰ δύο: Lk. 10:1. These all have the distributive idea, 'two by two.'

   There are four examples of ἀνὰ μέσον followed by the genitive. Here, it is a sort of compound prepositional phrase, meaning 'between,' 'up along the middle.' Cf. Mt. 13:25.

   There is one example of ἀνὰ μέρος: I Cor. 14:27, which means 'in turn.'

3. ἀντί, 'at the end of.' This is the locative case of the Sanskrit anta, and out of the meaning 'at the end of,' we get 'in front of,' 'opposite.' Every usage, both

---

⁹² A clear case of the accusative case of a noun becoming a preposition.

as a preposition and in compounds, should be explained starting with this fundamental idea of 'facing.'

Out of the idea 'facing' comes quite naturally the idea of 'substitution,' 'instead of,' the common meaning in the New Testament: ἡ κόμη ἀντὶ περιβολαίου (I Cor. 11:15), 'the hair (is) instead of a mantle.' Cf. Mk. 10:45. In χάριν ἀντὶ χάριτος (Jn. 1:16), some scholars insist that ἀντί should be taken in the sense of 'upon,' or 'in addition to.' This undoubtedly gives the general sense of the passage. But an equally suggestive translation, and possibly more correct, is 'grace instead of grace,' i. e., as we receive a grace and use it, another takes its place. As God's mercies are new every morning, so his acts of grace come to us in endless succession, each taking the place of its predecessor.

This word occurs as a preposition, twenty-two times in the New Testament. It is always used with the genitive case.

4. ἀπό, 'off,' 'away.' Moulton[93] says that all of the uses of this word start from the notion of separation. It is regularly used in the New Testament with the ablative case to make clearer the case-idea of separation.

Once, it is used in the nominative: ἀπὸ ὁ ὢν καὶ ὁ ἦν καὶ ὁ ἐρχόμενος (Rev. 1:4), 'from the one who is, who was and who is to come.' Dionysius[94] said that this "idiotism" was used "to express the unchangeableness of God." It is perfectly clear that the author knew that ἀπό should be followed by the ablative case (Rev. 1:5). Probably the whole expression was regarded as indeclinable.

a. It is of very frequent occurrence in the New Testament, usually expressing the simple idea of separation: βάλε ἀπὸ σοῦ (Mt. 5:29), 'cast (it) from thee.'

b. Occasionally, it may have a causative force: ἀπὸ τῆς χαρᾶς (Lk. 24:41), 'because of the joy' the disciples found it difficult to believe in the resurrection of Jesus.

[93] *A Grammar of New Testament Greek*, Vol. II, p. 297.
[94] Robertson, *A Grammar of the Greek New Testament in the Light of Historical Research*, p. 135.

c. It may express agency: ἀπὸ θεοῦ πειράζομαι (Jas. 1: 13), 'I am tempted from God.' Here, God is viewed, not as the direct agent, but as the source of 'temptation.'

d. Sometimes, it occurs in the New Testament as a sort of 'translation Hebraism' after verbs of fearing or taking precaution: μὴ φοβηθῆτε ἀπὸ τῶν ἀποκτεννόντων τὸ σῶμα (Lk. 12:4), 'do not fear those killing the body.'

Often, in the LXX, the preposition מִן is translated by ἀπό to express such an idea as fearing or taking precaution, but at least once, in the papyri where no Jewish influence could be claimed, we have the same construction: βλέπε σατὸν ἀπὸ τῶν Ἰουδαίων (B. G. U. 1079, A. D. 41), 'beware of the Jews.' The writer was warning his friend against Jewish money lenders. Deissmann[95] thinks that surely no Jew wrote that.

e. Some phrases with this preposition merely express the 'partitive genitive' idea: ἐκλεξάμενος ἀπ' αὐτῶν δώδεκα (Lk. 6:13), 'having selected twelve from them.'

5. διά. The root idea seems to be 'two' (δύο): δια-κόσιοι, δί-δραχμα, κ. τ. λ. As a preposition, it developed two distinct meanings which may easily be recognized in the two cases with which the preposition is used.

a. With the genitive, the primary idea is 'through.'

(1) It may express 'interval' of either time or space. The former is not so common, but does occur: δι' ὅλης νυκτός (Lk. 5:5), 'through all (the) night.' It is very common to express 'passing through space': διὰ τῆς Σαμαρίας (Jn. 4:4), 'through Samaria.'

(2) It may express 'secondary agency,' as contrasted with ὑπό and the genitive to express 'primary agency': ὑπὸ κυρίου διὰ τοῦ προφήτου (Mt. 1:22), 'by the Lord through the prophet.'

[95] *Light from the Ancient East*, p. 120.

(3) With inanimate objects, it may express means:
διὰ πίστεως (Eph. 2:8), 'by means of faith'; or
manner: διὰ παραβολῆς (Lk. 8:4), 'by the parabolic
method.'

b. With the accusative, it expresses the ground or
reason for an act, with the idea of 'because of,' 'for
the sake of,' 'on account of.' In διὰ φθόνον παρέδωκαν
αὐτόν (Mt. 27:18), 'because of envy they had
delivered him up,' the preposition tells us that envy
was the reason why the chief-priests and scribes
delivered Jesus to Pilate.

The aim or purpose of an act may be expressed
also: τὸ σάββατον διὰ τὸν ἄνθρωπον ἐγένετο καὶ οὐχ ὁ
ἄνθρωπος διὰ τὸ σάββατον (Mk. 2:27), i. e., the aim in
establishing the Sabbath was to benefit man, not
that man should serve the Sabbath.

6. ἐν, 'in,' 'withinness.' Originally, ἐν and εἰς were the
same word, and could be used with either the locative
or the accusative case; εἰς is simply a later form,
shortened from ἐνς.

In the New Testament, ἐν is used only with the locative case. The primary idea is very simple, 'within,'
but the preposition became a 'maid-of-all-work,' and
so a variety of ideas may be expressed.

a. The simplest is the local idea of place: ἐν τῇ ἀγορᾷ
(Mt. 20:3), 'in the market place.'

b. In the expression of time, it is very common: ἐν τῇ
ἐσχάτῃ ἡμέρᾳ (Jn. 6:44), 'in (on) the last day.'

The preposition may quite properly be omitted in
expressions of time: κἀγὼ ἀναστήσω αὐτὸν τῇ ἐσχάτῃ
ἡμέρᾳ (Jn. 6:54), 'and I will raise him up on the
last day.'

c. With plural nouns, it may have the idea of 'among':
ἐν τοῖς ἔθνεσιν (Gal. 1:16), 'among the nations.'

d. Where a single individual is selected as a specimen
or striking illustration, it may mean 'in the case of':
ἐν ἐμοί (Gal. 1:16), 'in the case of me.'

e. Sometimes, it may express the idea of 'occasion,' 'in the sphere of,' 'amounting to': ἔφυγεν ἐν τῷ λόγῳ τούτῳ (Acts 7:29), 'He fled at this word.' Here, the preposition gives the occasion of Moses' flight. In ἐν τῷ εὐαγγελίῳ (Rom. 1:9), 'in the gospel,' it gives the sphere of Paul's ministry. In Mk. 4:8, εἰς . . . ἐν . . .ἐν, it has the idea of 'amounting to.'

f. Sometimes, it may express 'accompanying circumstances': ἐν δέκα χιλιάσιν ὑπαντῆσαι (Lk. 14:31), 'to meet (a king) accompanied by ten thousand (soldiers).'

g. The dative idea seems to be expressed by it: τοῖς ἐν θεῷ πατρὶ ἠγαπημένοις (Jude 1), 'to those beloved by (dear to) God the father.' This should not surprise us in the light of the wide usage of ἐν and the fact that the locative and dative forms are the same.

In modern Greek, the regular way of expressing the dative idea is εἰς and the accusative.

h. The instrumental idea is sometimes expressed: πολεμήσω ἐν τῇ ῥομφαίᾳ (Rev. 2:16), 'I will fight with a sword.'

The correct meaning of this preposition can be gotten only in the light of the context.

7. εἰς, 'into.' Originally, this preposition was used without any thought of motion. In the New Testament, it will usually have the idea of 'up to and within,' and is used with verbs of motion: ἐλθόντες εἰς τὴν οἰκίαν (Mt. 2:11), 'having come into the house.'

a. There are a few instances where it does not seem to differ from ἐν in meaning: ὁ εἰς τὸν ἀγρόν (Mk. 13:16); ὁ ἐν τῷ ἀγρῷ (Mt. 24:18). Both expressions occur in parallel passages and seem to have identical meaning: 'in the field.'

b. In expressions of time, it either marks the limit or accents the duration of the time: φυλάξαι εἰς ἐκείνην τὴν ἡμέραν (II Tim. 1:12), 'to guard up until that day.'

In such expressions as εἰς τὸν αἰῶνα (Mt. 21:19), 'unto the age,' the preposition does not really add much to the force of the accusative case, which itself gives the idea of duration.

c. The dative idea may be expressed by it and the accusative: λειτουργὸν . . . εἰς τὰ ἔθνη (Rom. 15:16), 'a minister . . . to the nations.'

d. Sometimes, the context makes it clear that it implies 'aim' or 'purpose': τοῦτο ποιεῖτε εἰς τὴν ἐμὴν ἀνάμνησιν (I Cor. 11:24), 'do this to remember me (in remembrance of me).'

e. There is another use, called the predicative, where the preposition is followed by the accusative, when the usual construction would have been the nominative: ἔσεσθέ μοι εἰς υἱοὺς καὶ θυγατέρας (II Cor. 6:18, quoted from the LXX), 'ye shall be sons and daughters to me.' This construction was good *koine* Greek, but in the New Testament, it is usually due to the quoting of the LXX where the Hebrew preposition, ל, is translated.

8. ἐκ (ἐξ), 'out of,' 'from within.' In the New Testament, this preposition is used only with the ablative. The writings of John (Gospel, Epistles and Revelation) use it much more frequently than any other New Testament books.

a. In expressions of place, the sphere from which something comes: φωνὴ ἐκ τῶν οὐρανῶν (Mt. 3:17), 'a voice out of the heavens.' This is by far the commonest usage in the New Testament.

b. In expressions of time, it gives the point of time from which departure is taken: ἐκ νεότητος (Mk. 10: 20), 'from youth.' Other adverbial phrases with a metaphorical meaning have a kindred origin: ἐξ ἀνάγκης (II Cor. 9:7), 'from necessity.'

c. It may accent the idea of separation: ἐλεύθερος ἐκ πάντων (I Cor. 9:19), 'free from all.'

d. It may express the idea of origin or source: οὐκ εἰμὶ ἐκ τοῦ κόσμου (Jn. 17:14), 'I am not from the world.'

e. It may express cause or occasion: ἐμασῶντο ἐκ τοῦ πόνου (Rev. 16:10), 'they gnawed (their tongues) because of the pain.'

f. It may express the partitive idea: μή τις ἐκ τῶν ἀρχόντων ἐπίστευσεν; (Jn. 7:48), 'Have any of the rulers believed?' John is especially fond of this idiom.

9. ἐπί, 'upon.' This preposition differs from ὑπέρ, 'over,' in that it implies an actual state of 'resting upon.' The very simplicity of the idea gives a wide range of uses. It occurs with at least three cases: accusative, four hundred and sixty-four times; genitive, two hundred and sixteen times; locative, one hundred and seventy-six times (some of these are regarded as dative).

a. With the accusative, it means 'upon.' By coupling this meaning with the idea of 'extension' or 'motion toward' in the case itself, one gets the resultant idea: περιεπάτησεν ἐπὶ τὰ ὕδατα (Mt. 14:29), 'he walked upon the waters'; σκότος ἐγένετο ἐπὶ πᾶσαν τὴν γῆν (Mt. 27: 45), 'darkness came upon all the land.'

There are other uses growing out of this primary use.

(1) The metaphorical use: φόβος ἐπέπεσεν ἐπ' αὐτόν (Lk. 1:12), 'fear fell upon him.' The local idea easily gives rise to the metaphorical.

(2) The idea of 'as far as' may grow out of the context: ἔρχονται ἐπὶ τὸ μνῆμα (Mk. 16:2), the women 'came as far as the tomb,' not 'upon' it. Cf. Jn. 6:16; Acts 8:36.

(3) The idea of aim or purpose may be expressed: ἐρχομένους ἐπὶ τὸ βάπτισμα (Mt. 3:7), the Pharisees and the Sadducees came to be baptized.

(4) One's emotions may be expressed with verbs describing mental processes: τοῖς πιστεύσουσιν ἐπὶ τὸν

ἐγείραντα Ἰησοῦν ... ἐκ νεκρῶν (Rom. 4:24), 'to those believing upon the One who raised Jesus ... from the dead'; ἐλπίσατε ἐπὶ τὴν φερομένην ὑμῖν χάριν ἐν ἀποκαλύψει Ἰησοῦ Χριστοῦ (I Pet. 1:13), 'hope upon the grace being borne to you in the revealing of Jesus Christ'; σπλαγχνίζομαι ἐπὶ τὸν ὄχλον (Mt. 15: 32), 'I have compassion on the crowd.'

(5) In personal relations, hostility may be implied: ὡς ἐπὶ λῃστὴν ἐξήλθατε; (Mt. 26:55), 'Have you come out as against a thief?' Cf. Mk. 3:24, 26.

(6) With expressions of time, it may merely fill out the accusative: ἐπὶ ἔτη τρία (Lk. 4:25), 'for three years.'

In interpreting this preposition and the accusative, start with the root ideas of the preposition and of the case; then ask yourself what is the complete idea in the light of the context.

b. With the genitive, it has a wide range of uses. The simple meaning 'upon' will interpret most examples: ἐπὶ κλίνης (Mt. 9:2), 'upon a bed.'

The following uses grow out of this fundamental meaning:

(1) An ellipsis in thought: ἐπὶ τοῦ βάτου (Mk. 12:26), 'in the passage about the bush.'

(2) The idea of 'in the vicinity of': ἐπὶ τῆς θαλάσσης (Jn. 21:1), 'by the sea.'

In Mt. 21:19, ἐπὶ τῆς ὁδοῦ, the meaning is that the figtree was 'near' the path, not 'in' it or 'on' it.

(3) With persons, it often means 'in the presence of,' or 'before': ἐπὶ ἡγεμόνων (Mk. 13:9), 'before governors.' This construction must be watched, for sometimes it means 'in the time of': ἐπὶ Κλαυδίου (Acts 11:28), 'during the reign of Claudius.' Cf. Lk. 3:2; 4:27; Mk. 2:26.

(4) The idea of 'basis': ἐπ' ἀληθείας (Lk. 4:25), 'upon the basis of truth.'

(5) A metaphorical use with the idea 'over,' in the sense of ruling, grows quite naturally out of

'upon': ὁ ὢν ἐπὶ πάντων (Rom. 9:5), 'the one who is over (rules) all things.'

c. With the locative, the idea expressed is more simple, although there are still a variety of uses:

  (1) The purely local idea: ἐπὶ πίνακι (Mt. 14:8), 'upon a platter.'

  (2) The idea of contiguity: ἐπὶ θύραις (Mt. 24:33), 'at (the) doors.'

  (3) In expressions of time, it is used very sparingly: ἐπὶ συντελείᾳ τῶν αἰώνων (Heb. 9:26), 'at the end of the ages.'

  (4) The idea of cause or occasion: ἐφ' ᾧ πάντες ἥμαρτον (Rom. 5:12), 'because all have sinned.'

  (5) The idea of aim or purpose seems to be expressed: ἐπὶ ἔργοις ἀγαθοῖς (Eph. 2:10), 'for the purpose of good works.'

d. There seem to be a few examples where it is used with the dative. Robertson[96] cites διὰ τὴν ὑπερβάλλουσαν χάριν τοῦ θεοῦ ἐφ' ὑμῖν (II Cor. 9:14), 'on account of the surpassing grace of God to you,' as seemingly a "clear case." This does seem to suit well, but it is the context which yields the dative idea. Cf. Lk. 12:52f.

10. κατά. The root idea seems to be 'down.' In the New Testament, this preposition is used with three cases: accusative, genitive, and ablative.

a. With the accusative, it means 'down along': Lk. 10:4. Out of this simple local idea, several metaphorical uses have developed:

  (1) One of the commonest is the idea of 'standard' or 'rule of measurement': κατὰ τὸ εὐαγγέλιόν μου (Rom. 16:25), 'according to my gospel.' Cf. κατὰ τὸν νόμον (Lk. 2:22), 'according to the law'; κατὰ φύσιν (Rom. 11:21), 'according to nature'; κατὰ χάριν (Rom 4:4), 'according to grace'; κατὰ ὀφείλημα (Rom. 4:4), 'according to debt.'

---

[96] *A Grammar of the Greek New Testament in the Light of Historical Research*, p. 605.

(2) The distributive idea: κατ' ἔτος (Lk. 2:41), 'from
year to year,' 'annually'; κατὰ τὰς συναγωγάς (Acts
22:19), 'from synagogue to synagogue.'

Some interpreters consider κατά with the accusative in late Greek a mere circumlocution for the
genitive. But in such a phrase as τὴν καθ' ὑμᾶς πίστιν
(Eph. 1:15), the idea is 'faith like yours.' It is a
little stronger than the genitive would be.

b. With the genitive, it means 'down upon': ἡ κατὰ
βάθους πτωχεία (II Cor. 8:2), 'poverty down to the
depth.'

Out of this general idea, three resultant meanings developed:

(1) The idea of 'against': νύμφην κατὰ πενθερᾶς (Mt.
10:35), 'bride against mother-in-law.' The idea of
hostility grows out of the context. Cf. our 'down
on' one.

(2) The idea of 'throughout': καθ' ὅλης τῆς περιχώρου
(Lk. 4:14), 'throughout all the surrounding country.' This idiom occurs only in the writings of Luke,
and the adjective, ὅλος, is always present in the
construction.

(3) With verbs of swearing, it has the idea of 'by':
ἐξορκίζω σε κατὰ τοῦ θεοῦ (Mt. 26:63), 'I adjure thee
by God.'

In I Cor. 15:15, ἐμαρτυρήσαμεν κατὰ τοῦ θεοῦ is
thought by some to mean 'we have testified by
God,' and by others, 'we have testified against
God.' The context suggests the latter meaning:
as false witnesses against God 'we have testified
against Him.'

c. With the ablative, it means 'down from.' The root
idea of the preposition and the idea of the case
combine to give this meaning.

In Acts 27:14, ἔβαλεν κατ' αὐτῆς ἄνεμος τυφωνικός,
where αὐτῆς refers to the island, Crete, it means that
this tempestuous wind hurled itself down on the ship
from the direction of the island, Crete. Cf. Mk. 5:13,

where the herd of swine rush 'down from' the cliff into the sea, not 'down upon' it.

11. μετά. The root idea seems to be 'mid,' 'midst.' It is from μέσος. It is used with both the accusative and the genitive cases.

   a. With the accusative, in the New Testament, it always has the resultant notion of 'after,' except in one example: μετὰ τὸ δεύτερον καταπέτασμα (Heb. 9:3), 'beyond the second veil.' In this instance, the thought is that, having passed through the midst of the veil, one is now 'beyond' it. In all of the other instances the reference is to time, not space.

     It seems that the idiom arose out of the feeling that, having passed through a series of events, one could now look back on them. This gives rise to the idea of 'after': μετὰ δύο ἡμέρας (Mt. 26:2), 'after two days.'

   b. With the genitive, the usual notion is 'with.'

     (1) The commonest idea is that of accompaniment: οὐκ ἀκολουθεῖ μεθ' ἡμῶν (Lk. 9:49), 'he does not follow with us.'

     (2) The idea of fellowship may quite naturally grow out of the notion of accompaniment: μετὰ πάντων ἀνθρώπων εἰρηνεύοντες (Rom. 12:18), 'being at peace with all men.'

     (3) The notion of fellowship may easily develop into that of followers or partisans: ὁ μὴ ὢν μετ' ἐμοῦ (Mt. 12:30), 'the one not being with me.'

     (4) Conversation with another is quite naturally expressed by this construction: μετὰ γυναικὸς ἐλάλει (Jn. 4:27), 'he was talking with a woman.'

     (5) Some examples approach the instrumental idea: μετὰ ἐπιθέσεως τῶν χειρῶν (I Tim. 4:14), 'with the laying on of hands.'

     (6) The metaphorical use is fairly common: μετὰ σπουδῆς (Mk. 6:25), 'with haste'; μετὰ δακρύων (Heb. 12:17), 'with tears.' This idiom is practically equivalent to an adverb: 'hastily'; 'tearfully.'

12. παρά. The root idea is 'beside,' 'alongside.' Cf. the English, 'parallel.' It is used with three cases: locative, ablative, and accusative.

a. With the locative, it is usually used with persons: παρὰ Σίμωνι (Acts 10:6), 'at Simon's house.'

Once only, it occurs with a thing: ἱστήκεισαν παρὰ τῷ σταυρῷ (Jn. 19:25), 'they stood by the cross.' Here, it describes Mary, the mother of Jesus, and other women, who had taken their stand by the cross.

b. With the ablative, it occurs only with persons: παρὰ τοῦ πατρός[97] (Jn. 16:27), 'from the side of the Father.'

(1) The notion of authorship occurs: ἡ παρ' ἐμοῦ διαθήκη (Rom. 11:27), 'the covenant from me.'

(2) The idea of agent is sometimes expressed by it and a verb in the passive voice: ἀπεσταλμένος παρὰ θεοῦ (Jn. 1:6), 'sent from God.' Here, the source of the action is chiefly stressed.

In the papyri, οἱ παρ' αὐτοῦ is very common for one's agents.[98] Cf. Mk. 3:21, where the phrase probably refers to the disciples.

(3) The idea of one's property or resources may be expressed: τὰ παρ' αὐτῶν (Lk. 10:7), 'the things they possess.' This could mean 'the things which they provide.'

c. With the accusative, it is found both with verbs of rest and verbs of motion. The increase in the use of the accusative case accounts for the replacing of the locative with verbs of rest, by the accusative. The idea is 'along side of': ἦλθεν παρὰ τὴν θάλασσαν (Mt. 15:29), 'he came along side of the sea.'

(1) After comparative forms, it may have the notion of 'beyond,' or 'excelling': διαφορώτερον παρ' αὐτούς (Heb. 1:4), 'excelling them.'

(2) The notion of comparison may easily pass over into opposition: ἐλάτρευσαν τῇ κτίσει παρὰ τὸν κτίσαντα (Rom. 1:25), where the idea is that the Gentile

[97] Nestle reads θεοῦ instead of πατρός.
[98] Moulton, *Prolegomena*, p. 106.

world worshipped the creature 'rather than' the Creator. Setting the two side by side in their minds, they 'passed by' the Creator and bestowed their worship on the creature. The next step was hostility to the Creator. See Rom. 8:7.

An interesting use of κατά and παρά is seen in II Cor. 8:3, where Paul says that the Corinthians came up to the full measure of their power, κατὰ δύναμιν, and went on beyond it, παρὰ δύναμιν, in their voluntary giving.

13. περί. The root meaning is 'around,' 'on all sides.' In the New Testament, it is used with two cases, possibly three: genitive, ablative (?), and accusative.

   a. The genitive is by far the commonest usage, nearly three hundred examples. Cf. I Jn. 2:2, where it occurs three times. The idea is 'concerning' or 'about': περὶ ὧν ἐγράψατε (I Cor. 7:1), 'concerning which things ye wrote.'

   b. The accusative occurs thirty-eight times. The primary idea is 'around.'

      It is used of place: σκάψω περὶ αὐτήν (Lk. 13:8), 'I will dig around it'; of time: περὶ τρίτην ὥραν (Mt. 20:3), 'around the third hour'; of persons: περιαστράψαι . . . περὶ ἐμέ (Acts 22:6), 'to flash . . . around me.'

   c. The ablative is very rare and there seems to be some doubt if it occurs. In Rom. 8:3, περὶ ἁμαρτίας, 'concerning sin,' may mean 'for the removal of sin.'

In some instances, περί and ὑπέρ seem to have essentially the same meaning: δεήσει περὶ πάντων τῶν ἁγίων, καὶ ὑπὲρ ἐμοῦ (Eph. 6:18, 19), 'in prayer for all the saints, and for me.' "The ablative with ὑπέρ renders more probable this ablative use of περί."[99]

14. πρό. The original meaning is 'fore,' 'before.' It is used, in the New Testament, only with the ablative case. This is due, no doubt, to the idea of comparison involved in the word. It occurs forty-eight times.

[99] Robertson, *A Grammar of the Greek New Testament in the Light of Historical Research*, p. 618.

a. It may express the idea of place: πρὸ τῶν θυρῶν (Jas. 5:9), 'before the doors.' There are only four such examples in the New Testament: Acts 12:6, 14; 14:13.

b. It may express time: πρὸ τοῦ κατακλυσμοῦ (Mt. 24:38), 'before the flood.' This is by far the commonest usage. It occurs with the infinitive in a temporal clause, in the sense of 'before,' nine times.

c. The notion of superiority or primary in importance may be expressed: πρὸ πάντων (Jas. 5:12), 'before all things.'

15. πρός. The root meaning, according to Delbrück, is 'near,' 'near by.' Brugmann inclines to 'towards.' This preposition is, in the New Testament, practically confined to two cases: the accusative and the locative.

There is one example (Acts 27:34) where it is used either with the genitive or the ablative: τοῦτο γὰρ πρὸς τῆς ὑμετέρας σωτηρίας ὑπάρχει. If σωτηρίας is ablative, the phrase means, 'for this is from the point of view of your deliverance'; if genitive, the preposition would mean 'on the side of.'

a. There are more than six hundred examples of it with the accusative.

(1) With verbs of motion, it is very commonly used with the sense of 'toward': ἔρχονται πρὸς ὑμᾶς (Mt. 7:15), 'they come to you.'

(2) With verbs of speaking, λαλέω, λέγω, κ. τ. λ., it is frequently used to express living relationship or intimate converse: ὡμίλουν πρὸς ἀλλήλους (Lk. 24:14), 'they were talking to one another.' Cf. Lk. 24:17; Mk. 14:49.

(3) With verbs of rest, it often means 'face to face': ἐνδημῆσαι πρὸς τὸν κύριον (II Cor. 5:8), where it expresses the face to face converse with his Lord to which Paul looks forward. Cf. ὁ λόγος ἦν πρὸς τὸν θεόν (Jn. 1:1), 'the Word was face to face with God.'

(4) In expressions of time, it is occasionally used: πρὸς καιρόν (Lk. 8:13), 'for a time.' The idea of extension is the prominent point here.

(5) In the metaphorical uses, the notion of 'the disposition toward a person' is often expressed by this construction. This may be friendly: μακροθυμεῖτε πρὸς πάντας (I Th. 5:14), 'be ye longsuffering toward all'; or hostile: ἐν ἔχθρᾳ ὄντες πρὸς αὐτούς[100] (Lk. 23:12), 'being at enmity with one another.' In Eph. 6:12, πρός occurs five times in the sense of 'against.' Paul is speaking of the Christian's wrestling against spiritual evil. The context must decide the sense in such instances.

(6) Sometimes, it expresses essentially the dative idea. Cf. Lk. 3:14, where some manuscripts read εἶπεν αὐτοῖς, and others read, εἶπεν πρὸς αὐτούς. This usage is found especially with verbs of saying.

(7) With adjectives, it may express the idea of fitness: ἀγαθὸς πρὸς οἰκοδομήν (Eph. 4:29), 'good (fit) for edifying.'

(8) The idea of comparison may be expressed: οὐκ ἄξια τὰ παθήματα τοῦ νῦν καιροῦ πρὸς τὴν μέλλουσαν δόξαν ἀποκαλυφθῆναι (Rom. 8:18), 'the sufferings of this present time are not worthy to be compared with the glory about to be revealed.'

(9) The idea of purpose may be expressed by πρός and the infinitive: πρὸς τὸ θεαθῆναι αὐτοῖς (Mt. 6:1), 'in order to be seen by them.'

Cf. Mt. 19:8, where πρὸς τὴν σκληροκαρδίαν seems to express result: Moses as a result of the hardness of your hearts permitted divorce.

These usages may seem like a bewildering variety, but if the interpreter will start with the primary idea of the preposition and the case, the context should guide him to a correct interpretation of the construction.

b. With the locative, it occurs in the New Testament, seven times. These all refer to place. Four of these examples are in John's writings. Cf. Jn. 20:12, ἕνα

---

[100] The reflexive pronoun is used here for the reciprocal.

πρὸς τῇ κεφαλῇ καὶ ἕνα πρὸς τοῖς ποσίν, 'one at the head and one at the feet.' Cf. also Mk. 5:11; Jn. 20:11.

Only one of the seven examples is used with a verb of motion: ἐγγίζοντες (Lk. 19:37).

The normal meaning in all of these is 'near' or 'facing.'

16. σύν, 'together with.' It is used only with the associative-instrumental case, and the basic idea of association is always present. Even where the idea is 'help,' it grows naturally out of the idea of association.

Twice, it is used with ἅμα: I Th. 4:17; 5:10. This is really a redundancy, and shows the beginning of the retreat of σύν before ἅμα.

In modern Greek, σύν has been entirely displaced by μετά (μέ) and ἅμα.

17. ὑπέρ is the same in origin as the Latin *super* and the English *over* or *upper*. It is the comparative form of ὑπό. It is used in the New Testament, with the accusative and ablative cases.

a. With the accusative, it has the general sense of 'beyond': ὑπὲρ δύναμιν (II Cor. 1:8), 'beyond ability'; or 'more than': ὁ φιλῶν πατέρα ἢ μητέρα ὑπὲρ ἐμέ (Mt. 10:37), 'the one loving father or mother more than me.'

In the metaphorical use, it may express the idea of 'superior to': οὐκ ἔστιν μαθητὴς ὑπὲρ τὸν διδάσκαλον (Mt. 10:24), 'a pupil is not superior to his teacher.'

The context will make the various shades of meaning clear.

b. With the ablative, there are a variety of uses. There are one hundred and twenty-six examples with the ablative, as against nineteen with the accusative.

(1) The most common usage is to express the general notion of 'in behalf of,' 'for one's benefit.' "This grows easily out of the root idea of 'over' in the sense of protection or defence."[101] As to the

[101] Robertson, *A Grammar of the Greek New Testament in the Light of Historical Research*, p. 630.

bearing of this meaning on the doctrine of the substitutionary atonement, it should be said that it is the nature of the act related, rather than the meaning of the preposition, that determines whether or not the deed was substitutionary. A. T. Robertson[102] points out that in Euripides' Alcestis, he used ὑπέρ seven times for the substitutionary death of Alcestis for her husband. The notion of substitution is quite clear in εἷς ὑπὲρ πάντων (II Cor. 5:15), 'one in behalf of all.' Jesus' death was due to the fact that all had died in sin; He died to prevent their suffering the second death. The use of ἀντίλυτρον ὑπὲρ πάντων should be noted in I Tim. 2:6. The use of ἀντί in Mk. 10:45 and Mt. 20:28 should also be noted here. Cf. ἀντί.

(2) The resultant notion of 'for the sake of' is also fairly frequent: ὑπὲρ τῆς δόξης τοῦ θεοῦ (Jn. 11:4), 'for the sake of the glory of God.' Cf. Rom. 15:8.

(3) The more general idea of 'about' or 'concerning' is also expressed: ὑπὲρ ὑμῶν (II Cor. 7:14), 'concerning you.'

c. Once, it is used as a simple adverb: ὑπὲρ ἐγώ (II Cor. 11:23), 'I more.' This construction occurred also in Homer, where it is called *tmesis*.[103] It is simply the original usage.

18. ὑπό. The original meaning seems to have been 'upwards' or 'from under.' Later the idea of 'under' prevailed. In the New Testament, it is used with the accusative and ablative cases.

a. With the accusative, it is used both with verbs of rest and of motion. The idea is simply 'under': ὄντα ὑπὸ τὴν συκῆν (Jn. 1:48), 'being under the figtree'; τιθέασιν αὐτὸν ὑπὸ τὸν μόδιον (Mt. 5:15), 'they place it under the peck-measure.'

There is only one instance of it with an expression of time: ὑπὸ τὸν ὄρθον (Acts 5:21), where it means 'about dawn.'

[102] *Ibid.*, pp. 630, 631.
[103] *Ibid.*, pp. 555, 558, 629.

b. With the ablative, it is very frequently used with the passive voice to express the direct agent: ἐβαπτί- ζοντο ὑπ᾿ αὐτοῦ (Mt. 3:6), 'they were being baptized by him.'

The secondary agent is usually expressed by διά and the genitive.

It is well to recall that ἀπό, ἐκ, and παρά may be used with the ablative to express agent where the SOURCE of the act rather than the DOER of the act is emphasized.

Prepositions in Composition[104]

1. ἀμφί, the primary meaning, 'on both sides,' is seen in the following verbal compounds: ἀμφιβάλλω (Mk. 1:16), 'I cast on both sides'; ἀμφιέννυμι (Mt. 6:30; 11:8; Lk. 7:25), 'I put on clothing' (the late form of this verb, ἀμφιάζω, occurs in Lk. 12:28; DLT read ἀμφιέζω).

The noun compounds have parallel meanings: ἀμφί- βληστρον (Mt. 4:18), 'a net for casting on both sides' of a boat; Ἀμφίπολις (Acts 17:1), 'a city on both sides' of the river; ἄμφοδον (Mk. 11:4; Acts 19:28), 'a road around (?).'

The adjective, ἀμφότερος, 'both,' occurs in the New Testament, fourteen times: Lk. 6:39.

There are no other compounds of ἀμφί in the New Testament.

2. ἀνά, 'upwards.' There are about seventy verbal compounds in the New Testament. The preposition has various meanings in these compounds.

a. The local force, 'up,' occurs in thirteen of these compounds: ἀναβαίνω (Mt. 20:17), 'I go up.'

b. The sense of 'again,' 'back,' occurs in twenty-six of these: ἀναζάω (Rom. 7:9), 'I live again,' 'I revive'; ἀναχωρέω (Jn. 6:15), 'I retire,' 'draw back.'

[104] For further discussion of the preposition in composition, see Moulton, *A Grammar of New Testament Greek*, Vol. II, pp. 294-328.

c. The sense of the English prefix, 'un-': ἀνακαλύπτω (II Cor. 3:14), 'I uncover,' 'reveal.' There are very few of these. Cf. ἀνακύπτω (Lk. 21:28), 'I unstoop,' 'I lift myself up'; ἀνασκευάζω (Acts 15:24), 'I disfurnish,' 'I unsettle.'

d. In some verbs, it has more than one meaning: ἀναπέμπω (Acts 25:21; Lk. 23:7), 'I send up' or 'I send back'; ἀναβλέπω (Mk. 6:41; 10:51), 'I look up' or 'I regain my sight.' There are some ambiguous compounds: ἀνέχομαι (I Cor. 4:12; Eph. 4:2), may mean 'I hold myself up' (endure), or 'I hold myself back' (refrain).

e. A considerable number have the perfective force: ἀναδείκνυμι (Acts 1:24), 'I show up'; ἀναδέχομαι (Acts 28:7), 'I take up' an acquaintance.

There are about thirty noun compounds but, in general, they are analogous in meaning to the verbs.

3. ἀντί, 'opposite.' There are twenty of these verb compounds.

a. In the sense of 'opposite' or 'against' we have ten verbs: ἀνταγωνίζομαι (Heb. 12:4), 'I strive against.' In μὴ ἀντιστῆναι τῷ πονηρῷ (Mt. 5:39), 'resist not the evil (one),' it has the notion of hostility.

An interesting compound is ἀντι-παρ-έρχομαι (Lk. 10:31, 32), 'I pass by on the opposite side.' There are three other double compounds in the sense of opposite: ἀντ-απο-κρίνομαι (Rom. 9:20), 'I answer by contradicting'; ἀντι-δια-τίθεμαι (II Tim. 2:25), 'I place myself in opposition'; ἀντι-καθ-ίστημι (Heb. 12:4), 'I stand against,' 'I resist.' These double compounds retain the force of both prepositions, as well as the idea of the simple verb.

b. Reciprocal action may also be expressed: ἀντιλοιδορέω (I Pet. 2:23), 'I revile in return.'

There are two double compounds which express the reciprocal idea: ἀντ-ανα-πληρόω (Col. 1:24), 'I fill up in turn'; ἀντ-απο-δίδωμι (Lk. 14:14), 'I give back in turn.' These illustrate how the force of both prepositions is retained.

c. The local force survives in some verbs: ἀντέχομαι (Mt. 6:24), 'I hold myself over against another,' 'I hold to.'

The compound ἀντιλαμβάνομαι (Acts 20:35) means 'I grasp (take hold) while squarely facing another,' 'I help.' The double compound συν-αντι-λαμβάνομαι (Rom. 8:26), has the additional notion of co-operation, due to σύν in the compound.

There are about a dozen noun compounds. In general, all of these prepositional compounds effect the meaning of nouns in essentially the same way that they do verbs.

4. ἀπό, 'off,' 'away.'[105] All the uses of this word start from the notion of separation. There are about ninety verbal compounds in the New Testament.

a. The local force: ἀπόκοψον αὐτήν (Mk. 9:43), 'cut it off.' There are about forty of these.

Some of these shade off into the perfective force: ἀποθησαυρίζω (I Tim. 6:19), 'I store away,' 'I store up.' Cf. ἀπάγχομαι (Mt. 27:5), 'I choke off.'

The simple meaning 'off,' 'away,' produces different nuances according to the meaning of the verb root. Sometimes, the starting point is the subject, and sometimes, the object: ἀπαγγέλλω (Acts 12:17), 'I bring news,' 'I announce,' starts with the messenger; ἀποδέχομαι (Acts 2:41), 'I welcome,' starts with the recipient.

The double compound ἀποσυνάγωγος (Jn. 9:22) seems to give the local force to ἀπό.

b. The perfective force. Although something has been said under 'a' of this, a further word is necessary. There are thirty-four compounds that have distinctly a perfective force: ἀπαρνέομαι (Mt. 16:24), 'I renounce,' 'I deny utterly.' Sometimes, the perfect-

[105] Cf. ἀπό with the cases, p. 116.

ivizing preposition produces the transitive force when the simplex of the verb is intransitive: ἀφυστερέω (Jas. 5:4), 'I withdraw,' 'I hold back,' from ὑστερέω, 'I come late.'

The perfective force is seen in the double compounds ἀπεκδέχομαι (I Pet. 3:20), 'I wait assiduously,' from ἐκδέχομαι, 'I wait'; and ἀπεκδύομαι (Col. 2:15), 'I wholly strip off from myself,' or 'I despoil' another. The cognate noun, ἀπέκδυσις (Col. 2:11), means 'a complete putting off of clothing.'

c. The idea of 'back' is found in eight compounds. A development of the local force yields ἀποδίδωμι (Mt. 16:27), 'I give back what belongs to another,' and looks at the transaction from the standpoint of the receiver and not the giver. The verb might mean 'I give away,' but usage carried its development along the other line.

The noun ἀπαύγασμα (Heb. 1:3), from ἀπαυγάζω, could mean 'a ray of light flashed back as a reflection,' or 'a ray of light flashed from an object as an emission of light.' The problem of the interpreter then is, does the writer mean to say that Jesus is the 'effulgence' of God's glory, or the 'refulgence?' Only usage can decide this point. Philo's usage is divided. Calvin took it in the sense of 'refulgence.' The Greek Fathers are unanimous for 'radiance,' 'effulgence,' in this passage.

There are three double compounds meaning 'back': ἀποκαθίστημι (Acts 1:6), 'I restore to its former estate'; ἀποκατάστασις (Acts 3:2), 'a restoration'; ἀποκαταλλάσσω (Col. 1:20, 21; Eph. 2:16), 'I change back to a former state of harmony.' Possibly this last compound is perfective. If so, it means, 'I reconcile completely.'

d. In another class of verbs, it reverses the action of the verb. There are seven of these: ἀπαλγέω (Eph. 4:19), 'I have pain off,' i. e., 'I am past feeling'; ἀπελπίζω (Lk. 6:35), 'I cease hoping,' 'I despair'; ἀποδοκιμάζω (Mt. 21:42), 'I disapprove,' 'I reject';

ἀποκαλύπτω (Rom. 1:17), 'I take the cover off,' 'I unveil'; ἀποστεγάζω (Mk. 2:4), 'I take the roof off'; ἀποφορτίζομαι (Acts 21:3), 'I unburden myself'; ἀπο-ψύχω (Lk. 21:26), 'I cease breathing,' 'I expire.'

There are seventeen noun compounds. In general, they are analogous to the verbs in meaning.

5. διά, 'through,' from the root δύο, 'two.' Moulton[106] notes that outside Greek this adverb does not become a preposition. It forms seventy-nine verbal compounds in the New Testament. About three-fifths of these are in Luke and Acts.

   a. There are about sixteen compounds where it has the sense of 'per.' They express the idea of 'carrying an action through' to an accomplished result. These perfective compounds are usually spatial: διαβαίνω (Acts 16:9), which describes a journey to a goal; metaphorical: διηγέομαι (Mk. 5:16), 'I lead (a narrative) through to the end'; διαφεύγω (Acts 27:42), 'I flee through,' 'I escape'; temporal: διαφυ-λάσσω (Lk. 4:10), 'I guard as long as danger lasts.' The idea of thoroughly is seen in διασείω (Lk. 3:14), 'I shake thoroughly,' hence 'I extort by intimidation.' Cf. the English, 'shake down.'
   There are three double compounds where the idea is perfective: διακατελέγχομαι (Acts 18:28, only here), 'I confute completely'; διαπαρατρίβη (I Tim. 6:5, only here), 'constant irritation,' 'incessant wrangling'; διενθυμέομαι (Acts 10:19, only here), 'I have thoroughly in mind,' 'I consider.'

   b. There are a few compounds where it has the sense of 'inter':διαγίνομαι (Mk. 16:1), 'I intervene.'

   c. There are a number of compounds where it has the sense of 'trans,' 'across': διαβάλλω (Lk. 16:1), 'I toss across.' From this usage the idea of 'traduce,' 'slander,' arises. Another example is: διερμηνεύω (Lk. 24:27), 'I interpret across,' 'I interpret.'

[106] *A Grammar of New Testament Greek*, Vol. II. p. 300.

d. There are several compounds where it intensifies the idea of the verb: διαβεβαίομαι (I Tim. 1:7), 'I strongly affirm'; διαμαρτύρομαι (Acts 18:5), 'I solemnly declare'; διϊσχυρίζομαι (Lk. 22:59), 'I confidently assert.' These compounds do not necessarily imply a result; one may 'solemnly declare' a thing without convincing one's hearers.

e. There are about twelve compounds where it has the sense of δίς, 'between': διακρίνομαι (Mk. 11:23), 'I judge between (to and fro),' 'I distinguish.' The middle voice of this verb, 'I distinguish for myself,' naturally develops into 'I hesitate' by stressing the force of 'dis.' διαδίδωμι (Jn. 6:11), 'I give here and there,' 'I distribute,' illustrates another step in the development of the idea 'between.'

Akin in thought to this usage is the local idea 'through' seen in two double compounds: διεξέρχομαι (Acts 28:3), 'I go out through something'; διέξοδος (Mt. 22:9), 'a way out through.'

f. There are several compounds where it has a mediating force: διαλλάσσω (Mt. 5:24), 'I make a change between persons at variance,' 'I reconcile'; διαδέχομαι (Acts 7:45), 'I receive through another,' 'I succeed.' See the noun, διάδοχος, 'successor.'

In the compound nouns, the preposition has, in general, about the same sense as in the compound verbs. Occasionally, the force will be different in the noun from that of the cognate verb. In such cases, a good lexicon must be consulted.

6. εἰς, 'into,' developed out of the form ἐνς, which still survived before vowels in the Cretan dialect.[107] A shorter form, ἐς, was used before consonants. In Hellenistic Greek, ἐς was obsolete, appearing in the New Testament only in ἔσω (II Cor. 4:16) and ἔσοπτρον (I Cor. 13:12).

εἰς and ἐν are from the same root, and some grammarians treat them together. The Boeotian, Thessa-

---

[107] Moulton, *A Grammar of New Testament Greek*, Vol. II. p. 304.

lian and Northwest Greek used only ἐν.[108] In the Attic, they are always clearly differentiated. In the *koine*, the distinction is not always observed, but is so generally observed that they should be treated separately.

There are only ten verbal compounds of εἰς in the New Testament. The idea is quite simple, 'in,' or 'into': εἰσάγω (Jn. 18:16), 'I lead in'; εἰσκαλέομαι (Acts 10:23), 'I invite in.' The compound εἰσέρχομαι (Rev. 3:20), 'I go into,' occurs in the New Testament, one hundred and ninety-one times. The other nine compounds occur only about fifty times all together.

In εἰσακούω (Heb. 5:7; Mt. 6:7), the simple idea has developed into 'I attend to,' 'I heed.'

Double compounds, such as ἐπ-εισ-αγή (Heb. 7:19), 'a bringing in, in addition to,' and παρ-είσ-ακτος (Gal. 2:4), 'one led in at the side,' preserve the primary meaning of εἰς.

There is only one simple noun compound in the New Testament: εἴσοδος (Heb. 10:19), 'entrance.' This noun occurs five times in the New Testament.

7. ἐκ, 'out,' forms ninety-five verb compounds in the New Testament.

   a. In about fifty cases, the local force is clear. The simple local force is seen in verbs of 'going': ἐξέρχομαι (Jas. 3:10), 'I go out.'

   In many compounds by a little adaptation the meaning 'out' can be seen to underlie the derived meaning.

   In the double compounds ἐξανατέλλω (Mt. 13:5), 'I cause to arise'; ἐξανίστημι (Acts 15:5), 'I rise up'; ἐξαποστέλλω (Lk. 1:53), 'I send away,' the local force is probably the prominent idea.

   Often, a metaphorical meaning grows out of the local idea: ἐξαγγέλλω (I Pet. 2:9), 'I announce publicly.'

   b. In a few compounds, it is intensive, 'out and out': ἐκθαμβέομαι (Mk. 9:15), 'I am very much astonished'; ἐκταράσσω (Acts 16:20), 'I greatly disturb.'

[108] Robertson, *A Grammar of the Greek New Testament in the Light of Historical Research*, pp. 584, 585.

c. In some compounds, it is perfective, the local force having disappeared entirely or almost so. A particularly good example is found in II Cor. 4:8, where ἀπορούμενοι means 'being perplexed' and ἐξαπορούμενοι means 'being perplexed unto despair.' The apostle freely admits that his sufferings have brought perplexity, but they have not brought despair.

ἐκζητέω seems always to mean that the seeker either 'finds' or exhausts his powers in searching: ἐκζητήσας (Heb. 12:17). In this case, Esau's quest was frustrated, but nevertheless intense.

δαπανάω (II Cor. 12:15), 'I spend,' compounded with ἐκ, comes to mean 'I spend wholly,' i. e., 'I exhaust my resources,' (II Cor. 12:15).

There are about thirty noun compounds, in general, analogous in meaning to the verbs.

8. ἐν, 'within,' forms only fifty-five[109] compounds, but these are very frequently used. They are about equally divided between the force of ἐν, 'in,' and εἰς, 'into.' Usually the choice between the two is easily made. Sometimes, it is not necessary to make the distinction.

Sometimes, these compounds acquired a bad connotation: ἐγκαλέω (Rom. 8:33), 'I call in,' very easily came to mean to 'call a man in to accuse him.'

Such compounds as ἐμβριμάομαι (Mk. 1:43; Jn. 11:33), 'I have strong feeling within myself,' 'I am indignant,' and ἐνδέχομαι (Lk. 13:33), 'I accept in myself,' 'I admit,' have clearly the idea 'within.'

In the double compound, ἐγ-κατα-λείπω (II Cor. 4:9), the κατά is perfective (καταλείπω, meaning 'I leave utterly,' 'I abandon'), while ἐν calls attention to the plight in which the victim is left.

There is only one other double compound in the New Testament: ἐνπεριπατέω (II Cor. 6:16), 'I walk about in one.'

[109] With the noun, ἐν is by far the commonest preposition in the New Testament. In fact, it was so frequently used that it tended to lose its distinctive meaning, so we find it expressing both the dative and instrumental ideas. Cf. p. 142.

There are about twenty-five noun compounds with meanings analogous to that of the verbs.

9. ἐπί, 'upon.' There are ninety-nine verb compounds in the New Testament, a total exceeded only by κατά and σύν, the most frequent perfectivizing prefixes.

a. The local sense is very clear in many verbs. This is the oldest and simplest meaning: ἐπιπίπτω (Mk. 3:10), 'I fall upon.' About a third of the noun compounds come in here: ἐπίσημος (Rom. 16:7), 'with a sign upon it,' 'notable,' 'conspicuous.'

b. The directive sense, closely akin to the local sense, indicates the concentration of the verb's action upon some object: ἐπάρατος (Jn. 7:49), 'accursed,' has the object in view when cursing; ἐπιδείκνυμαι (Acts 18:28; Heb. 6:17), 'I display,' 'I point out,' 'I prove,' 'I demonstrate,' calls attention to the object displayed.

Some of these compounds have a hostile sense: ἐπ-αν-ίστημι (Mt. 10:21), 'I rise up against'; ἐπιτιμάω (Jude 9), 'I lay a penalty on,' 'I censure.'

c. The sense of 'in addition to' is sometimes expressed: ἐπιγαμβρεύω (Mt. 22:24), 'I make a new marriage connection'; ἐπίγνωσις (Col. 1:9), 'additional knowledge,' 'full knowledge.'

In I Cor. 13:12, ἄρτι γινώσκω ἐκ μέρους, τότε δὲ ἐπιγνώσομαι καθὼς καὶ ἐπεγνώσθην, there is a clear contrast between γινώσκω and ἐπιγνώσκω, 'Now I know in part, but then shall I know fully even as I also was fully known.' The AV flattens out the distinction until it is completely lost. Cf. γνῶσις and ἐπίγνωσις in Paul.

There are fourteen double compounds beginning with ἐπί. In most of these, ἐπί supplies the idea of 'in addition to': ἐπισυντρέχω (Mk. 9:25), 'I run together in addition to others already gathered.'

There are fifty-five noun compounds with meanings analogous to the verb compounds.

10. κατά, 'down.' There are one hundred and seven verb compounds in the New Testament.

a. A perfective force is expressed by about two-thirds of these compounds: καταδιώκω (Mk. 1:36), 'I hunt down'; κατέφαγον (Lk. 8:5), 'I ate up,' 'I devoured.'

b. The local force is quite common: καταβαίνω (Rev. 3:12, 'I go down.' See κατεπατήθη (Lk. 8:5), 'it is trodden down.'

c. The hostile sense 'against' occurs in about fourteen compounds: κατακρίνω (II Pet. 2:6), 'I condemn'; κατακυριεύω (Mk. 10:42; Acts 19:16), 'I exercise lordship over,' 'I overpower.'

There are no double compounds of verbs or nouns introduced by κατά. There is one improper preposition, κατ-έν-αντι, which means 'over against.'

The meaning of the noun compounds is analogous to that of the verbs.

11. μετά, 'mid,' 'midst.' As a preposition, the primary meaning is 'with.' The idea of 'after' comes from the idea of crossing the 'mid' space. There are twenty-one verb compounds in the New Testament.

a. The idea of change, the Latin, 'trans,' is expressed by sixteen compounds: μετανοέω (Mt. 3:2), 'I change my mind (I accept the will of God, instead of my own, as regnant in my life)'; μετατίθημι (Gal. 1:6), 'I transfer.'

b. The idea of sharing action, accounts for three compounds: μεταδίδωμι (Eph. 4:28), 'I give a share of,' 'I distribute'; μεταλαμβάνω (II Tim. 2:6), 'I partake of'; μετέχω (I Cor. 9:10), 'I hold with another,' 'I have a share of.'

c. The idea of crossing over to a goal is expressed: μετακαλοῦμαι (Acts 7:14), 'I call for,' 'I summon'; μεταπέμπομαι (Acts 11:13), 'I send for.'

There are sixteen noun compounds with similar meanings to those of the verbs.

12. παρά, 'beside.' There are about fifty verbal compounds in the New Testament.

   a. The local sense 'beside,' 'close to,' is found in a number: παροικέω (Lk. 24:18), 'I dwell by,' 'I sojourn'; παρακολουθέω (Lk. 1:3), 'I follow closely.' Sometimes, these compounds seem to have a perfective force: παρατηρέω (Mk. 3:2), 'I watch by (closely).'

   b. The meaning 'to the side of,' the idea of motion affecting the sense, is also common: παρακαλοῦμαι (Mt. 14:36), 'I call to my aid,' 'I beseech'; παραδίδωμι (Acts 16:4), 'I hand on to another.' Cf. παράδοσις in the sense of 'tradition.'

      Often, the idea of treachery developed in παραδίδωμι (Mt. 26:46), where it is used of Judas' betrayal of Jesus. But it is used in Rom. 1:24, 26, 28, of God handing man over to his self-chosen way; and in Rom. 8:32, of God giving his Son for the sinning world, with no suggestion of treachery in either case. It is the context which supplies the idea of treachery, when this idea occurs.

      παρασκευάζω (I Cor. 14:8), 'I prepare,' is almost identical with σκευάζω, but suggests a 'presentation' of the object prepared.

   c. The idea of 'going past' develops in several compounds: παραβαίνω (Mt. 15:2), 'I go by,' 'I transgress'; παραφέρω (Jude 12), 'I carry on by.'

   d. The idea of 'aside,' developing into 'mis-,' is found in five compounds: παραθεωρέω (Acts 6:1), 'I overlook'; παραιτέομαι (Lk. 14:18), 'I ask aside,' 'I beg off'; παρακούω (Mt. 18:17), 'I hear aside' (mis-hear), 'I ignore,' in some contexts it seems to mean 'I overhear'; παραπίπτω (Heb. 6:6), 'I fall aside,' 'I lapse' (cf. παράπτωμα); παραλογίζομαι (Col. 2:4), 'I reason aside,' 'I miscalculate,' 'I delude another with my reasoning.'

   e. The idea of separation (ablative idea) occurs a few times: παραδέχομαι (Acts 15:4), 'I receive from.'

In παραλαμβάνω (I Cor. 11:23), 'I receive from,' the source is suggested; in παραδίδωμι (I Cor. 11:23), 'I give from,' the giver is suggested. In the former word, the usual meaning is 'to take to one's side' (Mt. 1:20; 2:13).

f. The idea of motion onward appears: παραγγέλλω (Lk. 9:21), 'I pass a message on.' Cf. παραζηλόω (Rom. 10:19), 'I provoke to jealousy'; παροργιῶ (Rom. 10:19), 'I will arouse to wrath,' 'I exasperate.'

The idea of stealth appears in three of these: παρεισάγω (II Pet. 2:1), 'I bring in at the side'; παρεισδύω (Jude 4), 'I creep in'; παρεισέρχομαι (Gal. 2:4), 'to enter secretly as by stealth.' In Rom. 5:20, it means 'to come in in addition to.'

There are six double compound verbs beginning with παρά. In one of these double compounds, παρά adds the idea of 'besides,' 'in addition to': παρεισφέρω (II Pet. 1:5), 'I bring in besides,' 'I contribute in addition to.' In παρεμβάλλω (Lk. 19:43), 'I cast up alongside'; and in παρενοχλέω (Acts 15:19), 'I cause trouble by one,' the idea is local. There are three double compound nouns with analogous meanings.

There are twenty-six compound nouns with analogous meanings to the verb compounds.

13. περί, 'around.' There are thirty-two compound verbs in the New Testament.

a. The idea of 'around,' 'round about,' occurs in about four-fifths of these compounds: περιπατέω (Rom. 6:4), 'I walk about'; περιφέρω (Mk. 6:55), 'I carry about.'

b. The ablative idea, separation, appears in a few: περιαιρέω (II Cor. 3:16), 'I take from around,' 'I remove a veil'; περιΐστημι (II Tim. 2:16; Tit. 3:9), 'I stand myself around,' 'I avoid.'

c. Miscellaneous ideas are expressed: περιέχω (Lk. 5:9), 'I hold around,' 'I contain'; περιφρονέω (Tit. 2:15), 'I think around' (out-think), and therefore 'despise';

περιεργάζομαι (II Th. 3:11), 'I work around,' 'I overdo the matter,' and therefore 'become a busybody.' Here, Paul says that those who 'work around' (περιεργάζομαι) 'work not at all' (μηδὲν ἐργάζομαι). It seems that one may be busy here and there, and not really busy anywhere. A hint to the ministry!

There are no double compounds beginning with περί, in the New Testament.

There are ten noun compounds, with analogous meanings, linked with the verb compounds.

14. πρό, 'forwards,' 'before,' may be used of either time or place. There are forty-nine verbal compounds in the New Testament.

a. The idea of time, 'before,' is expressed in twenty-eight compounds: προγινώσκω (Rom. 8:29), 'I get to know beforehand.' There are four double compounds in the New Testament, all of which have the temporal idea: προενάρχομαι (only in II Cor. 8:6, 10), 'I begin before'; προεπαγγέλλομαι (only in Rom. 1:2; II Cor. 9:5), 'I promise before'; προκαταγγέλλω (only in Acts 3:18; 7:52), 'I announce beforehand'; προκαταρτίζω (only in II Cor. 9:5), 'I prepare before.'

b. The idea of place, 'before,' is expressed by eleven compounds: προέρχομαι (Lk. 22:47), 'I go before.'

c. The idea of either time or place may be expressed by a few compounds: προγράφω (Rom. 15:4; Gal. 3:1), 'I write previously,' 'in front of,' 'I placard.'

d. The sense of 'forward,' 'forth,' may be expressed: προπέμπω (I Cor. 16:6), 'I send forth,' or 'forward'; προτείνω (Acts 22:25), 'I stretch forth'; προφέρω (Lk. 6:45), 'I bear forth.' The metaphorical usage also occurs here: προτίθημι (Rom. 1:13), 'I set forth,' 'I propose.' Cf. προφήτης, 'a spokesman for another.'

e. The idea of preference may be expressed: προαιρέομαι (II Cor. 9:7), 'I choose deliberately,' i. e., in preference to something else.

f. The idea of protection or care also appears: προ-ΐσταμαι (I Tim. 3:4), 'I stand in front,' i. e., 'I protect.'

There are a number of noun compounds which have analogous meanings. The only one which adds a new idea is πρόδηλος (I Tim. 5:24), where 'openly' seems to be the idea.

15. πρός, 'near,' is used much more frequently as a preposition than as a preverb. There are forty-four compounds in the New Testament, if we include προσαχέω (Acts 27:27, B), and προσεγγίζω (Mk. 2:4, ACEΩ).

a. The idea is directive in thirty-six compounds, as in πρός with the accusative case: προσάγω (Mt. 18:24), 'I lead to,' 'I bring'; προσκολλάω (Eph. 5:31), 'I join myself closely to one.' Contrast προσεύχομαι, the usual New Testament term for Christian prayer, with εὔχομαι, 'pagan prayer,' in Acts 27:29.

In προσδέομαι (Acts 17:25), 'I need' or 'lack,' the verb is followed by the ablative case. The case implies 'from' and the preposition adds 'to oneself.'

The locative idea appears in προσμένω (Acts 18:18), 'I remain in,' 'I persist in.'

b. The idea of 'addition' is expressed by the other compounds: προστίθημι (Gal. 3:19), 'I place to,' 'I add'; προσδαπανάω (Lk. 10:35), 'I spend besides.'

There are five double compounds, all of which have the idea of 'in addition to': προσαναβαίνω (Lk. 14:10), 'I go up further (higher)'; προσαναλίσκω (Lk. 8:43), 'I expend besides'; προσαναπληρόω (II Cor. 9:12), 'I fill up by adding'; προσανατίθημι (Gal. 1:16), 'I lay upon in addition' (The middle voice in this last example means 'I consult'); προσανέχω (Acts 27:27), 'I hold up besides.'

There are sixteen noun compounds in the New Testament, analogous in meaning to the verbs.

16. σύν, 'together.' There are one hundred and twenty-three verb compounds in the New Testament.

a. The associative idea is expressed in ninety-nine of
these compounds. See χαίρω . . . συνχαίρω . . . χαίρετε
. . . συνχαίρετε, in Phil. 2:17, 18, where a strong sense
of Christian fellowship is expressed by σύν. A study
of the σύν compounds in Paul is a very fruitful
experience.

There are various shades of the idea of 'with,'
all starting from the idea of 'together': συνέχω (II
Cor. 5:14), 'I hold together,' 'I concentrate'; συνεργέω
(II Cor. 6:1), 'I co-operate with.'

There are twenty-five double compounds, such as:
συναναβαίνω (Mk. 15:41), 'I ascend together with';
συνκατεψηφίσθη (Acts 1:26), 'he was numbered along
with'; συνεπιμαρτυροῦντος (Heb. 2:4), 'testifying
along with in addition to,' i. e., God rendered a testimony in addition to and in co-operation with that
of the hearers of Jesus. This confirmatory testimony consisted in signs and wonders and various
kinds of miracles. See συναντιλαμβάνομαι (Rom. 8:
26), 'I take hold over against along with,' as a
description of the work of the Holy Spirit.

b. The perfective idea is expressed by twenty-four
compounds: συγκλείω (Rom. 11:32), 'I conclude,' 'I
shut together,' hence 'shut up'; συλλαμβάνω (Mt. 26:
55), 'I arrest.'

In the noun compounds, this preposition acts very
much as with the verbs. There are eighteen words and
groups of words which form these compounds.

17. ὑπέρ, 'over.' There are fourteen verb compounds in
the New Testament. The idea of 'over' passes easily
into 'across' or 'beyond.'

a. The idea of 'surpassing,' 'magnifying': ὑπερνικάω
(Rom. 8:37), 'I score a heavy victory'; ὑπεραυξάνω
(II Th. 1:3), 'I grow exceedingly'; ὑπερπλεονάζω (I
Tim. 1:14), 'I abound exceedingly'; ὑπερυψόω (Phil.
2:9), 'I elevate greatly,' 'I exalt greatly.'

The double compounds ὑπερπερισσεύω (Rom. 5:20),
'I overflow exceedingly'; ὑπερεκχύννω (Lk. 6:38), 'I

pour out beyond measure,' express the idea of 'surpassing.'

b. The idea of 'excess': ὑπερφρονέω (Rom. 12:3), 'I have high notions,' 'I am overweening'; ὑπερβάλλω (Eph. 3:19), 'I overshoot'; ὑπερβαίνω (I Th. 4:6), 'I go beyond,' 'I transgress.' The double compound, ὑπερεκτείνω (II Cor. 10:14), 'I stretch out beyond the prescribed bounds,' expresses the idea of 'excess.'

Whether or not the idea of 'magnifying' or 'excess' results from the compound is determined by the verb and the context.

c. The idea of 'in behalf of' is expressed by the double compound ὑπερ-εν-τυγχάνω (Rom. 8:26), 'I intercede.'

The noun compounds run parallel in meaning with the verbs.

Of all the ὑπέρ compounds in the New Testament, eighty-eight percent occur in the Pauline writings. This fact is probably due, in part, to his intense nature, but largely to his sense of the supreme significance of the Christian faith.

18. ὑπό, 'under.' The original idea was 'upwards from under.' The starting point became isolated from the rest of the idea, and the meaning 'under' became fixed. There are twenty-seven verb compounds in the New Testament.

a. The literal sense 'under': ὑποζόννυμι (Acts 27:17), 'I undergird.'

b. The idea of submission: ὑπακούω (Mt. 8:27), 'I obey'; ὑποτάσσω (I Cor. 14:32), 'I subject.'

c. The idea of 'underhand': ὑποβάλλω (Acts 6:11), 'I suborn'; ὑποκρίνομαι (Lk. 20:20), 'I act a part,' 'I pretend.'

d. The idea of 'away,' 'back': ὑποχωρέω (Lk. 5:16), 'I withdraw'; ὑποστέλλω (Acts 20:20), 'I withdraw.' The idea of cowardice may occur in the latter word: Heb. 10:38.

e. The idea of 'up': ὑπολαμβάνω (III Jn. 8), 'I take up,' 'I receive hospitably.'

f. The idea of 'behind': ὑπολείπω (Rom. 11:3; 9:27), 'I leave behind'; ὑπομένω (Lk. 2:43), 'I tarry behind.' In I Cor. 13:7, ὑπομένω means 'I endure,' 'I undergo.'

There are no double compounds of ὑπό in the New Testament.

In general, the noun compounds run parallel in meaning to the verb compounds.

THE CONJUNCTION

It is often desirable to link words to words, phrases to phrases, and clauses to clauses. This need gave rise to a class of connective words called conjunctions (from con-iungo). There is a great wealth of conjunctions in the Greek language which join not only words, phrases, clauses, and even sentences, but link also paragraphs to paragraphs. The conjunction serves to make clear the relation between the two elements united.

There are two general classes of conjunctions: those that unite elements of equal prominence in the sentence, called paratactic[110] or co-ordinating conjunctions; and those that unite elements of unequal rank, called hypotactic or subordinate conjunctions.

Paratactic or Co-ordinating Conjunctions

These conjunctions unite elements of equal rank, but the relationship between the elements may be different. This gives rise to five classes of paratactic conjunctions.

1. Copulative. Several conjunctions simply 'couple together,' without stating the relationship between the elements united.

a. καί connects in a loosely defined manner, and hence

---

[110] From παρα-τάκ-τικος, which is from παρατάσσω, 'I arrange beside.'

is by far the most frequently used of any conjunction in the New Testament. There are three main uses that it has in the New Testament, as well as in other Greek.

(1) The mere connective, 'and.' This is the most frequent and the simplest use. Any number of words may be linked together: it is used four times in Phil. 4:9; five times, Rom. 9:4; six times, Rev. 7:12.

The context may give other turns of meaning to the central idea 'and.' In Jn. 3:19; 4:20; 6:49; 7:30; I Jn. 2:9, the idea seems to be 'and yet.' This is probably due to the influence of the Hebrew connective, ۱. This usage is a characteristic of John's style.

In Lk. 12:24, it seems to draw a contrast, like ἀλλά. Here, it is the context again which shades the meaning.   In Mk. 15:25, it seems to have almost the meaning of ὅτε, 'when': ἦν ὥρα τρίτη καὶ ἐσταύρωσαν, 'it was the third hour when they crucified (him).'

(2) The adjunctive use, 'also.' This usage is not a co-ordinating conjunctive, but it is treated here so that the student may learn to distinguish between these two usages of the same word.

In the sense of 'also,' it occurs with nouns: καὶ οἱ μαθηταί σου (Jn. 7:3), 'thy disciples also'; with pronouns: καὶ γὰρ ἐγὼ ἄνθρωπος ὑπὸ ἐξουσίαν (Mt. 8:9), 'for I also am a man under authority.' The καὶ recognizes that the sick boy and the centurion are in similar situations: the centurion knows what it is to obey orders when he does not see the one issuing them, and so he is sure Christ can achieve His will through the paralytic boy without going to see him.

It may also occur with verbs, adverbs, or even other conjunctions.

(3) The ascensive use, 'even.' This use is climactic. Something unusual is introduced by it: καὶ τελῶναι

(Mt. 5:46), points out that 'even publicans' love those who love them, and therefore this standard of love can not be accepted as adequate for children of the Father in heaven. The force of this use depends wholly on the context.

The use of 'even if,' καὶ εἰ, belongs here, in part, but it must be discussed under conditional sentences also, so it will be left until then. Cf. I Cor. 8:5.

b. τέ, 'and.' This indicates a somewhat closer unity than καί. Usually, it follows the word or words united. It is rare in the New Testament, except in Acts, where it occurs one hundred and seventy-five times.

Various combinations, such as τε καί (Acts 1:1); τε καὶ . . . τε (Acts 9:15), occur. These are correlative, 'both . . . and.'

c. δέ, 'and,' 'but.' The earliest usage seems to have been a 'continuative' use in narrative with the meaning 'in the next place.' In this sense, it is used mainly in the historical books in the New Testament, especially in Matthew and Luke.

A good passage illustrating the mere copulative force is the genealogical table: Mt. 1:2-16.

The adversative use, 'on the other hand,' 'but,' will be discussed under adversative conjunctions.

d. ἀλλά. The most frequent use of this conjunction is adversative, 'but.' This, however, does not seem to have been the original usage, and certainly is not the only usage: πόσην κατειργάσατο ὑμῖν σπουδήν, ἀλλὰ ἀπολογίαν, ἀλλὰ ἀγανάκτησιν, ἀλλὰ φόβον, ἀλλὰ ἐπιπόθησιν, ἀλλὰ ζῆλον, ἀλλὰ ἐκδίκησιν (II Cor. 7:11), 'what earnest care it wrought in you, yea what clearing of yourselves, yea what indignation, yea what fear, yea what longing, yea what zeal, yea what avenging.' Clearly these are not adversative, but confirmatory and continuative uses of ἀλλά.

To take ἀλλά in Jn. 8:26 as 'but' is very awkward, but taken in the continuative sense, it is not hard to see the meaning. "Like δέ, the thing introduced by ἀλλά is something new; but not essentially in contrast."[111]

2. **Adversative.** Not all of these imply antithesis. The context will make clear how strong the contrast is, when there is any.

   a. δέ is often adversative: μὴ θησαυρίζετε . . . θησαυρίζετε δέ (Mt. 6:19), 'quit laying up treasure . . . but keep on laying up.'

   In Jas. 1:13, it is continuative, but in verse 14, it is adversative.

   In ἐγὼ ἐβάπτισα ὑμᾶς ὕδατι, αὐτὸς δὲ βαπτίσει ὑμᾶς Πνεύματι Ἁγίῳ (Mk. 1:8), 'I baptized you with water, but he shall baptize you with the Holy Spirit,' the δέ contrasts the agents, the media and the time of John's and Jesus' baptism.

   Often, the contrast is made more manifest by the use of μέν: ἐγὼ μὲν . . . ὁ δὲ ὀπίσω μου ἐρχόμενος (Mt. 3:11), 'I on the one hand . . . but on the other hand, the one coming after me.'

   b. ἀλλά is often used to introduce another object in contrast with the preceding.

   When used with οὐ, as in οὐ Μωϋσῆς . . . ἀλλὰ ὁ πατήρ (Jn. 6:32), 'not Moses . . . but the Father,' the antithesis is quite sharp. Cf. οὐχί, ἀλλὰ κληθήσεται Ἰωάννης (Lk. 1:60), 'no, but he shall be called John.'

   c. πλήν, as a conjunction, is always adversative: Lk. 6:24; 12:31. It is almost confined to Luke's writings.

   Blass[112] considered that Paul used it at the end of an argument to single out the essential point: I Cor. 11:11; Eph. 5:33; Phil. 3:16; 4:14. Here, it has the meaning 'only,' 'in any case.'

   Sometimes, πλήν is used as a preposition: Mk. 12:32.

   d. μέντοι is a combination of two intensive particles, μέν and τοί, and is used in the sense of 'however':

---

[111] Robertson, *A Grammar of the Greek New Testament in the Light of Historical Research*, p. 1185.

[112] *Grammar of New Testament Greek*, p. 268.

Jn. 4:27; 12:42. It occurs in the New Testament, only eight times.

e. ὅμως occurs only three times in the New Testament. Twice, it is used with participles: I Cor. 14:7; Gal. 3:15; and once, with μέντοι: Jn. 12:42. It means 'nevertheless.'

f. εἰ μή, 'except.' This phrase marks an exception: εἰ μὴ τοῖς ἱερεῦσιν μόνοις (Mt. 12:5), 'except for the priests only'; εἰ μὴ ὁ υἱὸς τῆς ἀπωλείας (Jn. 17:12), 'except the son of destruction.'

In I Cor. 14:5; 15:2; and I Tim. 5:19, it is emphasized by ἐκτός.

3. Disjunctive. These conjunctions unite two objects in one's thoughts by separating them.

a. ἤ is the simplest disjunctive, meaning 'or.' It occurs singly in Mt. 5:17, and four times in Mk. 13:35. In the latter example, it means 'either . . . or.'

b. εἴτε . . . εἴτε (ἐάντε . . . ἐάντε) is a conditional disjunctive, 'whether . . . or.' In I Cor. 10:31, it occurs three times; in I Cor. 3:22, it occurs eight times.

c. οὔτε . . . οὔτε. This is simply a negative copulative conjunction, 'neither . . . nor.' In Rom. 8:38, 39, it occurs ten times.

With essentially the same meaning οὐδὲ . . . οὐδέ occurs in Rev. 9:4; μηδὲ . . . μηδέ, Mt. 10:10; μήτε . . . μήτε, Mt. 5:34-36.

4. Illative or inferential conjunctions are used to draw a conclusion from a truth just stated: οὖν (Rom. 7:13) concludes from the statement in verse 12 that the 'law was holy and the commandment was holy and just and good.' For the sake of the argument Paul represents his opponent as concluding then that the 'good' may work death to one. He immediately repudiates this conclusion with μὴ γένοιτο.

The conclusion may be drawn from a single statement or from a long argument, e. g., Rom. 12:1, where οὖν looks back over the preceding eleven chapters.

a. οὖν, 'therefore,' is the commonest inferential conjunction in the New Testament, occurring about four hundred times. But a warning is necessary here. It does not always draw a conclusion, e. g., in John, where it occurs some two hundred times (mostly in the narrative portions), it is often merely a transitional particle, 'then,' carrying on the narrative. For an illustration of this statement, examine chapter eleven in John. The non-inferential use should not surprise us, for in Homer, it is often a transitional particle, loosely stringing clauses and sentences together by way of confirmation.[113]

b. ἄρα is nearly always inferential, in the New Testament. It means 'accordingly,' 'therefore,' and gives point to a conclusion already apparent.

In the older Greek, it was a post-positive, but in the New Testament, it is not always so: ἄρα ἔφθασεν (Mt. 12:28), 'then (it) has arrived.'

Several times, the intensive particle, γε, is added to it: εἰ ἄρα γε (Acts 17:27), 'if therefore indeed.' Cf. Mt. 7:20; 17:26f.

Paul is particularly fond of ἄρα οὖν: Rom. 5:18; 7:3, 25; etc. Once, he has ἄρα νῦν: Rom. 8:1.

These compound illatives have something of an intensifying effect on the conclusion.

c. There is a miscellaneous group, each occurring at least once:
  (1) τοιγαροῦν, 'therefore': Heb. 12:1; I Th. 4:8.
  (2) τοίνυν, 'so': Lk. 20:25.
  (3) ἀνθ᾽ ὧν, 'because': Lk. 12:3.

5. The causal co-ordinating conjunction is γάρ, 'for.' It is a compound of γε+ἄρα, and is always post-positive.

It quite frequently gives the reason for a statement just made: αὐτὸς γὰρ σώσει (Mt. 1:21) tells why the Child is to be called 'Jesus.'

[113] Robertson, *A Grammar of the Greek New Testament in the Light of Historical Research*, p. 1191.

In Rom. 1:16, 17, it occurs three times: the first instance introduces the reason for Paul's eagerness to preach the gospel in Rome; the second, his reason for not being ashamed of the gospel; the third, the reason for the dynamic of the gospel.

Sometimes, it is merely explanatory: ἦν γὰρ ἐτῶν δώδεκα (Mk. 5:42) does not tell why the girl stood, it is simply an explanatory remark by the author.

Asyndeton

Sometimes, the conjunction is not used where an English reader would expect it. This is called asyndeton (ἀ-privative+σύν, 'together,'+δετος, 'bound,' i. e., 'not bound together').

1. When asyndeton occurs between words or phrases in a sentence, it suggests excitement, rapidity of thought, urgency, or some other kindred idea. The context will make clear the exact nature of the force of asyndeton. Cf. Rom. 1:29-31; I Cor. 15:42-44a; Mk. 6:38; I Tim. 3:16.

It may also occur between sentences, with much the same force.

2. When asyndeton occurs between paragraphs, it usually indicates that a new subject is taken up. Cf. Rom. 9:1; 13:1.[114]

Parenthesis and Anacolouthon

Related roughly to asyndeton, but yet distinctly different, are parenthesis and anacolouthon.

1. Parentheses are usually thrown in by way of interpretation—they are the author's exegetical remarks, e. g.,

[114] See Abbott, *Johannine Grammar*, pp. 70f., for a discussion of asyndeton in John's gospel.

ἐν ᾧ ἔχομεν τὴν ἀπολύτρωσιν (Col. 1:14), 'in whom we have redemption,' is interpreted by τὴν ἄφεσιν τῶν ἁμαρτιῶν, 'the remission of sins.' The parenthesis enables the writer quickly and concisely to remind his readers that he is not referring to Gnostic 'redemption' from matter, but Christian redemption from sin.

Parenthetical remarks may be used to translate an unintelligible word or phrase: ὁ ἐστιν μεθερμηνευόμενον Τὸ κοράσιον, σοὶ λέγω, ἔγειρε (Mk. 5:41), 'which is being interpreted, Damsel, I say unto thee Arise,' translates for Greek readers the Aramaic Ταλιθὰ κούμ.

The editors do not always agree as to what constitutes a parenthesis, but in spite of that fact they are quite important in interpreting.

2. Anacoloutha are produced by the mind of the writer or speaker taking a direction different from that at the beginning of the sentence. These changes of direction may be accidental or intentional. The more alert a man's mind and the more his emotions are stirred, the more likely is he to use anacoloutha in his speech or writing. This accounts no doubt for the large number in Gal. and II Cor.: a man of great mental activity is writing under great emotional stress.

a. A common form of anacolouthon is the 'hanging nominative.'[115] This is quite characteristic of Rev.: ὁ νικῶν . . . δώσω αὐτῷ (Rev. 2:26), 'the one overcoming . . . I will give to him.' Cf. Rev. 3:12, 21. But in Rev. 2:7, 17, the author uses τῷ νικῶντι δώσω αὐτῷ. It is also found in a careful writer like Luke: Ταῦτα ἃ θεωρεῖτε, ἐλεύσονται ἡμέραι ἐν αἷς οὐκ ἀφεθήσεται λίθος ἐπὶ λίθῳ ὃς οὐ καταλυθήσεται (Lk. 21:6), 'These things which ye behold—days will come in which there shall not be left stone upon stone, which shall not be cast down.' Cf. Acts 7:40; II Cor. 12:17.

b. Digression is another form of anacolouthon that is fairly common in the New Testament. The author's

[115] See p. 28

remark: καὶ ταῦτα εἶπεν αὐτῇ (Jn. 20:18), 'and these things he said to her,' fits on quite loosely to Mary's statement: ἑώρακα τὸν κύριον, 'I have seen the Lord.' In reality, it is a side remark about Jesus' words to Mary in verse 17. For other examples see Gal. 2:6; II Cor. 7:5.

c. The participle is frequent in anacoloutha: καταρτίζετε τὸν τοιοῦτον . . . σκοπῶν σεαυτόν (Gal. 6:1), 'restore such a one . . . considering thyself.' The change from a plural verb to a singular participle serves to remind the individual of his responsibility.

In Rom. 12:9-21, a series of hortatory participles and adjectives is interrupted by imperatives (vs. 14) and infinitives (vs. 15), with imperatives again in vss. 17, 19-21.

In Acts 15:22f., the dative τοῖς ἀποστόλοις καὶ τοῖς πρεσβυτέροις is in logical (but not grammatical) agreement with the accusative ἐκλεξαμένους and with the nominative γράψαντες.

d. The 'Pindaric construction' is another form taken by anacoloutha, i. e., several subjects may be linked together but followed by a singular verb: καὶ ὁ ἄνεμος καὶ ἡ θάλασσα ὑπακούει αὐτῷ (Mk. 4:41), 'the wind and the sea obey him.'

Hypotactic or Subordinate Conjunctions

These conjunctions introduce clauses subordinate to the principal clause. There is a great variety of these subordinating conjunctions. They introduce clauses which stand in one of three relations to the main clause.

1. Noun clauses always stand in a case relation to a verb of the main clause, i. e., either its subject or object: ὅτι ἐπαίχθη (Mt. 2:16) is the direct object of the participle, ἰδών. Cf. II Tim. 1:12.

2. Adjective clauses describe some substantive, usually the subject or object of the verb in the main clause: ὅς ἐστιν ἐν δεξιᾷ τοῦ θεοῦ (Rom. 8:34) is a description of

Χριστὸς Ἰησοῦς. Another descriptive relative clause follows immediately. It should be noted that the participles, ὁ ἀποθανών and ἐγερθείς, are used parallel to these two relative clauses, and that they stand in essentially the same relation to Χριστὸς Ἰησοῦς.

3. Adverbial clauses modify some part of the main clause. They express a great variety of ideas, such as time, place, comparison.

All of these subordinate clauses and conjunctions will be discussed more fully under each class of clause, such as relative, temporal, local, comparative, final (purpose), purport (subfinal), consecutive (result), causal, conditional, etc.

THE PARTICLE

Some scholars use the term 'particle' to include adverbs, prepositions, conjunctions, and interjections. We are using it in a more restricted sense.

Negative Particles

There are two simple negative particles in Greek, οὐ[116] and μή. They are used in the New Testament much as they are in Attic Greek.

1. οὐ. This negative is used for a positive, clear-cut denial. It is the natural one to use with the indicative mode. This will hold true everywhere except in protases of conditions of the second class, where μή is used: εἰ μὴ ἦν οὗτος παρὰ θεοῦ (Jn. 9:33), 'if this man were not from God.' There is one exception to this use of μή in second class conditions: εἰ οὐκ ἐγεννήθη ὁ ἄνθρωπος ἐκεῖνος (Mt. 26:24; Mk. 14:21), 'if that man had not been born.'

a. Uses of οὐ.

---

[116] This negative appears as οὐκ before vowels with smooth breathing and οὐχ before the rough breathing.

(1) The commonest use is to negative a statement: οὐκ οἴδαμεν (Mt. 21:27), 'We do not know.'

(2) It is used to introduce questions where an affirmative answer is expected: οὐχ οἱ δέκα ἐκαθα-ρίσθησαν; (Lk. 17:17), 'Were there not ten cleansed?'

When the emphatic form, οὐχί, introduces a question, it insists on an affirmative answer: οὐχὶ κρατήσει αὐτὸ καὶ ἐγερεῖ; (Mt. 12:11), 'Will he not seize it and lift (it out)?' Jesus' point is, 'Of course, a man will rescue his sheep on the Sabbath. Why should I not rescue a man?'

(3) It is used with the future indicative to express prohibitions: οὐκ ἐπιορκήσεις (Mt. 5:33), 'Thou shalt not perjure thyself.' Cf. οὐ φονεύσεις (Mt. 5:21), and οὐ μοιχεύσεις (Mt. 5:27).

(4) It is used with μή to emphasize the negative idea: οὐ μὴ ἀφεθῇ ὧδε λίθος ἐπὶ λίθον (Mt. 24:2), 'There shall not, in any wise, be left here stone upon stone.' Note that the aorist subjunctive is used here.

This double negative is used especially when quoting the LXX or the words of Jesus. The origin of this construction has never been satisfactorily explained, but it is clearly emphatic.

(5) The emphatic form, οὐχί, is used for a strong denial: οὐχί, ἀλλὰ κληθήσεται Ἰωάνης (Lk 1:60), 'Most assuredly not, but he shall be called John.' This example illustrates also another usage, where οὐ and ἀλλά are used for a sharp contrast between two things. Here, the contrast is between the proposed name, 'Zacharias,' and the accepted name, 'John.'

b. Compounds of οὐ.

There are a number of compounds, such as οὐδείς (οὐθείς is the form that had considerable vogue in the first centuries, B. C. and A. D.), οὐδέ, οὔτε, οὐκέτι, κ. τ. λ.

2. μή. This negative is used for hypothetical, hesitant or indefinite denial. It is subjective: ὅτι μὴ πεπίστευκεν εἰς τὸ ὄνομα (Jn. 3:18), 'because he has not believed on the name.' The hypothetical μή is used here with the indicative because this is a supposed case. Contrast the clear-cut denial made by οὐ: ὅτι οὐ πεπίστευκεν εἰς τὴν μαρτυρίαν (I Jn. 5:10), 'because he did not believe the testimony.'

It is quite natural that μή should be used with the subjunctive, imperative, and optative modes, the infinitive and the participle. There are about twenty examples of οὐ with the participle in the New Testament. Luke and Paul account for about three-fourths of the total. It is always used for a definite denial: τὴν οὐκ ἠγαπημένην (Rom. 9:25), 'the one not beloved.' Cf. II Cor. 4:8, 9.

a. Uses of μή.

(1) It is used to negative a hypothetical statement: Cf. Jn. 3:18, above.

(2) It is used to introduce questions expecting a negative answer: μὴ κατὰ ἄνθρωπον ταῦτα λαλῶ; (I Cor. 9:8), 'Do I speak these things after the fashion of man?' The answer is 'No.' Cf. the following question.

A touch of doubt may be added to the answer which is expected by τι: μήτι ἐγώ; (Mk. 14:19), 'It isn't I, is it?' The disciples are not quite sure of themselves.

The Samaritan woman, convinced of the Messiahship of Jesus, uses μήτι to avoid a controversy, but at the same time to arouse curiosity: μήτι οὗτός ἐστιν ὁ Χριστός; (Jn. 4:29), 'This isn't the Christ, is it?' By using μήτι, she, in effect, said to her fellow-townsmen, 'Here is the evidence, what do you think?'

(3) It is used with the aorist subjunctive and the present imperative to express prohibitions.

(a) With the aorist subjunctive, it has the ingressive force and means 'don't begin': μὴ νομίσητε (Mt. 5:17), 'don't begin to think.'

(b) With the present imperative, it is linear and either means 'stop' what you are doing, or 'don't get the habit' of doing it. If the act is already in progress, the former is the meaning: μὴ θησαυρίζετε (Mt. 6:19), 'stop hoarding treasure.' If the act has not begun, it would mean, 'don't get into the habit of hoarding treasures on earth.' The great majority of instances come under the first head. Cf. Mt. 7:1; Jn. 6:20.

An interesting use of μὴ οὐκ occurs: μὴ οὐκ ἔχομεν ἐξουσίαν ἀδελφὴν γυναῖκα περιάγειν; (I Cor. 9:4), 'Do we not have authority to lead about a sister as a wife?' Here, μή negatives the question, and οὐ negatives the verb. The answer is: 'We certainly do.'

b. Compounds of μή.

There are a number of compounds, such as μηδέ, μηδείς, μηθείς (see οὐθείς), μηδέπω, κ. τ. λ.

3. A succession of compound negatives strengthen each other: μηδενὶ μηδὲν ὀφείλετε (Rom. 13:8), 'owe no one anything.'

Intensive Particles

These often express fine shades of thought or emotion and are practically untranslatable into English.

1. γε (enclitic), 'at least.' It adds nothing to the meaning of the word with which it occurs, but serves to intensify the idea: ὅς γε τοῦ ἰδίου υἱοῦ οὐκ ἐφείσατο (Rom. 8:32), 'who, at least, spared not his own son.'

2. δή, 'surely.' This is always (six times) a post-positive in the New Testament. It has a note of urgency in it. The context must decide the English word or words used to express this idea: δοξάσατε δὴ τὸν θεὸν ἐν τῷ σώματι ὑμῶν (I Cor. 6:20), 'glorify now then God in your body.'

3. εἰ μήν, 'assuredly.' This is an itacism for ἦ μέν and is an asseverative particle: εἰ μὴν εὐλογῶν εὐλογήσω σε (Heb. 6:14), 'assuredly, in blessing I will bless thee.'

4. μέν, 'indeed.' This is by far the most common intensive particle in the New Testament. It is a weakened form of μήν. It was originally used alone with no thought of a corresponding δέ. This use is frequent in the New Testament: Acts 1:1, 18; 3:13, 21; II Cor. 11:4; etc.

Where there is contrast with δέ, the contrast may be slight: μὲν ... δὲ ... δέ (Mt. 25:14f) ; or decided: μὲν ... δὲ ... δὲ ... δέ (I Cor. 1:12).

5. ναί, 'yes,' 'verily.' This affirmative particle occurs, in the New Testament, about thirty times. It is used in the sense of 'yes': Mt. 13:51; in the sense of 'verily': Mt. 11:9.

6. νή, 'by.' This particle occurs in the New Testament, once: νὴ τὴν ὑμετέραν καύχησιν (I Cor. 15:31), 'by the glorying in you.' It is used for a strong affirmation. It is possibly a variant of ναί.

7. περ (enclitic), 'thoroughly.' This is probably a shortened form of περί. It is extensive as well as intensive. It occurs in a number of compounds: διόπερ (I Cor. 8:13) ; ἐάνπερ (Heb. 3:14) ; εἴπερ (Rom. 8:9) ; ἐπειδήπερ (Lk. 1:1) ; καθάπερ (sixteen times in Paul and once in Heb. 4:2) ; καθώσπερ (Heb. 5:4) ; καίπερ (Heb. 12:17) ; ὥσπερ (thirty-six times, e. g., Mt. 6:2) ; ὡσπερεί (only once in the New Testament: I Cor. 15:8). It is never used in the simplex. The idea added by περ is always 'thoroughly.'

8. τοί, 'on this account.' This occurs only in compounds, in the New Testament: καίτοι (Acts 14:17) ; τοιγαροῦν (Heb. 12:1) ; etc.

PART IV

CLAUSES

RELATIVE CLAUSES

Relation to the Main Clause

The relative clause will be introduced by a relative pronoun. It may bear either of two relations to the main clause:

1. It may be adjectival: ὃν ἤγειρεν ἐκ νεκρῶν Ἰησοῦς (Jn. 12:1), 'whom Jesus had raised from the dead.' This clause describes Λάζαρος of the principal clause. The aorist tense, ἤγειρεν, tells that it had happened before the feast at which both Jesus and Lazarus were present. Cf. ὃν φιλεῖς ἀσθενεῖ (Jn. 11:3), '(he) whom Thou lovest is sick,' where ὃν φιλεῖς describes the unexpressed antecedent, the subject of the verb, ἀσθενεῖ.

2. It may be substantival: ὃς οὐ λαμβάνει τὸν σταυρὸν αὐτοῦ καὶ ἀκολουθεῖ ὀπίσω μου, οὐκ ἔστιν μου ἄξιος (Mt. 10:38), 'who does not take his cross and follow after me, is not worthy of me.' The subject of the principal verb, ἔστιν, is the ὅς clause.

Types of Relative Clauses

Every relative clause is either 'definite' or 'indefinite.'

1. The definite relative clause describes a particular individual or group, like the English 'who': ἐποίησεν δώδεκα οὓς καὶ ἀποστόλους ὠνόμασεν[1] (Mk. 3:14), 'He appointed twelve whom he also called apostles.' The relative clause describes the Twelve.

   Generally, definite clauses are introduced by ὅς, but occasionally by ὅστις: εἰσίν τινες ὧδε τῶν ἑστηκότων οἵτινες

---

[1] The relative clause is omitted in ADL it. vg. pesh. κ. τ. λ.; it is read by אBC* WΔΘ cop. κ. τ. λ.

οὐ μὴ γεύσωνται θανάτου (Mk. 9:1), 'there are some of those standing here who shall not in any wise taste death.'

In Rom. 6:2, οἵτινες ἀπεθάνομεν τῇ ἁμαρτίᾳ, 'we the very ones who died to sin,' has an argumentative note. In a sense, the relative refers to a definite group, in that they all have died to sin; in another sense, it is indefinite, in that any one may become a member of that group by dying to sin.

A relative clause may imply purpose: ὃς κατασκευάσει τὴν ὁδόν σου (Mk. 1:2), 'who shall prepare thy way,' i. e., the messenger comes in order to prepare the way of the Lord. This was a common idiom in Attic Greek, but not so frequent in the New Testament. The future tense of the verb was regularly used in such clauses of purpose.

2. The indefinite relative clause pictures anyone in general, without any particular individual in mind, like the English 'whoever': ὅστις γὰρ ὅλον τὸν νόμον τηρήσῃ (Jas. 2:10), 'whoever keeps the whole law.' The idea of the clause is, 'anyone who keeps the whole law.'

Usually, indefinite relative clauses are introduced by ὅστις, but occasionally, ὅς may be so used: ὃς ἔχει ὦτα ἀκούειν ἀκουέτω (Mk. 4:9), 'who (ever) has ears to hear let him hear.' Probably ἀκούειν ἀκουέτω should be regarded as a Semitism, reflecting the Hebrew infinitive absolute. If so, this should be rendered: 'Whoever has ears let him hear attentively.' Cf. εἴ τις ἔχει ὦτα ἀκούειν ἀκουέτω (Mk. 4:23), where the conditional clause is used as the equivalent of the relative clause in Mk. 4:9.

In the New Testament, ὅστις is confined almost entirely to the nominative case.

The context must be consulted for the exact meaning of the relative clause.

3. For the qualitative relatives, οἷος (I Th. 1:5) and ὁποῖος (Jas. 1:24); the quantitative, ὅσος (Mt. 7:12); and the

quantitative correlative, ἡλίκος (for age, Jn. 9:21; or for stature, Mt. 6:27), see the section on Pronouns.[2]

The Use of ἄν (ἐάν) in the Relative Clause

This particle practically always emphasizes the indefiniteness of the clause: ὃς ἂν ὁμολογήσῃ (Lk. 12:8), 'whoever shall confess.' In one example, ὅσοι ἂν ἥψαντο αὐτοῦ ἐσώζοντο (Mk. 6:56), 'Whoever touched him were made whole,' some grammarians think that it makes the idea more definite. Cf. ὅσοι ἥψαντο (Mt. 14:36). It seems to be more correct to say that, in this case, it emphasizes that the virtue lay in the touch, rather than in the person doing the touching.

The Negative in the Relative Clause

The negative in the relative clause is usually οὐ. Such matters are always determined by the mode and not by the relative.

TEMPORAL CLAUSES

The temporal clause stands in an adverbial relation to the predicate of the principal clause. Like the purely relative clause, the temporal clause may be either definite or indefinite. The particle, ἄν, is used to make a temporal clause indefinite: ὅταν (ὅτε+ἄν) εἰσφέρωσιν (Lk. 12:11), 'whenever they bring in.'

Either the indicative or the subjunctive mode may be used, depending on the shade of thought to be expressed.

There are three general types of temporal clauses:

1. Clauses introduced by a conjunction;

2. Clauses using an infinitive;

3. Temporal circumstantial participles.

Clauses Introduced by a Conjunction

These fall into two classes: those expressing the idea

[2] Pp. 44f.

of 'when' or 'while,' and those expressing the idea of 'until.'

1. 'When' or 'while.'
   a. ὅτε (definite, 'when') and ὅταν (indefinite, 'whenever') are the most frequent temporal conjunctions in the New Testament.

   (1) ὅτε may be used with any tense of the indicative, but usually refers to past time: ὅτε ἐτέλεσεν (Mt. 7:28), 'when he finished.'
   Occasionally, it refers to present time: ὅτε ζῇ (Heb. 9:17), 'while he lives.'

   (2) ὅταν is quite frequent with the subjunctive for indefinite future time. The tense is usually aorist: ὅταν ἴδητε (Mt. 24:33), 'whenever ye see.'
   The present subjunctive occurs when the idea of repetition is present: ὅταν ἄρτον ἐσθίωσιν (Mt. 15:2), 'whenever they eat bread.'
   Once, the idea of duration is expressed: ὅταν ἐν τῷ κόσμῳ ᾦ (Jn. 9:5), 'as long as (while) I am in the world.'

   (3) ὅταν with the indicative occurs occasionally:
   (a) With the future: ὅταν δώσουσιν (Rev. 4:9), 'whenever they shall give.' This is a rather natural usage, since the aorist subjunctive and the future indicative have a rather close kinship in meaning.
   (b) With the present: ὅταν στήκετε (Mk. 11:25), 'whenever ye stand,' i. e., 'at any time when you pray.' Cf. Rom. 2:14.
   (c) With the imperfect: ὅταν αὐτὸν ἐθεώρουν προσέπιπτον αὐτῷ (Mk. 3:11), 'Whenever they saw Him, they fell before Him.' Here, it gives the clause the notion of indefinite repetition.
   (d) With the aorist: ὅταν ὀψὲ ἐγένετο (Mk. 11:19), 'whenever evening came.' Probably here, it calls attention to the repeated return of evening. But in Rev. 3:1, ὅταν ἤνοιξεν τὴν σφραγῖδα τὴν ἑβδόμην

it is certainly definite, 'when' not 'whenever,' i. e., 'when he opened the seventh seal.'

b. ἕως. The usual meaning is 'until,' but with the present indicative, it means 'while.'

It may refer to a contemporaneous event: ἕως αὐτὸς ἀπολύει τὸν ὄχλον (Mk. 6:45), 'while he dismisses the crowd'; or it may draw a future event into the present for the sake of vividness: ἕως ἔρχομαι (Jn. 21:22), 'while I am coming.' Cf. I Tim. 4:13.

Sometimes, ὅτου is added: ἕως ὅτου εἶ μετ' αὐτοῦ ἐν τῇ ὁδῷ (Mt. 5:25), 'while thou art with him in the way.' This word, ὅτου, really adds nothing to the meaning.

The particle, ἕως, must be watched closely, for it is more often a preposition than a conjunction. As a preposition, it denotes the *terminus ad quem:* ἕως τοῦ ἐλθεῖν αὐτὸν εἰς Καισαρίαν (Acts 8:40), 'until he came to Caesarea.' Here, it is followed by the infinitive in the the genitive case.

c. ἐπειδή and ἐπάν, 'when' and 'whenever.'
The temporal use of ἐπεί has disappeared from the New Testament, but these two compounds have not quite disappeared.

ἐπειδή occurs once: ἐπειδὴ ἐπλήρωσεν πάντα τὰ ῥήματα αὐτοῦ (Lk. 7:1), 'when he had finished all his words.'

ἐπάν occurs three times: ἐπὰν ... νικήσῃ αὐτόν (Lk. 11:22), 'whenever ... overcomes him'; Mt. 2:8; Lk. 11:34. It is always used with the subjunctive.

d. ἡνίκα, 'when.'
This conjunction, originally a pronoun, occurs in the New Testament, only twice. Both instances refer to the future.

Once, it is used with the present subjunctive and ἄν: ἡνίκα ἂν ἀναγινώσκηται Μωϋσῆς (II Cor. 3:15), 'whenever Moses is read.'

Once, it occurs with the aorist subjunctive and ἐάν: ἡνίκα ἐὰν ἐπιτρέψῃ (II Cor. 3:16), 'whenever it turns.'

The present tense in the first example calls attention to the customary reading of Moses. while the aorist in the second example calls attention to the single act of turning in conversion.

e. ἐφ' ὅσον, 'for so long a time as,' 'as long as,' 'while.' This phrase implies the word χρόνον: ἐφ' ὅσον μετ' αὐτῶν ἐστιν ὁ νυμφίος (Mt. 9:15), 'for so long a time as the bridegroom is with them.'
Several variations of this phrase occur:

(1) ὅσον χρόνον (Mk. 2:19).

(2) ἐφ' ὅσον χρόνον (Rom. 7:1).

(3) ὅσον ὅσον (Heb. 10:37). This example is a Hebraism, from the LXX, Isa. 26:20. It is due to translation.

f. ἐν ᾧ, 'while,' 'in which time.'
This phrase also implies χρόνῳ. It is not strictly a conjunction, but is a phrase so used: ἐν ᾧ ἔρχομαι (Jn. 5:7), 'while I am coming.'
In Rom. 2:1 and 14:21, it introduces a local phrase. In Rom. 8:3, it is causal.

2. 'Until.' There is quite a variety of this usage.

a. ἄχρι (ἄχρις).

This particle is more frequently used as a preposition, e. g., ἄχρι καιροῦ (Lk. 4:13), than as a conjunction.

As a conjunction, it occurs, e. g., ἄχρι τελεσθήσονται οἱ λόγοι τοῦ θεοῦ (Rev. 17:17), 'until the words of God shall be completed.'

(1) It is used with the relative pronoun a number of times to form a compound conjunction: ἄχρι οὗ ἀνέστη (Acts 7:18), 'until (he) arose.' The meaning is not changed by this compound. The aorist indicative refers to a past event.

(2) When used with ἄν, the time of the clause becomes indefinite: ἄχρις ἄν ἔλθῃ (Gal. 3:19), 'until there come.' The subjunctive refers to a future event. Cf. I Cor. 15:25.

b. ἕως.
(1) When an actual past event is referred to, it is used with the aorist indicative: ἕως ἦλθεν (Mt. 24: 39), 'until (it) came.'
(2) With the subjunctive, a future event is referred to: ἕως ἔλθῃ (Mt. 10:23), 'until there come.'
ἄν makes such a clause indefinite: ἕως ἂν ἀποδῷς (Mt. 5:26), 'until you pay.'
(3) With the present tense, see under 'when' and 'while.'
(4) When used with τοῦ, οὗ and ὅτου, χρόνου is implied. The sense is substantially the same as when used alone. There is only one example with τοῦ in the New Testament: ἕως τοῦ ἐλθεῖν (Acts 8: 40), 'until he come.'

c. μέχρι (μέχρις).
This word occurs only three times, as a conjunction.
Once, it is alone: μέχρι καταντήσωμεν (Eph. 4:13), 'until we attain.'
Twice, it is μέχρις οὗ: ὠδίνω μέχρις οὗ μορφωθῇ Χριστὸς ἐν ὑμῖν (Gal. 4:19), 'I am in travail until Christ be formed in you'; Mk. 13:30.

d. πρίν.
There are only two examples of this, as a conjunction, in the sense of 'until.'
One example is in Acts 25:16, and one is in Lk. 2:26[3]: πρὶν ἢ ἂν ἴδῃ, 'until he see.' In each instance ἢ follows. In each case, it is used with a finite verb after a negative sentence. In Acts 25:16, the optative follows πρίν, and in Lk. 2:26, the subjunctive.

e. ἀφ' οὗ, 'from which time,' 'since.'
This hardly belongs here, but since it sometimes approaches ἕως in meaning, it is included. This phrase implies χρόνου.
(1) It is used with the present indicative: τρία ἔτη ἀφ' οὗ ἔρχομαι (Lk. 13:7), 'three years since I have been coming.'

[3] Some manuscripts do not have ἄν in this construction in Luke. Aleph reads ἕως ἄν here.

(2) It is used with the subjunctive and ἄν: ἀφ' οὗ ἄν ἐγερθῇ (Lk. 13:25), 'when he has risen.'

The Infinitive in Temporal Clauses

1. πρίν or πρὶν ἤ, 'before.'
This occurs, with the infinitive, eleven times in the New Testament. The article is not used in this construction: πρὶν 'Αβραὰμ γενέσθαι ἐγὼ εἰμί (Jn. 8:58), 'before Abraham became I am.'

Usually, these examples refer to future time, and use the aorist infinitive: κατάβηθι πρὶν ἀποθανεῖν τὸ παιδίον μου (Jn. 4:49), 'come down before my child die.'

2. πρὸ τοῦ, 'before.'
This occurs, with the infinitive, nine times. It is used with the aorist infinitive, eight times: πρὸ τοῦ ὑμᾶς αἰτῆσαι αὐτόν (Mt. 6:8), 'before you ask him.' It is used with the present infinitive, once: πρὸ τοῦ τὸν κόσμον εἶναι (Jn. 17:5), 'before the world was.'

3. ἐν τῷ, 'while,' 'when.'
This construction is much more common in Luke than in any other New Testament writer.[4] This is due to the fact that the LXX influenced his style more profoundly than any other New Testament writer, in spite of his literary style. (It occurs in the LXX about five hundred times).

a. With the present infinitive, it means 'while': ἐν τῷ ἱερατεύειν αὐτόν (Lk. 1:8), 'while he was serving as priest.'

b. With the aorist, it means 'when': ἐν τῷ εἰσαγαγεῖν τοὺς γονεῖς τὸ παιδίον 'Ιησοῦν (Lk. 2:27), 'when the parents brought the child Jesus.'

4. μετὰ τό, 'after.'
There are fifteen instances of this idiom: μετὰ τὸ

[4] See the infinitive, p. 109.

παραδοθῆναι τὸν Ἰωάνην (Mk. 1:14), 'after John was delivered up.'

Luke uses this idiom more than any other New Testament writer.

The Temporal Participle[5]

1. The present temporal participle usually describes simultaneous action, and means 'while': Ἰακὼβ ἀποθνήσκων[6] ἕκαστον τῶν υἱῶν Ἰωσὴφ εὐλόγησεν (Heb. 11: 21), 'Jacob while he was dying blessed each of the sons of Joseph.'

2. The aorist participle normally describes action antecedent to that of the main verb, and means 'when' or 'after': πωλήσας ἤνεγκεν (Acts 4:37), 'when he had sold he brought.'

    Occasionally, the aorist participle expresses simultaneous action: σπεύσας κατάβηθι (Lk. 19:5), 'come down in a hurry.'

    There is an aorist participle of identical action: ἀποκριθεὶς εἶπεν, 'answering he said.' This is of such frequent occurrence as to make it hardly necessary to give examples. Cf. Mk. 10:51; 11:14.

LOCAL CLAUSES

1. There are three conjunctions which introduce local clauses. They are all derived from the relative pronouns.

    a. ὅθεν (ὅ+θεν), 'whence.'
    This is commonly used to express the local idea of source. It is used only with the indicative: ὅθεν ἐξῆλθον (Lk. 11:24), 'whence I came out.'

    In the Epistle to the Hebrews, it is used several times as an inferential particle: ὅθεν ὤφειλεν κατὰ πάντα τοῖς ἀδελφοῖς ὁμοιωθῆναι (Heb. 2:17), 'wherefore

---

[5] For more on this idiom, see the circumstantial participle, p. 101.
[6] This participle may have a slight concessive force here.

it behooved him to be made in all things like unto his brethren.' This usage is a characteristic of the style of Hebrews, and is found elsewhere in the New Testament only in Acts 26:19.

b. οὗ (gen. of ὅ), 'where.'

This is fairly common.

With verbs of rest, it means 'where': οὗ ἦν τὸ παιδίον (Mt. 2:9), 'where the child was.'

With verbs of motion, it means 'whither'[7]: οὗ ἤμελλεν αὐτὸς ἔρχεσθαι (Lk. 10:1), 'whither he himself was about to go.'

Once, ἐάν occurs with it and the subjunctive: οὗ ἐὰν πορεύωμαι (I Cor. 16:6), 'whithersoever I go.' This effect of ἐάν is to make the clause indefinite.

c. ὅπου, 'where.'

This is the usual local conjunction, in the New Testament.

With verbs of rest, it means 'where': ὅπου ἦν (Mk. 2:4), 'where he was.'

With verbs of motion, it means 'whither'[8]: ὅπου ἐγὼ ὑπάγω (Jn. 8:21), 'whither I go.'

With this conjunction, ὅπου, ἄν (ἐάν) occurs several times: ὅπου ἂν εἰσπορεύετο (Mk. 6:56), 'wherever he was entering.' This particle produces its usual effect of indefiniteness here.

Sometimes, this conjunction occurs in metaphorical clauses: ὅπου γὰρ διαθήκη (Heb. 9:16), 'for where (there is) a testament.'

2. ἐν ᾧ, 'in what.'

This prepositional phrase may be used to express the local idea. Most of these examples are metaphorical: ἐν ᾧ κρίνεις (Rom. 2:1), 'in what thou judgest.'

The temporal use occurs in Jn. 5:7, and the causal in Rom. 8:3.

---

[7] In classical Greek, οἷ was used to express the idea of whither.' This form does not occur in the New Testament.

[8] In classical Greek, ὅποι was used to express the idea of 'whither.' This form does not occur in the New Testament.

COMPARATIVE CLAUSES

The conjunctions introducing comparative clauses all had their origin in the relative pronoun.

1. ὡς (from ὅς), 'as.'
This is a very common conjunction to introduce comparative clauses, but it has other uses which must be watched. There are, at least, ten distinct uses of this particle in the New Testament. This seems to be the best place to list them:

a. It is a temporal conjunction: ὡς ἐπλήσθησαν αἱ ἡμέραι τῆς λειτουργίας αὐτοῦ (Lk. 1:23), 'as the days of his ministration were fulfilled.'

b. Once, it introduces a purpose clause: ὡς τελειώσω τὸν δρόμον μου (Acts 20:24), 'that I may finish my course.'

c. Once, it is exclamatory: ὡς ὡραῖοι οἱ πόδες (Rom. 10: 15), 'how beautiful are the feet.'

d. It may be used after a verb of saying in the sense of declarative ὅτι: ὡς ἔχρισεν αὐτὸν ὁ θεὸς πνεύματι ἁγίῳ καὶ δυνάμει (Acts 10:38), 'that[9] God had anointed him with the Holy Spirit and with power.'

e. It is used twice with the infinitive.
In ὡς ἑτοιμάσαι (Lk. 9:52), 'to make ready,' it expresses purpose. Nestle reads ὥστε in this verse.
In ὡς ἔπος εἰπεῖν (Heb. 7:9), 'so to speak a word,' or 'so to speak,' it introduces a hesitant statement. It indicates that the writer does not want to be understood literally.

f. It is used with superlative adverbs in the sense of 'as . . . as possible': ὡς τάχιστα (Acts 17:15), 'as quickly as possible.'

g. It is used with numbers in the sense of 'about': ὡς δισχίλιοι (Mk. 5:13), 'about two thousand.'

h. It is used with participles to give an alleged reason

---

[9] This would make good sense, as expressing manner, 'how.' It is so translated in the ARV.

for an act: ὡς μέλλων τι ἀκριβέστερον πυνθάνεσθαι περὶ αὐτοῦ (Acts 23:20), 'as about to inquire somewhat more accurately concerning him.'

i. It may introduce a result clause: ὡς ὤμοσα ἐν τῇ ὀργῇ μου (Heb. 3:11), 'so I swore in my wrath.' Cf. also Heb. 4:3. Some interpreters take these as examples of the comparative use.

j. The comparative use is by far the most common. Mention of this usage has been left until last, because it is the one in which we are interested here. The examples are many: ὡς οἱ ὑποκριταί (Mt. 6:5), 'as (or 'like') the hypocrites'; ὡς καὶ εἰώθει πάλιν ἐδίδασκεν αὐτούς (Mk. 10:1), 'and as he had been accustomed he was teaching them again.'

Sometimes, it is used with the subjunctive in comparative clauses: ὡς ἄνθρωπος βάλῃ (Mk. 4:26), 'as (if) a man should cast'; ὡς καιρὸν ἔχωμεν (Gal. 6:10), 'as we may have opportunity.'

Some grammarians cite as a causal use: ὡς καὶ ἡμεῖς ἀφήκαμεν τοῖς ὀφειλέταις ἡμῶν (Mt. 6:12), 'because we also have forgiven our debtors.' It seems more natural to take this example in the comparative sense: 'as we also have forgiven our debtors.' The correlative for ὡς is οὕτως: ὡς ἀμνὸς ἐναντίον τοῦ κείροντος αὐτὸν ἄφωνος οὕτως οὐκ ἀνοίγει τὸ στόμα αὐτοῦ (Acts 8:32), 'as a lamb before his shearers is dumb so he opened not his mouth.'

These numerous uses will seem quite confusing if one attempts to memorize them. The best method is to keep in the mind the general facts and let the context determine the exact meaning of each example.

2. Compounds of ὡς.

a. ὡσεί, 'as if.'

This comparative conjunction never has a verb used with it, in the New Testament: καταβαῖνον ὡσεὶ περιστεράν (Mt. 3:16), 'descending as a dove'; ἐρριμμένοι ὡσεὶ πρόβατα μὴ ἔχοντα ποιμένα (Mt. 9:36), 'scattered as sheep not having a shepherd.'

b. ὥσπερ, 'as indeed,' is simply ὡς+ the intensive particle, πέρ.

It is used with the indicative: ὥσπερ οἱ ὑποκριταὶ ποιοῦσιν (Mt. 6:2), 'as indeed the hypocrites do.'

It is used without a verb: ὥσπερ οἱ ἐθνικοί (Mt. 6:7), 'as the Gentiles.'

It is used with the participle: ὥσπερ φερομένης πνοῆς βιαίας (Acts 2:2), 'as a rushing mighty wind.'

c. ὡσπερεί, 'as if indeed,' is from ὡς+πέρ+εἰ.

It occurs only once in the New Testament: ὡσπερεὶ τῷ ἐκτρώματι (I Cor. 15:8), 'as if indeed to one born out of season.'

3. Compounds of κατά with the relative.

a. καθό (κατά+ὅ), 'according to what.'

This occurs in the New Testament, four times. Three examples use the indicative: καθὸ δεῖ (Rom. 8:26), 'according to what is necessary'; II Cor. 8:12; I Pet. 4:13. One example occurs with the subjunctive: καθὸ ἐὰν ἔχῃ εὐπρόσδεκτος (II Cor. 8:12), 'according to whatever one may have is he acceptable.' The next clause, using the indicative, οὐ καθὸ οὐκ ἔχει (II Cor. 8:12), 'not according to what he actually does not have,' supplies a good illustration of the difference between the subjunctive and the indicative mode. The subjunctive is hypothetical; the indicative is positive.

b. καθά (plural of καθό).

This occurs once: καθὰ συνέταξεν (Mt. 27:10), 'according to what things (the Lord) commanded.'

c. καθάπερ (κατά+ἅ+πέρ), 'according to which very things.'

This occurs seventeen times, counting three passages where there is a textual confusion with καθώς. It is simply καθά+πέρ (the intensive particle): καθάπερ γέγραπται (Rom. 3:4), 'precisely as it stands written.'

d. καθότι (κατά+ὅτι), 'according to what.'

It is well to note that ὅτι is simply the indefinite relative, whereas ὅ is definite, so this is essentially the same construction as 'a,' 'b,' and 'c' above.

There are only two examples of this as a comparative (all of the others are causal) conjunction: καθότι ἄν τις χρείαν εἶχεν (Acts 2:45; 4:35), 'according as any one might have need.' The indefinite is used in each of these identical passages.

e. καθώς (κατά+ὡς), 'according as.'

This is very frequent with the indicative: καθὼς ἠγάπησα ὑμᾶς (Jn. 13:34), 'according as (or 'even as') I have loved you.'

Sometimes, it seems to shade off into the causal idea: καθὼς οὐκ ἐδοκίμασαν τὸν θεὸν ἔχειν ἐν ἐπιγνώσει παρέδωκεν αὐτοὺς ὁ θεὸς εἰς ἀδόκιμον νοῦν (Rom. 1:28), 'because they did not approve having God in (their) knowledge God gave them up to a reprobate mind.' If the comparative idea should be kept here, then it means: 'In proportion as (according as) they did not approve having God in their knowledge, God gave them up to a reprobate mind.'

f. καθώσπερ (κατά+ὡς+πέρ), 'according (even) as indeed.'

This occurs in the New Testament, only once: καθώσπερ καὶ Ἀαρών (Heb. 5:4), 'even as indeed Aaron also.'

This, as well as 'e' above, is also a compound of ὡς, as well as of κατά.

4. ὅσος, 'as great as.'

In a comparative clause, this quantitative relative normally had the correlative, τοσοῦτος, with it in classical Greek. In the New Testament, this full idiom occurs only in Hebrews: τοσούτῳ κρείττων γενόμενος τῶν ἀγγέλων ὅσῳ διαφορώτερον παρ' αὐτοὺς κεκληρονόμηκεν ὄνομα (Heb. 1:4, 'having become by so much better than the angels as he had inherited a better name than they.'

In Heb. 9:27, the correlative is οὕτως: καθ' ὅσον ἀπόκειται τοῖς ἀνθρώποις ἅπαξ ἀποθανεῖν . . . οὕτως καὶ ὁ Χριστὸς

ἅπαξ προσενεχθείς, 'as it is appointed to man to die once
. . . so also the Christ was once for all offered.'

In Heb. 10:37, ὅσον ὅσον is a Hebraism from the
LXX (Isa. 26:20). In Mk. 7:36, ὅσον occurs in a comparative clause, but has no correlative.

CAUSAL CLAUSES

Paratactic or Co-ordinating Clauses

These are introduced by γάρ: τὸ γὰρ θέλειν παράκειταί
μοι τὸ δὲ κατεργάζεσθαι τὸ καλὸν οὔ (Rom. 7:18), 'for the
desiring the good is present with me, but the accomplish-
ing of it is not.' This gives Paul's reason for knowing
that no good thing dwells in his flesh.

But γάρ is not always causal; it is often merely explanatory: ἦσαν γὰρ ἁλιεῖς (Mt. 4:18), 'for they were fisher-
men.' This clause does not tell why Peter and Andrew
were casting a net into the sea; it is merely an explanatory note.

Hypotactic or Subordinating Clauses

1. ὅτι and its compounds.
   a. ὅτι is by far the most frequent causal conjunction.
   It always takes the indicative mode: ἐπαίνω δὲ ὑμᾶς
   ὅτι πάντα μου μέμνησθε (I Cor. 11:2), 'But I praise
   you because ye remember me in all things.'

   If a negative is used in the causal clause, it is
   regularly οὐ: ὅτι οὐ πεπίστευκεν (I Jn. 5:10), 'because
   he has not believed.'

   There is one exception where μή is used: ὅτι μὴ
   πεπίστευκεν (Jn. 3:18), 'because he has not believed.'

   These last two examples illustrate the difficulty
   in translating the difference between οὐ and μή. The
   first example deals with an actual case of disbelief,
   and the second, with a supposed case.

   ὅτι is, however, not always a causal conjunction;
   it has many other uses:

   (1) Sometimes, it introduces a direct quotation:
   τότε ἤρξατο καταθεματίζειν καὶ ὀμνύειν ὅτι Οὐκ οἶδα
   τὸν ἄνθρωπον (Mt. 26:74), 'Then began he to curse

and to swear "I do not know the man."' Here, ὅτι is practically equivalent to quotation marks in English, and is not translated. This usage is called recitative ὅτι.

(2) It often introduces an indirect quotation: ἀγνοῶν ὅτι τὸ χρηστὸν τοῦ θεοῦ εἰς μετάνοιάν σε ἄγει (Rom. 2: 4), 'not knowing that the goodness of God leadeth thee to repentance.' This type of clause is the direct object of a verb, and is in the accusative case. It follows verbs of thinking, saying, perceiving, hoping, knowing, declaring, etc. This usage is called declarative ὅτι.

(3) It may introduce a clause which is the subject of a verb: οὐ μέλει σοι ὅτι ἀπολλύμεθα; (Mk. 4:38), 'Is it not a care to thee that we perish?' The ὅτι clause is the subject of the verb, μέλει, and is in the nominative case. Cf. ἵνα clauses used as the subject of the verb.

(4) It may introduce a clause which is in apposition with a noun in the preceding clause: αὕτη ἐστὶν ἡ μαρτυρία τοῦ θεοῦ ὅτι μεμαρτύρηκεν περὶ τοῦ υἱοῦ αὐτοῦ (I Jn. 5:9), 'This is the testimony of God that He has borne testimony concerning His Son.' This ὅτι clause explains ἡ μαρτυρία τοῦ θεοῦ. This usage is called epexegetical ὅτι.

Often, the ὅτι clause is in apposition with οὗτος and ἐκεῖνος: λογίζῃ δὲ τοῦτο . . . ὅτι σὺ ἐκφεύξῃ τὸ κρίμα τοῦ θεοῦ (Rom. 2:3), 'Reckonest thou this . . . that thou shalt escape the judgment of God'; ἐκεῖνο δὲ γινώσκετε ὅτι εἰ ᾔδει ὁ οἰκοδεσπότης (Mt. 24: 43), 'but know this that if the Master of the house had known.'

(5) A few times, it is used to introduce a consecutive clause: τίς ἄρα οὗτός ἐστιν ὅτι καὶ ὁ ἄνεμος καὶ ἡ θάλασσα ὑπακούει αὐτῷ (Mk. 4:41), 'Who then is this one, that even the wind and the sea obey Him.' Abbott[10] considers ὅτι in Jn. 14:22, consecutive.

[10] *Johannine Grammar*, p. 534.

(6) Sometimes, it is simply the indefinite relative pronoun neuter singular, and will introduce a relative clause: ὅτι ἂν προσδαπανήσῃς . . . ἀποδώσω σοι (Lk. 10:35), 'Whatever thou spendest in addition . . . I will repay thee.'

(7) Sometimes, it is used with τί to introduce a question: τί ὅτι ἐζητεῖτέ με; (Lk. 2:49), 'Why are you seeking me?'

This long list of uses of ὅτι may seem quite confusing, but if the interpreter will keep in mind the basic meanings of the word, the context will make clear the meaning of individual instances of it.

b. διότι (διά+ὅτι), 'on account of which,' 'because.'
This conjunction is almost confined to the writings of Luke and Paul. Outside of Paul and Luke, διότι occurs twice in Hebrews, once in James, and three times in I Peter.
In Phil. 2:26, ἀδημονῶν, διότι ἠκούσατε ὅτι ἠσθένησεν, 'being homesick because ye had heard that he had become sick,' διότι is causal, and ὅτι is declarative.

c. καθότι (κατά+ὅτι), 'because that,' 'because.'
This conjunction occurs in a causal sense, five times: καθότι οὐκ ἦν δυνατόν (Acts 2:24), 'because it was not possible.'

2. ἐπεί and its compounds.

a. ἐπεί, 'since.'
This conjunction is not nearly so common as ὅτι, but is fairly frequent. It is always used with the indicative: ἐπεὶ ἦν παρασκευὴ ὅ ἐστιν προσάββατον (Mk. 15:42), 'because it was Friday which is the day before the Sabbath.'
The negative of this causal clause is always οὐ (cf. Lk. 1:34), except once: ἐπεὶ μή ποτε ἰσχύει ὅτε ζῇ ὁ διαθέμενος (Heb. 9:17), 'since it is not then in force while the testator lives.'

b. ἐπειδή (ἐπεί+δή), 'since indeed,' 'since.'
This conjunction occurs nine times, in the New

Testament: ἐπειδή . . . αἰτοῦσιν (I Cor. 1:22), 'since indeed . . . (they) ask.'

c. ἐπειδήπερ (ἐπεί+δή+πέρ), 'since indeed to be sure,' 'since.'
This word occurs only once, in the New Testament: ἐπειδήπερ πολλοὶ ἐπεχείρησαν ἀνατάξασθαι διήγησιν (Lk. 1:1), 'since indeed many have taken in hand to draw up a narrative.'

3. ὅθεν, 'whence.'
This conjunction usually introduces a local clause, but it is used several times in Hebrews in a causal sense: ὅθεν ὤφειλεν κατὰ πάντα τοῖς ἀδελφοῖς ὁμοιωθῆναι (Heb. 2:17), 'wherefore he was under obligation to be made in all respects like unto his brethren.' Cf. Heb. 3:1.

Introduced by Relative Pronouns

There are several prepositions used with the relative in a causal sense.

1. ἀνθ' ὧν, 'in return for which things,' 'because': ἰδοὺ ἔσῃ σιωπῶν . . . ἀνθ' ὧν οὐκ ἐπίστευσας τοῖς λόγοις μου (Lk. 1:20), 'Behold thou shalt be silent . . . because thou hast not believed my words.'

2. δι' ἣν αἰτίαν, 'for which reason,' 'for what cause': τρέμουσα ἦλθεν καὶ προσπεσοῦσα αὐτῷ δι' ἣν αἰτίαν ἥψατο αὐτοῦ ἀπήγγειλεν ἐνώπιον παντὸς τοῦ λαοῦ (Lk. 8:47), 'Trembling she came falling down before him and announced to all the people for what cause she touched him.'

3. διό (διά+ὅ), 'on account of which': διὸ προσώχθισα τῇ γενεᾷ (Heb. 3:10), 'because of which I became angry (disgusted) with this generation.'

4. διόπερ (διά+ὅ+πέρ), 'on account of which indeed': διόπερ εἰ βρῶμα σκανδαλίζει τὸν ἀδελφόν μου, οὐ μὴ φάγω

κρέα εἰς τὸν αἰῶνα (I Cor. 8:13), 'on account of which indeed, if eating meat makes my brother stumble, I will eat no flesh unto the age.'

5. οὗ χάριν, 'for the sake of which,' 'wherefore': οὗ χάριν λέγω σοι (Lk. 7:47), 'for the sake of which I say to thee.'

The 'preposition,' really a 'post-position,' is a good example of how the case-form of nouns became first adverbs, and then prepositions. χάριν is the accusative case of χάρις, 'grace.' See also τούτου χάριν (Eph. 3:1, 14).

6. ἐν ᾧ, 'in which thing,' 'in that.'

This occurs once as a causal conjunction: τὸ γὰρ ἀδύνατον τοῦ νόμου, ἐν ᾧ ἠσθένει διὰ τῆς σαρκός (Rom. 8:3), 'for the inability of the law, in that it was weak through the flesh.'

7. ἐφ' ὅσον, 'in as much as': ἀμὴν λέγω ὑμῖν, ἐφ' ὅσον ἐποιήσατε ἑνὶ τούτων τῶν ἀδελφῶν μου τῶν ἐλαχίστων, ἐμοὶ ἐποιήσατε (Mt. 25:40), 'Verily I say unto you, in as much as ye have done it unto one of the least of these my brethren, ye have done it unto me.' See also Mt. 25:45.

8. καθ' ὅσον, 'in as much as': καὶ καθ' ὅσον οὐ χωρὶς ὁρκωμοσίας (Heb. 7:20), 'and in as much as not apart from an oath.'

The Infinitive with διὰ τό to Express Cause

This is a common idiom for giving the cause or reason for an act: διὰ τὸ εἶναι αὐτὸν ἐξ οἴκου καὶ πατριᾶς Δαυείδ (Lk. 2:4), 'because he was from the house and lineage of David.'

In Jn. 2:24, διὰ τὸ αὐτὸν γινώσκειν, 'on account of his knowing,' is used parallel to a ὅτι causal clause in Jn. 2:25, ὅτι οὐ χρείαν εἶχεν, 'because he did not have need.'

The Participle to Express Cause

The circumstantial participle may imply cause: δίκαιος

ὧν καὶ μὴ θέλων αὐτὴν δειγματίζεσθαι ἐβουλήθη λάθρᾳ ἀπολῦσαι αὐτήν (Lk. 1:19), 'Being a righteous man and not wishing to make a spectacle of her, he was planning to divorce her privately.' The participles, ὤν and θέλων, tell why Joseph planned to put Mary away privately.

The force of ὡς with the participle is seen in ὡς διαστρέφοντα τὸν λαόν (Lk. 23:14), 'as disturbing the people.' The ὡς calls attention to the fact that Jesus was charged with an alleged crime, not an actual one.

PURPOSE,[11] PURPORT[12] AND RESULT[13] CLAUSES

These clauses are grouped together because they are often introduced by the same conjunctions. This fusing of the use of these conjunctions was due to two influences. In the first place, the infinitive, having a roughly analogous but much wider usage, seems to have encouraged the looser handling of these conjunctions. In the second place, in the final analysis, purpose and result are rather close akin. Purpose is simply intended result, and result is accomplished purpose. The interpreter must watch the context for the exact meaning of these clauses.

1. The ἵνα clause

By far the most frequent conjunction introducing purpose clauses is ἵνα. It occurs about eight times as often as ὅπως. So fixedly was it associated with purpose (design) in classical Greek that many exegetes refused for a long time to admit that it could ever express result. Meyer was the leader in an "heroic warfare" on the idea that ἵνα could ever express any idea but purpose. Meyer and others of his school were attempting to fix koine usage by Attic standards.

In the New Testament, the ἵνα clause has the following uses:

a. Purpose is the usual meaning of the ἵνα clause in koine.

[11] Other names for the purpose clauses are: final, design.
[12] Other names for the purport clauses are: sub-final, appositive.
[13] Other names for the result clauses are: consecutive, ecbatic.

(1) The mode of the verb is virtually always subjunctive.

(a) Both the aorist and the present tenses are frequent in these clauses: the aorist is timeless and punctiliar; the present is timeless and linear.

Occasionally, both tenses may occur in the same clause: τοῖς ἔργοις πιστεύετε, ἵνα γνῶτε καὶ γινώσκητε (Jn. 10:38), 'Believe the works in order that ye may come to know and keep on knowing.' This example supplies a good illustration of the difference in meaning of the two tenses in the subjunctive.

(b) Occasionally, the perfect subjunctive is found: ἡμεῖς δὲ οὐ τὸ πνεῦμα τοῦ κόσμου ἐλάβομεν ἀλλὰ τὸ πνεῦμα τὸ ἐκ τοῦ θεοῦ, ἵνα εἰδῶμεν τὰ ὑπὸ τοῦ θεοῦ χαρισθέντα ἡμῖν (I Cor. 2:12), 'But we did not receive the spirit of the world, but the Spirit of God, in order that we might know the things that are freely given us.' It should be remembered that the perfect subjunctive, εἰδῶμεν (from οἴδαμεν), has the force of the present tense.

Except for a few periphrastic subjunctives, οἶδα has the monopoly on perfect subjunctives in the New Testament, occurring ten times.

(2) The indicative mode occurs in a ἵνα clause of purpose, occasionally.

(a) The future indicative: καὶ καιρῷ ἀπέστειλεν πρὸς τοὺς γεωργοὺς δοῦλον, ἵνα ἀπὸ τοῦ καρποῦ τοῦ ἀμπελῶνος δώσουσιν αὐτῷ (Lk. 20:10), 'And in season he sent a servant to the husbandmen, in order that they should give him from the fruit of the vineyard.'

The future indicative was occasionally found in classical Greek after ὅπως to express purpose.[14] This probably led to its later use with ἵνα. There is no essential difference in meaning between the aorist subjunctive and the future indicative in these clauses. It is well here to

[14] See Goodwin, *Greek Grammar*, p. 291, sec. 1366.

recall the close historical connection between the future indicative and the aorist subjunctive.

(b) The present indicative: οἴδαμεν δὲ ὅτι ὁ υἱὸς τοῦ θεοῦ ἥκει, καὶ δέδωκεν ἡμῖν διάνοιαν ἵνα γινώσκομεν τὸν ἀληθινόν (I Jn. 5:20), 'But we know that the Son of God has come and has given to us understanding in order that we may know the truth.' There are two possible explanations of the present indicative, γινώσκομεν, in this ἵνα clause: the indicative mode may be used here to express the fact that Christ's purpose in coming into the world was realized; or, it might have been a misspelling for γινώσκωμεν (pres. subj.), although such confusions in spelling were rare. It is best not to be dogmatic in a case like this.

(3) The negative of the purpose clause is always μή: μὴ κρίνατε, ἵνα μὴ κριθῆτε (Mt. 7:1), 'Judge not, in order that ye be not judged.'

b. Purport may also be expressed by a ἵνα clause.
A purport clause differs from a purpose clause in that it is either the subject or the object of the verb in the principal clause.

(1) Subject clauses introduced by ἵνα are common: συμφέρει γάρ σοι ἵνα ἀπόληται ἓν τῶν μελῶν σου καὶ μὴ ὅλον τὸ σῶμά σου βληθῇ εἰς γέενναν (Mt. 5:29), 'For it is expedient for thee that one of thy members should be destroyed and not that thy whole body should be cast into Gehenna.' The entire ἵνα clause is the subject of the verb, συμφέρει.

(2) Object clauses introduced by ἵνα occur, in the New Testament, after verbs of saying, speaking, praying, etc.: καὶ προσηύχετο ἵνα εἰ δυνατόν ἐστιν παρέλθῃ ἀπ' αὐτοῦ ἡ ὥρα (Mk. 14:35), 'And he was praying that if possible the hour might pass from him.'

c. Result is expressed by the ἵνα clause in a few instances: τίς ἥμαρτεν, οὗτος ἢ οἱ γονεῖς αὐτοῦ, ἵνα τυφλὸς γεννηθῇ; (Jn. 9:2), 'Who sinned, this man or his parents, so that he should be born blind?' It is hardly conceivable that the parents or the unborn child should have committed some heinous sin with the intent that the child should be born sightless. But it is quite in keeping with the theology of the time to raise the question as to whose sin resulted in the child's blindness.

Sanday and Headlam,[15] without the aid of the new knowledge of *koine* Greek as exhibited in the papyri, argue on exegetical (not grammatical) grounds for the consecutive use of ἵνα in μὴ ἔπταισαν ἵνα πέσωσιν; (Rom. 11:11), 'Did they stumble so that they fell?' It is hardly conceivable that Israel stumbled in order to fall, but it is quite in keeping with Israel's history to say that she stumbled so (seriously) that she fell. See also Lk. 1:43; I Th. 5:4; Rev. 9:20; 13:13; I Jn. 1:9.

d. The epexegetical ἵνα clause.

(1) A considerable number of these clauses are in apposition with nouns in various cases. It is quite characteristic of the Johannine writings.

(a) Nominative: ἔρχεται ὥρα ἵνα πᾶς ὁ ἀποκτείνας ὑμᾶς δόξῃ λατρείαν προσφέρειν τῷ θεῷ (Jn. 16:2), 'An hour comes that (when) everyone who kills you will think that he offers service to God.' The ἵνα clause defines the word ὥρα. It is almost temporal in force.

(b) Ablative: μείζονα ταύτης ἀγάπην οὐδεὶς ἔχει, ἵνα τις τὴν ψυχὴν αὐτοῦ θῇ ὑπὲρ τῶν φίλων αὐτοῦ (Jn. 15:13), 'No man hath greater love than this, that one should lay down his life for his friends.' The ἵνα clause explains ταύτης.

(c) Locative: ἐν τούτῳ ἐδοξάσθη ὁ Πατήρ μου, ἵνα καρπὸν πολὺν φέρητε (Jn. 15:8), 'In this is my Father glorified, that ye should bear much fruit.' Here, the ἵνα clause explains ἐν τούτῳ.

(d) Accusative: ἴδετε ποταπὴν ἀγάπην δέδωκεν ἡμῖν ὁ Πατὴρ ἵνα τέκνα θεοῦ κληθῶμεν (I Jn. 3:1), 'Behold what manner of love the Father hath

[15] The Epistle to the Romans (I. C. C.)

bestowed upon us, that we should be called the children of God.' Here, the ἵνα clause explains ἀγάπην.

(2) Another type of epexegetical ἵνα clause is where a verb is explained: πληρώσατέ μου τὴν χαρὰν ἵνα τὸ αὐτὸ φρονῆτε (Phil. 2:2), 'Fulfill my joy, that ye think the same thing.'

2. The ὅπως clause.

a. Purpose clauses are introduced by ὅπως about fifty times in the New Testament. These are found chiefly in Matthew, seventeen times, and Luke-Acts, twenty times.

(1) The usual mode is the subjunctive: μὴ σαλπίσῃς ἔμπροσθέν σου, ὥσπερ οἱ ὑποκριταὶ ποιοῦσιν ἐν ταῖς συναγωγαῖς καὶ ἐν ταῖς ῥύμαις, ὅπως δοξασθῶσιν ὑπὸ τῶν ἀνθρώπων (Mt. 6:2), 'Do not sound a trumpet before thee as the hypocrites do in the synagogues and in the streets in order to be glorified by men.'

The future indicative, so common in ancient Greek, is almost gone in the New Testament, although it does occur a few times. Some grammarians take προσκυνήσω in the ὅπως clause of Mt. 2:8 as a future indicative. The form, however, is also a first aorist subjunctive.

(2) The use of ἄν in the ὅπως clause of purpose occurs four times in the New Testament: γινέσθω δὲ ὁ θεὸς ἀληθής, πᾶς δὲ ἄνθρωπος ψεύστης, καθάπερ γέγραπται, ὅπως ἂν δικαιωθῇς ἐν τοῖς λόγοις σου καὶ νικήσεις ἐν τῷ κρίνεσθαί σε (Rom. 3:4), 'But let God be true and everyman a liar, even as it is written, in order that thou mayest be justified in thy words and overcome in thy judging.' Note that the aorist subjunctive, δικαιωθῇς, and the future indicative, νικήσεις, are used co-ordinately in this clause.

The other examples are all in Luke's writings: Lk. 2:35; Acts 3:20; 15:17. Two of these four examples, Rom. 3:4 and Acts 15:17, are in quotations from the LXX. Since Luke's style was much

influenced by the LXX, the other two examples
may be due to that influence.

According to Goodwin,[16] this use of ὅπως ἄν
with the subjunctive in a purpose clause first
appeared in Aeschylus. The ἄν does not seem to
affect the meaning. Possibly, it adds a slight
touch of indefiniteness.

b. Purport clauses are introduced by ὅπως a few times.

(1) There are three examples of this idiom in the
New Testament after συμβούλιον ἔλαβον: Mt. 12:14;
22:15; Mk. 3:6.[17] There is a good deal of the flavor
of an indirect deliberative question in each of
these examples, as is seen in Mt. 22:15: τότε πορευ-
θέντες οἱ φαρισαῖοι συμβούλιον ἔλαβον ὅπως αὐτὸν παγι-
δεύσωσιν ἐν λόγῳ, 'Then the Pharisees having gone
took counsel to ensnare him in talk.' The problem
before the council was, 'How can we ensnare him?'
The sentence might well be rendered, 'The Pharisees having gone took counsel how they might
ensnare him in talk.'

(2) It occurs a number of times after several verbs
of beseeching: αἰτούμενοι . . . ὅπως (Acts 25:3);
προσηύξαντο . . . ὅπως (Acts 8:15); ἐρωτῶν . . . ὅπως
(Lk. 7:3); παρεκάλεσαν ὅπως (Mt. 8:34); δεήθητε
. . . ὅπως (Mt. 9:38).

c. The negative of ὅπως clauses of both purpose and
purport is μή: Acts 8:24; 20:16.

3. The μή clauses.

μή and its compounds all introduce negative clauses.

a. Purpose clauses.

(1) The purpose clause introduced by μή: γρηγορεῖτε
οὖν . . . μὴ . . . εὕρῃ ὑμᾶς καθεύδοντας (Mk. 13:35, 36),
'Watch therefore . . . lest he find you sleeping.'

In early Greek, μή was by far the commonest
way of introducing negative clauses of purpose,
but in the New Testament, it is almost crowded

---

[16] *Syntax of the Moods and Tenses of the Greek Verb*, sec. 313,3.
[17] Nestle reads ἐδίδουν instead of ἔλαβον in Mk. 3:6.

out by ἵνα μή and ὅπως μή. Only the subjunctive mode occurs in the μή clauses.

(2) Purpose clauses introduced by μήποτε (μή+ποτέ). The notion of time, ordinarily expressed by ποτέ, has disappeared, being replaced by the idea of contingency, 'lest perchance.'

In the New Testament, μήποτε occurs:

(a) With the subjunctive: μήποτε καὶ αὐτοὶ ἀντικαλέσωσίν σε (Lk. 14:12), 'lest perchance they also invite thee in return.'

(b) With the future indicative: μήποτε ἔσται (Mk. 14:2), 'lest perchance there shall be.'

(c) In some manuscripts with the aorist optative: μήποτε δώῃ αὐτοῖς ὁ θεὸς μετάνοιαν (II Tim. 2:25), 'lest perchance God should give repentance to them.' Other manuscripts read the subjunctive, δώῃ.

(3) μήπως (μή+πώς) is rare in purpose clauses, in the New Testament. The indefinite adverb, πώς, 'in some way,' introduces the idea of manner into the clause.

μήπως is used:

(a) With the subjunctive: μήπως . . . γένωμαι (I Cor. 9:27), 'lest in any way . . . I become.'

(b) Twice, with the aorist indicative, referring to a past event where the purpose is conceived as unfulfilled: μήπως . . . ἔδραμον (Gal. 2:2), 'lest somehow . . . I had run'; μήπως ἐπείρασεν (I Th. 3:5), 'lest somehow (he) had tempted.' This was an Attic idiom.

b. Purport clauses

μή and its compounds are sometimes used with verbs of fearing and taking caution, instead of ἵνα μή.[18]

(1) μή.

(a) It is usually used with the subjunctive: βλέπετε μή τις ὑμᾶς πλανήσῃ (Mt. 24:4), 'see to it

---

[18] These clauses are very closely akin to purpose clauses.

that no one lead you astray'; ἐφοβοῦντο τὸν λαὸν μὴ λιθασθῶσιν (Acts 5:26), 'they feared the people lest they be stoned.'

(b) Sometimes, it occurs with the future indicative: βλέπετε μή τις ἔσται ὁ συλαγωγῶν διὰ τῆς φιλοσοφίας καὶ κενῆς ἀπάτης (Col. 2:8), 'See to it that there shall not be any one making a prey of you through philosophy or vain deceit.' The indicative seems to suggest the likelihood that such will happen.

(c) Even the present indicative may occur, if the fear is about the present: σκόπει μὴ τὸ φῶς τὸ ἐν σοὶ σκότος ἐστίν (Lk. 11:35), 'look whether the light that is in thee is darkness.' The indicative adds a note of reality to the grounds for caution.

(2) μήποτε.

(a) It occurs a few times with the aorist subjunctive: προσέχειν ἡμᾶς τοῖς ἀκουθεῖσιν, μήποτε παραρυῶμεν (Heb. 2:1), 'that we take heed to the things heard lest perchance we be carried on by.'

(b) It occurs with the present subjunctive: φοβηθῶμεν μήποτε . . . δοκῇ τις (Heb. 4:1), 'let us be afraid lest perchance . . . any one seem.'

(c) It occurs with the future indicative: βλέπετε . . . μήποτε ἔσται (Heb. 3:12), 'look lest . . . there shall be.'

(3) μήπως.

(a) It occurs with the aorist subjunctive: βλέπετε μήπως γένηται (I Cor. 8:9), 'look out lest somehow (it) become.'

(b) If the fear is about the present or the past, the indicative is used: φοβοῦμαι . . . μήπως εἰκῇ κεκοπίακα (Gal. 4:11), 'I fear . . . lest somehow I have labored in vain.'

The infinitive after a verb of fearing means to hesitate to do a thing: ἐφοβήθη ἀπελθεῖν (Mt. 2:22), 'he feared to go away.'

4. Once, ὡς occurs in the text of WH introducing a purpose clause: ἀλλ᾽ οὐδενὸς λόγου ποιοῦμαι τὴν ψυχὴν τιμίαν
ἐμαυτῷ ὡς τελειώσω τὸν δρόμον μου (Acts 20:24), 'But I
hold not my life of any account as dear unto myself
in order that I may finish my course.' Some manuscripts read τελειῶσαι, the infinitive of purpose, instead
of τελειώσω.

Purport and result clauses are not introduced by ὡς.

5. Relative clauses implying purpose and result.

   a. Relative clauses implying purpose.

   (1) The future indicative is the usual verb form in
   these clauses: ἰδοὺ ἀποστέλλω τὸν ἀγγελός μου πρὸ
   προσώπου σου ὃς κατασκευάσει τὴν ὁδόν σου (Mk. 1:2),
   'Behold I send my messenger before thy face who
   shall prepare thy way.' Purpose is only implied
   by the relative clause, ὃς κατασκευάσει.

   (2) The subjunctive may be used: παρ᾽ ᾧ ξενισθῶμεν
   (Acts 21:16), 'with whom we were to lodge.'

   b. Relative clause implying result.
   This was a common idiom in ancient Greek, and
   there seem to be a few examples in the New Testament: ὅς γε τοῦ ἰδίου υἱοῦ οὐκ ἐφείσατο (Rom. 8:32),
   'who indeed spared not his own Son.' Cf. Mt. 10:26;
   24:2.

6. The infinitive to express purpose, purport, and result.

   a. The infinitive to express purpose.
   This is next to ἵνα in frequency, in the New Testament, to express purpose (two hundred and eleven
   examples).

   (1) The simple infinitive occurs: οὐκ ἦλθον καλεῖν
   (Mk. 2:17), 'I came not to call.'

   (2) The infinitive with the article, τοῦ: μέλλει γὰρ
   Ἡρῴδης ζητεῖν τὸ παιδίον τοῦ ἀπολέσαι αὐτό (Mt. 2:
   13), 'for Herod is about to seek the child to
   destroy it.'
   Not all of the instances of this idiom express

purpose. The majority are explanatory (epexegetical). Most of the examples expressing purpose
are in the writings of Luke and Matthew. Paul
uses it, in this sense, twice: Rom. 6:6; Phil. 3:10.

The infinitive with τοῦ seems to have become a
stereotyped phrase, for in Lk. 17:1 and Acts 10:
25, it is treated as if in the nominative case, and
made the subject of the verb.

(3) The infinitive with εἰς τό, to express purpose,
is very common (seventy-two times), in the New
Testament: εἰς τὸ εἶναι αὐτὸν πρωτότοκον ἐν πολλοῖς
ἀδελφοῖς (Rom. 8:29), 'that he might be the first-
born among many brethren.'

(4) The infinitive with πρὸς τό, to express purpose,
occurs twelve times: πρὸς τὸ θεαθῆναι (Mt. 23:5),
'to be seen.'

(5) The infinitive with ὡς is used once, to express
purpose: ὡς ἑτοιμάσαι (Lk. 9:52),[19] 'so as to make
ready.'

b. The infinitive to express purport.
This is a common use of the infinitive.

(1) It is used as the subject of the verb: ἐμοὶ γὰρ
τὸ ζῆν Χριστός (Phil. 1:21), 'for to me to live (is)
Christ.'

(2) It is used as the object of the verb: οὐχ ἁρπαγμὸν
ἡγήσατο τὸ εἶναι ἴσα θεῷ (Phil. 2:6), 'He did not
reckon being equal to God a prize to be clutched.'
In this example the verb has two objects: ἁρπαγμόν
and εἶναι.

c. The infinitive to express result.

(1) By far the most common way to express result
is ὥστε with the infinitive: καὶ ἐθεράπευσεν αὐτοὺς
ὥστε τὸν ὄχλον θαυμάσαι (Mt. 15:31), 'and he healed
them so that the crowd marveled.' The *koine*
does not, as a rule, observe the difference between
contemplated result and actual result. This construction may be used for both. There are two

---

[19] Nestle reads ὥστε here.

exceptions (Jn. 3:16; Gal. 2:13), where the indicative is used with ὥστε for actual result.

(2) The simple infinitive: ψεύσασθαι (Acts 5:3), 'so as to lie.'

(3) The infinitive with τοῦ: τοῦ μὴ εἶναι αὐτήν (Rom. 7: 3), 'so that she is not.'[20]

(4) The infinitive with εἰς τό seems to express result in some instances: εἰς τὸ παρακαλέσαι ἡμᾶς Τίτον (II Cor. 8:6), 'so that we besought Titus.' Cf. Rom. 1:20.

(5) The infinitive with πρὸς τό.
There is some doubt about this construction, but result is possible: πρὸς τὸ ἐπιθυμῆσαι (Mt. 5:28), 'so as to lust.'

7. The participle may express purpose.
This idiom is not frequent in the New Testament.

   a. It occurs with the future participle: ἐληλύθει προσκυνήσων (Acts 8:27), 'had come to worship.' Cf. Mt. 27:49.

   b. It occurs with the present participle: ἀπέστειλεν αὐτὸν εὐλογοῦντα ὑμᾶς (Acts 3:26), 'sent him blessing (to bless) you.'

8. ὅτι seems to introduce a result clause: ποταπός ἐστιν οὗτος ὅτι καὶ οἱ ἄνεμοι καὶ ἡ θάλασσα αὐτῷ ὑπακούουσιν; (Mt. 8:27), 'Who then is this one that even the winds and the sea obey him?' The ὅτι clause could be taken as an exclamation here. Cf. Lk. 8:25.

Summary

Purpose is most frequently introduced by ἵνα, but purport and result may also be introduced by ἵνα, in the New Testament. Often, ἵνα is epexegetical.

Purpose, purport and indirect discourse may be introduced by ὅπως.

---
[20]   See purpose clauses, p. 190.

Purpose and purport are introduced by μή and its compounds.

The relative clause may imply purpose and result.

The infinitive, in several constructions, may express purpose, purport and result. ὥστε with the infinitive is the most common way of expressing result in the New Testament.

The circumstantial participle may express purpose.

The interpreter of the New Testament must sense from the context the exact meaning of each of these constructions. No set of rules is adequate here. A clear understanding of the context is better than all the rules that could be devised.

PART V

SENTENCES

Conditional Sentences

There are two types of conditional sentences: determined and undetermined. The distinguishing feature of these types is the mode of the verb in the protasis (the conditional clause). Since the indicative is the mode of positive assertion, the indicative will always be found in the protases of the conditions that are determined. Either the subjunctive or the optative, being the modes of doubtful assertions, will be found in the protases of the undetermined conditions.

Conditions That Are Determined

These divide into two classes: those fulfilled, and those unfulfilled. They are known as first and second class conditions.

1. First class conditions.

   a. The protasis will always have the indicative mode, and will usually be introduced by εἰ (sometimes, by ἐάν or ἄν, due to a loss of distinction between these particles). It may use any of the tenses.

   b. The apodosis (conclusion) may have any tense and any mode.
   It may be a statement or a question.
   This is by far the most common of the conditional sentences. The protasis assumes the condition to be true and so states it by using the indicative mode. The protasis has to do with the way the statement is made, and not with the truth or falsity of it: εἰ ἐγὼ ἐν βεεζεβοὺλ ἐκβάλλω τὰ δαιμόνια οἱ υἱοὶ ὑμῶν ἐν τίνι ἐκβάλλουσιν; (Mt. 12: 27), 'If I by Beezeboul[1] cast out demons by whom do your sons cast them out?' For the sake of the argument, Jesus assumes as true the Pharisees' statement that he

[1] See Thayer's *Lexicon* for explanation of these forms.

195

casts out demons by Beelzebub[1] to prove them wrong.
He develops by means of the above conditional sentence
a sort of argument *ad hominem:* διὰ τοῦτο αὐτοὶ κριταὶ
ἔσονται ὑμῶν, 'on account of this they shall be your
judges,' i. e., either your charge is false or you are also
guilty of the same offense. He then makes an assumption based on fact: εἰ δὲ ἐν πνεύματι θεοῦ ἐγὼ ἐκβάλλω (vs.
28), 'but if by the Spirit of God I cast out (the demons).'
From this he concludes: ἄρα ἔφθασεν ἐφ᾿ ὑμᾶς ἡ βασιλεία
τοῦ θεοῦ (vs. 28), 'then is come upon you the kingdom
of God.' This last conclusion represents the truth of
the situation: the kingdom, having come upon them,
they should prepare for it by repentance (Mt. 4:17).

As an example of a first class condition introduced by
ἐάν, see νῦν ζῶμεν ἐὰν ὑμεῖς στήκετε ἐν κυρίῳ (I Th. 3:8),
'now we live, if ye stand in the Lord.' Here, the conclusion comes first in the sentence.

2. Second class conditions.

a. The protasis will always have the indicative mode,
and will be introduced by εἰ. The tense will always
be a past tense: imperfect, aorist, or pluperfect.

b. The apodosis will take a past tense of the indicative. Usually ἄν will occur in the apodosis to mark
this condition off from a first class condition. In
Jn. 15:22, ἄν is omitted, but it is clear from the
context that we have a second class condition: εἰ μὴ
ἦλθον καὶ ἐλάλησα αὐτοῖς, ἁμαρτίαν οὐκ εἴχοσαν,[2] 'If I
had not come and spoken to them, they would not
have had sin.' The point is that Jesus had come and
had spoken and they were guilty.

ἄν is often omitted in the apodosis of a second
class condition after verbs of propriety, fitness, possibility, or obligation: Mt. 26:24; Acts 26:32.

(1) If the condition refers to present time, the
imperfect is used: εἰ γὰρ ἐπιστεύετε Μωϋσεῖ, ἐπιστεύ-

---

[2] Note the unusual Boeotian form of the imperfect. See also the
same form in Jn. 15:24, and ἐδολιοῦσαν in Rom. 3:13 (quoted from
the LXX).

ετε ἄν ἐμοί (Jn. 5:46), 'For if ye believed Moses, ye would believe me.' The point of the condition is that if the Jews really believed Moses, whom they profess to believe, they would also believe Jesus.

(2) If the condition refers to past time, usually the aorist tense is used: εἰ ἐν Τύρῳ καὶ Σιδῶνι ἐγένοντο αἱ δυνάμεις αἱ γενόμεναι ἐν ὑμῖν, πάλαι ἄν ἐν σάκκῳ καὶ σποδῷ μετενόησαν (Mt. 11:21), 'If in Tyre and Sidon had come to pass the miracles which have come to pass among you, they would have repented long ago in sackcloth and ashes.'

(3) If it is desired to express continued action in past time, the imperfect must be used: καὶ εἰ μὲν ἐκείνης ἐμνημόνευον ἀφ' ἧς ἐξέβησαν, εἶχον ἄν καιρὸν ἀνακάμψαι (Heb. 11:15), 'And if indeed they had kept remembering that (land) from which they had gone out, they would continually have had opportunity to return.'

The context will make it clear when the imperfect in conditional sentences refers to past time. In Heb. 4:8, the aorist tense occurs in the protasis and the imperfect in the apodosis: εἰ γὰρ αὐτούς Ἰησοῦς κατέπαυσεν, οὐκ ἄν περὶ ἄλλης ἐλάλει μετὰ ταῦτα ἡμέρας, 'But if Jesus (Joshua) had given them rest, he (God) would not have kept speaking of another day (of rest) after these things (conditions).' Joshua's failure to give the people complete rest (undisputed settlement in their heritage) led to repeated promises of a rest yet to be realized.

Sometimes, the protasis will have the imperfect and the apodosis, the aorist: εἰ ἠγαπᾶτέ με, ἐχάρητε ἄν (Jn. 14:28), 'if ye loved (habitually) me, ye would have rejoiced.' The viewpoint is changed between the protasis and the apodosis, but both are still members of a second class condition. Cf. I Jn. 2:19 for the imperfect in the protasis and the pluperfect in the apodosis. These are not 'mixed conditions.'

Conditions That Are Undetermined

These divide into two classes: those that have probability of fulfilment, and those with remote possibility of fulfilment. These are called third and fourth class conditions.

1. Third class conditions.

   a. The protasis will always have the subjunctive mode, and will usually be introduced by ἐάν (ἄν) but occasionally, by εἰ (Phil. 3:12). Since the subjunctive mode alone is used, the tense is limited to present and aorist.

   b. The apodosis may have any mode or any tense. It may make a statement, ask a question, or give a command.

   The condition is stated as a matter of doubt, with some prospect of fulfilment.

   A first and a third class condition may be used side by side: εἰ ταῦτα οἴδατε μακάριοί ἐστε ἐὰν ποιῆτε αὐτά (Jn. 13:17), 'If you know these things (as you do) blessed are you if you do (as I hope you will) them.' A sharp distinction is drawn here between the first class and third class conditions. Jesus assumes that His disciples do 'know' the things He has been teaching and He expresses hope that they will do them. This is not a 'mixed condition,' but two protases of different classes.

   The third class condition is usually hopeful but hesitant: ἐὰν θέλῃς δύνασαί με καθαρίσαι (Mk. 1:40), 'If thou art willing, thou art able to cleanse me.' The leper is hopeful, but not certain, that Jesus wants to cleanse him. A first class condition would have indicated that the leper was confident that Jesus wanted to heal him.

2. Fourth class conditions.

   a. The protasis has the optative mode, and is introduced by εἰ. It may use either the present or the aorist tense.

b. **The apodosis has the optative mode, and the modal ἄν.**

This condition is even more doubtful than the third class. Had the leper of Mk. 1:40 used this condition, he would have been expressing pessimism as to Jesus' desire to heal him, and probably never would have come to him to be healed.

There is not a complete example of this condition in the New Testament. The nearest complete fragments are in I Peter: ἀλλ' εἰ καὶ πάσχοιτε διὰ δικαιοσύνην, μακάριοι (I Pet. 3:14), 'but although you should suffer on account of righteousness, happy (are you).' The apostle assumes it unlikely that Christians will suffer for their righteousness. Cf. I Pet. 3:17.

Other fragments occur in I Cor. 15:37; Acts 17:27; 27:39.

Mixed Conditions

In these mixed conditions, the protasis will belong to one class of conditions and the apodosis to another: εἰ ἔχετε πίστιν ὡς κόκκον σινάπεως, ἐλέγετε ἂν τῇ συκαμίνῳ ταύτῃ κ. τ. λ. (Lk. 17:6), 'If you have faith as a grain of mustard seed, you would say to this sycamine tree' etc. The protasis is first class, and the apodosis, second class. In Acts 8:31, we have a protasis of the first class, and an apodosis of the fourth class.

These mixed conditions arise from the fact that the writer changes his viewpoint between the protasis and the apodosis.

Elliptical Conditions

Often, the apodosis is expressed and the protasis is simply implied. The protasis may be implied in several ways.

1. By the participle: καὶ κρινεῖ ἡ ἐκ φύσεως ἀκροβυστία τὸν νόμον τελοῦσα σε (Rom. 2:27), 'and the naturally uncircumcised keeping the law (if they keep the law) will judge thee.' This is simply the conditional circumstantial participle. Other examples of the conditional

participle are: ἀμελήσαντες (Heb. 2:3), 'if we neglect'; μετατιθεμένης . . . τῆς ἱερωσύνης (Heb. 7:12), 'if the priesthood is changed'; λαμβανόμενον (I Tim. 4:4), 'if it is received.'

2. By a verb in the imperative mode: δεῦτε ὀπίσω μου, καὶ ποιήσω ὑμᾶς γενέσθαι ἁλεεῖς ἀνθρώπων (Mk. 1:17), 'Come ye after me, and I will make you to become fishers of men,' i. e., 'If ye come, I will make' etc. Cf. ὀργίζεσθε καὶ μὴ ἁμαρτάνετε (Eph. 4:26), 'Be ye angry and sin not,' i. e., 'If you are angry, do not sin.'

3. The protasis may be abbreviated to the vanishing point, as with εἰ μή in the sense of 'except': οὐδεὶς ἐπιγνώσκει τὸν υἱὸν εἰ μὴ ὁ πατήρ (Mt. 11:27), 'No one knows the Son except the Father,' i. e., 'If the Father does not know the Son, no one does.' Cf. ὡσεί (Mt. 3:16); ὡσπερεί (I Cor. 15:8); εἴπερ (Rom. 3:30); ἐκτὸς εἰ μή (I Tim. 5:19).

4. The apodosis may be omitted: εἰ ἔγνως καὶ σύ (Lk. 19:42), 'if thou hadst known, even thou.' Jesus does not complete the condition. The effect of this broken condition is to express sorrow and regret in a very dramatic way. It is as though Jesus hesitated to express the fate coming upon the city.

(1) There is a Hebraistic use of εἰ, a translation of the Hebrew אִם to introduce an oath: εἰ δοθήσεται τῇ γενεᾷ ταύτῃ σημεῖον (Mk. 8:12), 'if a sign shall be given to this generation,' i. e., 'it shall not be given.' Another example is: ὡς ὤμοσα ἐν τῇ ὀργῇ μου Εἰ εἰσελεύσονται εἰς τὴν κατάπαυσίν μου (Heb. 3:11), 'As I sware in my wrath, "If they shall enter into my rest," ' i. e., "They shall not enter into my rest."

(2) It is also used to ask a direct question: κύριε, εἰ ἐν τῷ χρόνῳ τούτῳ ἀποκαθιστάνεις τὴν βασιλείαν τῷ Ἰσραήλ; (Acts 1:6), 'Lord, wilt Thou at this time restore the kingdom to Israel?'
These are not conditional sentences.

Concessive Clauses

These are simply conditional clauses with the addition of καί. The participle may also express the concessive idea.

1. Clauses introduced by καί εἰ and καί ἐάν (κἄν), 'even if': καὶ ἐὰν κρίνω δὲ ἐγώ, ἡ κρίσις ἡ ἐμὴ ἀληθινή ἐστιν (Jn. 8:16), 'Even if I (do) judge, my judgment is true.' This construction is climacteric. The supposition (that Jesus will judge) is considered improbable, but if he should judge, it will be a true (correct) judgment. See I Cor. 8:5 for an example with καί εἰ. Here, Paul concedes that there may be those that are called gods . . . gods many and lords many, but for us there is one God, even the Father. A truth is stoutly affirmed in the face of one particular objection.

2. Clauses introduced by εἰ καί, 'if also,' 'although': εἰ γὰρ καὶ τῇ σαρκὶ ἄπειμι, ἀλλὰ τῷ πνεύματι σὺν ὑμῖν εἰμί (Col. 2:5), 'For although I am absent in the flesh, yet I am present in the Spirit.' The protasis concedes something to be true, but treats it as a matter of indifference. Sometimes, there is a tone of contempt in εἰ καί. This will be revealed by the context.

   Clauses introduced by εἰ καί are much more frequent than those introduced by καί εἰ.

3. Participles.
   The participle alone may express concession: λυπηθεὶς ὁ βασιλεὺς . . . ἐκέλευσεν (Mt. 14:9), 'the king although grieved . . . commanded.' Cf. the discussion of the circumstantial participle.

   In five passages in the New Testament, καίπερ is used to call attention to the concessive force of the participle: καίπερ ὢν υἱὸς ἔμαθεν ἀφ' ὧν ἔπαθεν τὴν ὑπακοήν (Heb. 5:8), 'although a son, He learned obedience from the things which he suffered.' See also καί γε (Acts 17:27); καί τοι (Acts 14:17); καίτοιγε (Jn. 4:2), as other particles calling attention to concessive clauses.

   Negative Particles in Conditional Clauses

1. In the first class protases, οὐ is practically always used: εἰ καὶ τὸν θεὸν οὐ φοβοῦμαι οὐδὲ ἄνθρωπον ἐντρέπομαι, διά γε τὸ παρέχειν μοι κόπον τὴν χήραν ταύτην ἐκδικήσω

αὐτήν (Lk. 18:4), 'Although I do not fear God nor regard man, because this widow troubles me, I will avenge her.'

There are only five examples where μή is used: Mk. 6:5; I Tim. 6:3.

2. In second class protases, μή is used to negative the condition itself: εἰ μὴ ἦν οὗτος κακὸν ποιῶν, οὐκ ἄν σοι παρεδώκαμεν αὐτόν (Jn. 18:30), 'If this fellow were not doing evil, we would not have delivered him over to thee.'

Once, οὐ is used when a very emphatic denial is desired: καλὸν ἦν αὐτῷ εἰ οὐκ ἐγεννήθη ὁ ἄνθρωπος ἐκεῖνος (Mt. 26:24=Mk. 14:21), 'It would have been well for that man, if he had not been born.'

3. In third class protases, μή is always used: ἐὰν μὴ μετανοῆτε (Lk. 13:3), 'except ye repent.'

4. There are no negatives in fourth class protases, in the New Testament.

INDIRECT DISCOURSE

As there are three kinds of direct discourse, so there are three kinds of indirect discourse: assertions, questions, and commands.

Indirect Assertions

There are three ways of turning a direct statement into an indirect statement.

1. The ὅτι clause.
   This is the usual idiom in the New Testament: θεωρῶ ὅτι προφήτης εἶ σύ (Jn. 4:19), 'I behold that thou art a prophet.'

   a. The mode of the direct statement is kept in the indirect. In classical Greek, after secondary tenses, the indicative and the subjunctive are often changed to the corresponding tense of the optative, but that is not used in the New Testament.

b. The tense is kept, as a rule, for the sake of vividness: ἐκεῖνοι δὲ ἔδοξαν ὅτι περὶ τῆς κοιμήσεως τοῦ ὕπνου λέγει (Jn. 11:13), 'but they thought he was speaking concerning the taking of rest in sleep.'

In English, after a past tense, we must change a present tense to the past.

c. The person often must be changed: ἐνόμισαν ὅτι πλεῖον λήμψονται (Mt. 20:10), 'they thought they would receive more.' In direct discourse, the verb was λημψόμεθα, 'we shall receive.'

In κἀγὼ δέ σοι λέγω ὅτι σὺ εἶ Πέτρος (Mt. 16:18), 'but I say to thee, that thou art Peter,' there is no need to change the person.

2. The infinitive.
Usually, the infinitive will be accompanied by a noun or pronoun in the accusative case (accusative of general reference): ἐν τῷ εἰσαγαγεῖν τοὺς γονεῖς τὸ παιδίον Ἰησοῦν (Lk. 2:27), 'when the parents brought the child Jesus.'

If the subject of the verb of the main clause is the same as that of the verb in the direct statement, the noun used with the infinitive may be in the nominative case: εἴ τις δοκεῖ θρησκὸς εἶναι (Jas. 1:26), 'if anyone thinks that he is religious.'

The infinitive may occur with no noun or pronoun: ἦλθον λέγουσαι καὶ ὀπτασίαν ἀγγέλων ἑωρακέναι (Lk. 24: 23), 'they came saying that they also had seen a vision of angels.'

In the New Testament, the infinitive to express indirect discourse is disappearing before the ὅτι clause. It is used much more frequently by Luke than any other New Testament writer. It is a mark of his literary style.

a. The present infinitive in indirect discourse represents the present or the imperfect in the direct:

πεπεισμένος γάρ ἐστιν Ἰωάνην εἶναι (Lk. 20:6), 'for (the people) are persuaded that John was a prophet.' Here, εἶναι represents ἦν.

b. The future infinitive represents the future indicative: χωρήσειν, for χωρήσει (Jn. 21:25), 'to contain' for 'it will contain.' In English, this is rendered by 'would.'

c. The perfect infinitive represents the perfect indicative: τεθνηκέναι, for τέθνηκε (Acts 14:19), 'to have died' for 'he has died.'

3. The participle.
   Verbs of knowing, perceiving, showing, etc. may have the participle in indirect discourse: ὁρῶ σε ὄντα (Acts 8:23), 'I see thee being.'

   a. The participle in indirect discourse describes an actual experience, while the infinitive and the ὅτι clause represent only an intellectual apprehension.

   b. The tense in the participle has its usual force: ἐθεώρουν τὸν Σατανᾶν . . . πεσόντα (Lk. 10:18), 'I was beholding Satan . . . fall.' The participle, πεσόντα, describes a punctiliar act. The present participle, πίπτοντα, would have pictured the process of falling, and the perfect, πεπτωκότα, would have called attention to the state after falling. Cf. ἐξεληλυθυῖαν (Lk. 8:46).

Indirect Questions

1. The most usual word to introduce indirect questions is τίς, τί. The classic use of ὅστις to introduce them has disappeared in the New Testament, except in Acts 9:6: λαληθήσεταί σοι ὅτι σε δεῖ ποιεῖν, 'it will be told thee what it is necessary for thee to do.'

2. Other ways of introducing indirect questions:

   a. The relative, ὅς, and the interrogatives became confused in Greek as in other Indo-European lan-

guages.[3] In the New Testament, we have: οὐκ ἔχω
ὃ παραθήσω αὐτῷ (Lk. 11:6), 'I do not have what I
may set before him.' The direct question is: τί
παραθήσω αὐτῷ;, 'What shall I set before him?'

b. There is a large group of interrogative words used:
ποῦ in the sense of 'where' (Mt. 2:4); πόθεν (Jn.
8:14); ποῦ in the sense of 'whither' (Jn. 8:14);
ποῖος (Rev. 3:3); πότε (Lk. 12:36); πῶς (Lk. 8:36);
πηλίκος (Gal. 6:11); πόσος (Mt. 16:9); ποταπός (Lk.
1:29).

c. The correlatives are also used: ὅπως (Lk. 24:20);
ὁποῖος (I Th. 1:9).

3. Changes occurring in the transfer from direct to
indirect questions.

a. The person often must be changed: μὴ μεριμνᾶτε . . .
τί φάγητε (Mt. 6:25), 'Stop worrying (about) . . .
what ye shall eat.' The direct question was: τί
φάγωμεν;, 'What shall we eat?' Cf. Mt. 6:31.

b. The tense is seldom changed: ἐθεώρουν ποῦ τέθειται
(Mk. 15:47), 'they were beholding where he had
been laid.'
Occasionally, the tense is changed: αὐτὸς γὰρ ἐγίνω-
σκεν τί ἦν ἐν τῷ ἀνθρώπῳ (Jn. 2:25), 'for he knew
what was in man.' The direct question would have
been: τί ἐστι ἐν τῷ ἀνθρώπῳ;, 'What is in man?'

c. The mode is seldom changed in the New Testament.
(1) The indicative remains indicative: ἦλθον ἰδεῖν τί
ἐστιν τὸ γεγονός (Mk. 5:14), 'They came to see
what it was that had happened.' The direct question, τί ἐστιν τὸ γεγονός;, 'What has happened?',
sought for information.
(2) The subjunctive remains subjunctive: οὐ γὰρ
ᾔδει τί ἀποκριθῇ (Mk. 9:6), 'For he did not know
what he was to answer.' The direct question, τί
ἀποκρίνωμαι, was deliberative.

[3] Blass, *Grammar of New Testament Greek*, p. 175.

(3) When the optative with ἄν occurs in the indirect
question, it was so in the direct question: τὸ τίς
ἂν εἴη μείζων αὐτῶν (Lk. 9:46), 'who of them should
be the greater.' The article, τό, simply singles out
the cause of the dispute.

Elsewhere, Luke followed the classic idiom, and
changed the indicative to the optative: ἤρξαντο
συζητεῖν . . . τὸ τίς ἄρα εἴη (Lk. 22:23), 'they began
to dispute . . . who then it should be.' In vs. 24,
he retains the indicative.

4. The article with the indirect question.
Luke is fond of the article with the indirect question:
1:62; 22:2, 4, 23, 24. It is seldom found elsewhere.

The effect of the article is to make plain that syntactically the subordinate clause is the object of the
verb of the main clause: ἐζήτουν τὸ πῶς ἀνέλωσιν (Lk.
22:2), 'they were seeking how they might destroy
him.' The clause is the direct object of the verb,
ἐζήτουν. The article points out this fact.

Indirect Commands

There are three ways by which a direct command can
be changed to the indirect.

1. The infinitive is the usual way: λέγων μὴ περιτέμνειν
αὐτοὺς τὰ τέκνα (Acts 21:21), 'saying not to circumcise their children.' This idiom must be distinguished
from the indirect statement. The direct quotation
was: μὴ περιτέμνετε τὰ τέκνα, 'Quit circumcising your
children.' Paul is charged with forbidding Jewish
parents to circumcise their children, not with report-
ing that they have quit the practice; so it is an
indirect command, not an indirect statement.

2. The conjunctions, ἵνα and ὅπως, are used with a finite
verb. These are really sub-final, or purport clauses.

a. ἵνα.
παρήγγειλεν αὐτοῖς ἵνα μηδὲν αἴρωσιν εἰς ὁδόν (Mk. 6:8),

'He commanded that they take nothing for the journey.'

b. ὅπως.

αἰτούμενοι . . . ὅπως μεταπέμψηται αὐτόν (Acts 25:3), 'begging that he summon him.'

3. The deliberative question.

A direct command, μὴ φοβηθῆτε (Lk. 12:4), 'fear ye not,' may be made indirect by the deliberative subjunctive after τίνα: ὑποδείξω τίνα φοβηθῆτε (Lk. 12:5), 'I will show you whom ye are to fear.'

DIRECT QUESTIONS

We are concerned here with two things: the means of introducing direct questions, and the mode used in them.

Introducing Questions

Questions may be introduced in a variety of ways, depending on the purpose of the speaker or writer.

1. Particles, implying the answer expected.

a. οὐ (οὐκ, οὐχ), οὐχί.

If an affirmative answer is expected, οὐ is used: οὐκ εἰμὶ ἀπόστολος; (I Cor. 9:1), 'Am I not an apostle?' The implication is: 'I certainly am.'

If one desired to emphasize the expectation of an affirmative answer, οὐχί, the emphatic form, was used: οὐχὶ ἡ ψυχὴ πλεῖόν ἐστιν τῆς τροφῆς καὶ τὸ σῶμα τοῦ ἐνδύματος; (Mt. 6:25), 'Is not indeed the life more than the food and the body than the clothing?' The thought is: 'Most assuredly, it is.'

b. μή, μήτι.

(1) If a negative answer is expected, μή is used: μὴ ἀπώσατο ὁ θεὸς τὸν λαὸν αὐτοῦ; (Rom. 11:2), 'Did God reject his people?' 'Surely not' is the idea.

(2) For a hesitant question, μήτι may be used: μήτι

οὗτός ἐστιν ὁ Χριστός; (Jn. 4:29), 'Might this be the Messiah?' The form suggests the negative answer, but the woman is convinced that he is probably the Messiah. The -τι leaves the matter for the people to decide. No doubt, her social position in the community would prompt her not to be too positive in such a matter. But she knows how to arouse the curiosity of her fellow-townsmen.

The context must decide the exact emotion that μήτι reveals in the one who asks the question. Cf. II Cor. 1:17; Mt. 26:22, 25.

Often, these particles, οὐ and μή, are calculated to influence the decision of the other party: μὴ καὶ ὑμεῖς πεπλάνησθε; (Jn. 7:47), 'Have you also been led astray?' The Sanhedrin, by this scornful question, seek to break down Nicodemus' wavering loyalty to Christ, and to keep him in line with the parties in power. An example with οὐ is seen in Jn. 18:37: οὐκοῦν (οὐκ+οὖν) βασιλεὺς εἶ σύ;, 'Then you are a king, are you not?' Pilate hopes to induce Jesus to commit himself.

2. Interrogative pronouns.

   a. τίς, τί.

   By far the commonest is τίς: τίς ὑπέδειξεν ὑμῖν φυγεῖν; (Mt. 3:7), 'Who warned you to flee?'

   Often, the neuter accusative singular, τί, is an adverb, 'why': τί με λέγεις ἀγαθόν; (Mk. 10:18), 'Why callest thou me good?' This is in keeping with the fact that all adverbs are a case-form of some noun or pronoun.

   There are several phrases formed with τί which are used in asking questions:

   (1) διὰ τί asks the reason for an action: διὰ τί μετὰ τῶν τελωνῶν καὶ ἁμαρτωλῶν ἐσθίει ὁ διδάσκαλος ὑμῶν; (Mt. 9:11), 'Why does your teacher eat with publicans and sinners?'

   (2) εἰς τί inquires the objective of an action: εἰς τί ἡ ἀπώλεια αὕτη τοῦ μύρου γέγονεν; (Mk. 14:4), 'Unto what end is the waste of this myrrh?'

(3) τί ὅτι inquires as to the reason for an action: τί ὅτι ἐζητεῖτέ με; (Lk. 2:49), 'Why were you seeking me?' It is difficult to explain why the ὅτι was used here.

b. ποῖος.
In the New Testament, this pronoun is losing its qualitative force. In modern Greek, it has almost displaced τίς, and hence has no qualitative force. But the qualitative force is not entirely gone in the New Testament: ἐν ποίᾳ ἐξουσίᾳ ταῦτα ποιεῖς; (Mt. 21:23), 'By what sort of authority do you do these things?' Both τίς and ποῖος occur in I Pet. 1:11. Blass considers this merely tautology for emphasis, but it seems rather strained to deny all qualitative force where an author makes a point of setting two words over against each other. It seems better to take τίς as inquiring as to the period of time, and ποῖος as to the nature of the Messianic reign. Both of these questions were problems to the Jews.

c. πόσος.
This interrogative is always quantitative: πόσους ἔχετε ἄρτους; (Mk. 6:38), 'How many loaves have you?'

d. ποταπός.
This interrogative developed from the older ποδαπός, 'of what country.' It is always qualitative in the New Testament: ποταπός ἐστιν οὗτος; (Mt. 8:27), 'What sort of person is this one?' The weakening of the sense of ποῖος caused ποταπός to take over the functions of that interrogative.

3. Interrogative adverbs.
There is quite a variety of these.

a. ἆρα expresses 'uncertainty,' 'bewilderment': ἆρά γε γινώσκεις ἃ ἀναγινώσκεις; (Acts 8:30), 'Do you then indeed know what you are reading?' Philip is not certain that the Ethiopian is reading with understanding. Another example is: ἆρα Χριστὸς ἁμαρτίας διάκονος; (Gal 2:17), 'Is Christ then the minister of

sin?' The confusion here lies in the conduct of
Paul's converts. He makes clear his own convictions
about Christ's involvement in sin by μὴ γένοιτο.

b. εἰ may introduce a direct question: εἰ ἔξεστιν τοῖς
σάββασιν θεραπεῦσαι; (Mt. 12:10), 'Is it lawful to heal
on the Sabbath?' Cf. Acts 1:6. This is a Hebraism.[4]

c. There is a miscellaneous group of adverbs introducing questions. Since there is nothing unusual
about them, we will merely name the more common
ones: πότε, ἕως πότε, ποῦ, πόθεν, ὅπως, ὅπου, μήποτε, κ. τ. λ.

4. Questions often may be asked without using any introductory word: συνήκατε ταῦτα πάντα; (Mt. 13:51), 'Did
you understand all these things?'

In some of these examples, there may be doubt as
to whether it is a question or a statement: μεμέρισται
ὁ Χριστός (I Cor. 1:13), 'Is Christ divided,' or 'Christ
is divided.' The context alone can decide. This, probably, should be taken as a rhetorical question.

The Mode

1. The most common mode in a question is the indicative.

2. Where there is uncertainty, the deliberative subjunctive is common: δῶμεν ἢ μὴ δῶμεν; (Mk. 12:15), 'Shall
we give or shall we not give?'

In τί ποιοῦμεν; (Jn. 11:47), 'What are we doing?',
the indicative is used to make a charge of inaction
against the rulers. The subjunctive would have raised
the question as to what should be done; the indicative rebukes them, because nothing is being done.

3. The optative with ἄν occurs in the apodosis of a
fourth class condition: τί ἂν θέλοι; (Acts 17:18), 'What
would he wish?' The whole thought here is what
would Paul like to say if he could, implying that it
would be very unlikely that he could say anything
worth hearing, even if he should succeed in saying it.
The tone of contempt is very strong.

[4] See under conditional sentences, p. 200.

OTHER WAYS OF EXPRESSING WISHES

The old idoms of εἴθε and εἰ γάρ, to express wishes, are not used in the New Testament. They have been replaced by ὄφελον (the aorist form of ὀφείλω, without the augment).

Wishes About the Past

1. These are expressed by ὄφελον and the aorist. There is only one example in the New Testament: ὄφελόν γε ἐβασιλεύσατε (I Cor. 4:8), 'Would that you had reigned.'

2. A polite wish about the past may be expressed by the imperfect: ηὐχόμην (Rom. 9:3), 'I was on the point of praying.' Cf. Gal. 4:20; Acts 25:22.

Wishes About the Present

1. These are expressed by ὄφελον and the imperfect. There are only two examples in the New Testament: ὄφελον ψυχρὸς ἦς ἢ ζεστός (Rev. 3:15), 'Would that thou wert either hot or cold'; ὄφελον ἀνείχεσθέ μου μικρόν τι ἀφροσύνης (II Cor. 11:1), 'Would that you did put up with me in a little foolishness.'

2. Of course, wishes about the present may be expressed by verbs of wishing, like θέλω (Jn. 12:21).

Wishes About the Future

1. These are expressed by ὄφελον and the future indicative. There is only one example in the New Testament: ὄφελον ἀποκόψονται (Gal. 5:12), 'would that they would cut themselves off' (mutilate themselves?).

2. The optative (present or aorist) can be used to express a wish about the future. The commonest of these is μὴ γένοιτο (Gal. 6:14), 'may it not happen.' This expression occurs in the New Testament, fifteen times; of these, fourteen are in Paul, with ten in Romans.

3. A courteous wish about the future can be expressed by the potential optative with ἄν: εὐξαίμην ἄν (Acts 26:29), 'I could wish.'

It is evident that wishes, as a separate idiom, are disappearing in *koine* Greek.

SEMITISMS IN THE NEW TESTAMENT

This is a much debated subject, and one requiring a highly technical investigation and discussion. Obviously, it can not be dealt with adequately in a brief discussion. A fair-minded and rather adequate treatment is given in Moulton and Howard, *A Grammar of New Testament Greek*, Vol. II, pp. 413-485.

Quite extreme views have been advocated. The truth probably lies somewhere between the extremes. Probably Deissmann admitted too few Semitisms, but this is only natural, since it was his great work to demonstrate that the language of the New Testament was not a "Judaeo-Greek jargon." Probably Welhausen, Torrey and others have found Semitisms, where they did not exist. James H. Moulton seems to have moved slightly away from Deissmann's position in his later writings.[5]

Attention has been called, in the body of this grammar, to some of these Semitic influences.[6]

In addition, the following should be mentioned:

1. The hanging nominative, so characteristic of the Johannine writings:

   a. ὅσοι δὲ ἔλαβον αὐτόν, ἔδωκεν αὐτοῖς ἐξουσίαν τέκνα θεοῦ γενέσθαι (Jn. 1:12), 'But to as many as received him, to them gave he the right to become sons of God.'

   b. ὁ νικῶν, ποιήσω αὐτὸν στῦλον ἐν τῷ ναῷ τοῦ θεοῦ μου (Rev. 3:12), 'The one overcoming, I will make him a pillar in the temple of my God.'

[5] Moulton and Howard, *A Grammar of New Testament Greek*, Vol. II, p. 413.
[6] Pp. 30, 37, 109, 117, 120, 149, 164, 168, 177, 200.

2.

   a. καὶ ἐγένετο (καί).

   b. ἐγένετο δέ.

These expressions are distinctive of the Lucan writings. They no doubt are reflections in Luke's style of the LXX, which use especially καὶ ἐγένετο καί with great frequency. In the Gospel, Luke used καὶ ἐγένετο slightly more frequently than ἐγένετο δέ (25/18). In the Acts, he used ἐγένετο δέ exclusively. This seems to indicate that Luke tended to get away from the distinctively translation Greek to more idiomatic language.

3. The infinitive absolute seems to be reflected in the New Testament in several passages:

   a. ἐπιθυμίᾳ ἐπεθύμησα τοῦτο τὸ πάσχα φαγεῖν μεθ' ὑμῶν (Lk. 22:15), 'With desire have I desired (i. e., I have very earnestly desired) to eat this passover with you.'

   b. προσευχῇ προσηύξατο τοῦ μὴ βρέξαι (Jas. 5:17), 'he prayed with prayer (i. e., he prayed very fervently) that it should not rain.'

   c. ὃς ἔχει ὦτα ἀκούειν ἀκουέτω (Mk. 4:9), 'Who has ears, let him hear attentively.'

4. Parallelism is sometimes reflected in the New Testament, e. g., I Cor. 13:12 furnishes a contrast between one state of imperfect knowledge, described under two figures, and a state of complete knowledge.

5. The frequent use of ἰδού (while in itself good Greek) suggests a Semitic habit of thought. James, although some of the best Greek in the New Testament, uses ἰδού six times, while the Pauline letters have only nine instances. Revelation has twenty-six occurrences, indicating the strong Semitic flavor of that document.

PART VI

THE PRINCIPAL PARTS OF SOME IMPORTANT NEW TESTAMENT VERBS

Pres.	Fut.	Aor. Act.	Perf. Act.	Perf. M. & P.	Aor. Pass.
ἀγγέλλω announce	ἀγγελῶ	ἤγγειλα	......	-ἤγγελμαι	-ηγγέλην[1]
ἄγω lead	ἄξω	ἤγαγον ἦξα	......	......	ἤχθην
αἱρέω take away	αἱρήσομαι -ελῶ	-εῖλον -εῖλα	......	-ἥρημαι	ᾑρέθην
αἴρω raise, lift up	ἀρῶ	ἦρα	ἦρκα	ἦρμαι	ἤρθην
ἀκούω hear	ἀκούσω	ἤκουσα	ἀκήκοα	......	ἠκούσθην
ἀλλάσσω change	ἀλλάξω	ἤλλαξα	......	-ἤλλαγμαι	-ηλλάγην
ἁμαρτάνω sin	ἁμαρτήσω	ἥμαρτον ἡμάρτησα	ἡμάρτηκα	......	......
ἀνοίγω open	ἀνοίξω	ἀνέῳξα ἠνέῳξα ἤνοιξα	ἠνέῳγα	ἠνέῳγμαι	ἀνεῴχθην ἠνεῴχθην ἠνοίχθην ἠνοίγην
ἀποκτείνω kill	ἀποκτενῶ	ἀπέκτεινα	......	......	ἀπεκτάνθην
ἀπόλλυμι destroy	ἀπολέσω	ἀπώλεσα	ἀπολωλώς (participle)	......	......
ἀρέσκω please	ἀρέσω	ἤρεσα	......	......	......
ἁρπάζω snatch	ἁρπάσω	ἥρπασα	-ηρπάκειν (pluperf.)	......	ἡρπάγην ἡρπάσθην
-βαίνω go	-βήσομαι	-έβην	-βέβηκα	......	......

[1] Forms preceded by a hyphen do not occur in the New Testament, except in compounds.

Pres.	Fut.	Aor. Act.	Perf. Act.	Perf. M. & P.	Aor. Pass.
βάλλω throw	βαλῶ	ἔβαλον ἔβαλα (once, Acts 16:37)	βέβληκα	βέβλημαι	ἐβλήθην
βαπτίζω baptize	βαπτίσω	ἐβάπτισα	......	βεβάπτισμαι	ἐβαπτίσθην
γίνομαι become	γενήσομαι	ἐγενόμην	γέγονα	γεγένημαι	ἐγενήθην
γινώσκω know	γνώσομαι	ἔγνων	ἔγνωκα	ἔγνωσμαι	ἐγνώσθην
διδάσκω teach	διδάξω	ἐδίδαξα	......	......	ἐδιδάχθην
δίδωμι give	δώσω	ἔδωκα -έδοσα (once, Lk. 1:2)	δέδωκα	δέδομαι	ἐδόθην
δύναμαι able, can	δυνήσομαι	......	......	......	ἠδυνήθην ἠδυνάσθην
εἰμί be	ἔσομαι	......	......	......	......
ἐλπίζω hope	ἐλπιῶ	ἤλπισα	ἤλπικα	......	......
ἔρχομαι go, come	ἐλεύσομαι	ἦλθον ἦλθα	ἐλήλυθα	......	......
εὑρίσκω find	εὑρήσω	εὗρον εὕρησα	εὕρηκα	......	εὑρέθην
ἔχω have	ἕξω	ἔσχον ἔσχα	ἔσχηκα	......	......
ζάω live	ζήσω	ἔζησα	......	......	......
ἥκω have come	ἥξω	ἦξα	ἧκα (T. R. in Mk. 8:36)	......	......
θνήσκω die	-θανοῦμαι	-έθανον	τέθνηκα	......	......

Pres.	Fut.	Aor. Act.	Perf. Act.	Perf. M. & P.	Aor. Pass.
ἵστημι ἱστάνω ἱστάω στήκω stand	στήσω	ἔστην ἔστησα	ἔστηκα	......	ἐστάθην
καλέω call	καλέσω	ἐκάλεσα	κέκληκα	κέκλημαι	ἐκλήθην
κερδαίνω gain	κερδανῶ κερδήσω	ἐκέρδησα	......	......	κερδηθήσομαι (fut. pass.)
κλίνω lean	κλινῶ	ἔκλινα	κέκλικα	......	ἐκλίθην
κρίνω judge	κρινῶ	ἔκρινα	κέκρικα	κέκριμαι	ἐκρίθην
κρύπτω hide	......	ἔκρυψα	......	κέκρυμμαι	ἐκρύβην
λαμβάνω receive, get	λήμψομαι	ἔλαβον	εἴληφα	-είλημμαι	-ελήμφθην
λέγω say	ἐρῶ	εἶπον εἶπα -ελεξάμην	εἴρηκα	εἴρημαι	ἐρρέθην ἐρρήθην -ελέχθην
λέγω collect	λέξω	ἔλεξα	......	-λέλεγμαι	......
μανθάνω learn	......	ἔμαθον	μεμάθηκα	......	......
μιμνήσκω remember	-μνήσω	-έμνησα	......	μέμνημαι	ἐμνήσθην
ὁράω see	ὄψομαι	ὠψάμην also εἶδον εἶδα	ἑώρακα ἑόρακα	......	ὤφθην
πείθω persuade	πείσω	ἔπεισα	πέποιθα	πέπεισμαι	ἐπείσθην

Pres.	Fut.	Aor. Act.	Perf. Act.	Perf. M. & P.	Aor. Pass.
πίμπλημι -πιμπλάω fill	......	ἔπλησα	......	πεπλησμένος (part.)	ἐπλήσθην
πίνω drink	πίομαι	ἔπιον	πέπωκα	......	-επόθην
πιπράσκω sell	......	......	πέπρακα	πέπραμαι	ἐπράθην
πίπτω fall	πεσοῦμαι	ἔπεσον ἔπεσα	πέπτωκα cf. πέπτωκες (N. W. Gk. Rev. 2:25)	......	......
πράσσω act, do	πράξω	ἔπραξα	πέπραχα	πέπραγμαι	......
σβέννυμι σβεννύω extinguish	σβέσω	ἔσβεσα	......	......	σβεσθήσομαι (fut. pass.)
σπείρω sow	......	ἔσπειρα	......	ἔσπαρμαι	ἐσπάρην
στέλλω send	στελῶ	-έστειλα	-έσταλκα	-έσταλμαι	-εστάλην
στρέφω turn	-στρέψω	ἔστρεψα	......	-έστραμμαι	ἐστράφην
σώζω save	σώσω	ἔσωσα	σέσωκα	σέσωσμαι	ἐσώθην
τάσσω arrange, fix	-τάξομαι	ἔταξα	τέταχα	τέταγμαι	-ετάγην -ετάχθην
τελέω accomplish	τελέσω	ἐτέλεσα	τετέλεκα	τετέλεσμαι	ἐτελέσθην
τίθημι τιθέω place	θήσω	ἔθηκα	-τέθεικα	τέθειμαι	ἐτέθην
τρέχω run	......	ἔδραμον	......	......	......
φέρω bear	οἴσω	-ήνεγκον ἤνεγκα	-ενήνοχα	......	ἠνέχθην

Pres.	Fut.	Aor. Act.	Perf. Act.	Perf. M. & P.	Aor. Pass.
φεύγω flee	φεύξομαι	ἔφυγον	-πέφευγα	......	......
φθείρω destroy	φθερῶ	ἔφθειρα	......	-ἔφθαρμαι	ἐφθάρην
χαίρω rejoice	......	......	......	......	ἐχάρην
χαρίζομαι show favor	χαρίσομαι	ἐχαρισάμην	......	κεχάρισμαι	ἐχαρίσθην

INDEX OF SCRIPTURE PASSAGES